Marketing Communication Policies

Rainer Busch · Margarete Seidenspinner
Fritz Unger

Marketing Communication Policies

With 91 Figures

 Springer

Prof. Dr. Rainer Busch
Ludwigshafen University of
Applied Sciences
East Asia Institute
Rheinuferstraße 6
67061 Ludwigshafen
Germany
rainer.busch@rainerbusch.de

Prof. Dr. Margarete Seidenspinner
Heilbronn University
Faculty of Economics 2 (W2)
Max-Planck-Straße 39
74081 Heilbronn
Germany
seidenspinner@hs-heilbronn.de

Prof. Dr. Fritz Unger
Ludwigshafen University of
Applied Sciences
Department of Management
Science II (BWII)
Ernst-Boehe-Straße 4
67059 Ludwigshafen
Germany
unger@fh-ludwigshafen.de

Library of Congress Control Number: 2006934070

ISBN 10 3-540-37322-5 Springer Berlin Heidelberg New York
ISBN 13 978-3-540-37322-3 Springer Berlin Heidelberg New York

Springer is a part of Springer Science+Business Media

springer.com

© Springer-Verlag Berlin Heidelberg 2007

Cover: Erich Kirchner, Heidelberg
Production: LE-TeX, Jelonek, Schmidt & Vöckler GbR, Leipzig

SPIN 11816478   Printed on acid-free paper – 43/3100 – 5 4 3 2 1 0

Preface

By summing up the authors' lectures on *Marketing Communications,* this work introduces its users to the fundamental knowledge that is indispensable in this complex and exciting field of Marketing.

It has been compiled especially for first-degree students of Business Administration and Marketing who take an interest in the international aspects of these disciplines.

At the same time, the sound grounding provided by this work is suitable for students pursuing Post-graduate Diploma or Master programmes in technological, scientific or IT-related areas.

The contents dealt with here meet the general requirements of *Communications Management* offering, as they do, an introduction to the generic issues of *Marketing Communications* as well as an overview of the information behaviour of targeted customer groups. The foundation laid in the initial chapters is followed up by more specific areas such as situational analysis and the development of communications strategies.

Subsequently, the students are introduced to the implementation of communication strategies in media planning and the appropriate choice of communication tools.

By way of conclusion, the authors investigate the principles of co-operation with communication agents and selected areas of International Marketing Communications.

Our thanks go to Regina Kalteis, who helped a great deal in the production of this book.

We wish all our users and readers an enjoyable and successful learning experience.

Meckesheim,
Altrip und
Oberstdorf

Rainer Busch
Margarete Seidenspinner
Fritz Unger

Contents

1 An overview

1.1 Introduction

Business organisations, which find themselves forced with progressive frequency to justify their competitive strategies to their stakeholders, are experiencing increasing difficulty in convincing their potential customers, i. e. an unreceptive unsympathetic public, and their relevant target groups in general, of the high level of quality of their business performance. Consequently, communication policies are becoming crucially important as organisations, seeking to meet rising stakeholder expectations, need to give due consideration to the growing impact of the respective societal and political environmental forces impacting on their future corporate perspectives.

Against this background, and in response to these rising stakeholder expectations, "integrated" and interlinked "business communications" can be defined as a strategy that is capable of providing businesses, and organisations in general, with a communication policy that succeeds to the greatest effect and with the greatest efficiency.

1.2 Didactic purpose and expected learning outcomes

This text has been tailored to the needs of students and professional people who are looking for an overview of the relevant concepts pertaining to communications management. Based on a sound theoretical grounding, which is supplemented by examples taken from managerial practice and detailed illustrations, this module addresses and outlines the key issues of communications management.

In addition, there are end-of-chapter self-review exercises (multiple choice questions) and other "student activities" that offer the opportunity for the learners of contributing their own experience and views.

A glossary of specific subject-related terms in the field dealt with here has been added to the final unit, and a number of German translations have been provided in order to highlight semantic complexity. This glossary will facilitate the understanding of the subject-related terms for informed students who, nonetheless, may not have the command of a native speaker. Moreover, it will provide them with specific ESP-skills and a high level of general linguistic proficiency.

On completing this unit,

1. you will be in a position to understand the multifarious array of communications at work in (business) organisations as an inter-correlated system which coordinates and aligns all individual communication measures. In particular, you will have learned how to contribute your own communication efforts to this system.
2. you will have acquired the competency, provided by the research of the social sciences, that is required for participation in the contemporary communication process, and you will comprehend the difference between long-term communication strategies and those communication measures that are, more or less, of a short-term nature.
3. This book, in particular, should enable you to integrate these short-term measures into long-term concepts, and to employ communication media in a way which produces the intended results.
4. Moreover, this unit will enable you, especially with a view to your potential function as a future business executive, to deal confidently with communication agencies (the majority of which will be advertising agencies). You will become familiar with their different approaches and will have learned how to benefit fully from the competency of consultants and agents.
5. Last but not least, you will be able to integrate your own personal selling techniques optimally into the wider communications concept of your (business) organisation.

1.3 Structure

Communications management is responsible for all decisions related to corporate communication policies. As with the process pursued in overall marketing planning, communication policies follow a mapped out planning route whose starting point, which also provides the structural platform for the contents of this module, constitutes a comprehensive analysis of the essential factors that are of significance to the communication process. This route further includes excursions into some of the specific theories on the impact of communications as well as into certain research aspects concerning advertising and strategic analysis. The following part contains a summary description of the procedures used in determining the target groups, the components of the Unique Communication Proposition (UCP) and the media goals. In addition, this unit will focus on the discussion of conceivable communication strategies, media planning and the instruments of marketing communications. By way of conclusion, a variety of possible media classes and media vehicles will be compared and evaluated.

2 The fundamental aspects of marketing communications

2.1 Introduction and learning objectives

The authors of this module will begin this first chapter by detailing their own understanding of communications. This will be followed by a brief explanation of the principal effects of marketing communications and an outline of the planning process used. In addition, a special focus will be placed on the question as to which corporate function and level is to assume responsibility for market communications.

On completing this chapter,

1. you will have learned that each impact made in marketing is the result of the sum total of all marketing functions.
2. you will be aware of those factors accountable for the impact achieved by marketing communications.
3. you will appreciate the systematic process which is pursued by efficient planning in marketing communications.
4. you will be familiar with the fundamental structure inherent in the overall communications concept to be found in a (business) organisation.
5. you will be able to identify the corporate function in charge of the organisation of marketing communications.

2.2 Communications and the marketing mix

The success of marketing communications cannot be measured simply in terms of the turnover achieved. Companies that wish to benefit from this experience in future need to know why they have succeeded or failed in the past. Each marketing effect achieved derives from the sum total of **all** marketing functions employed and from their multiple interaction with each other; in other words from the marketing mix.

Communications policies may also comprise personal selling, package design and brand techniques. However, these three items are traditionally associated with other corporate functions such as the distribution mix and

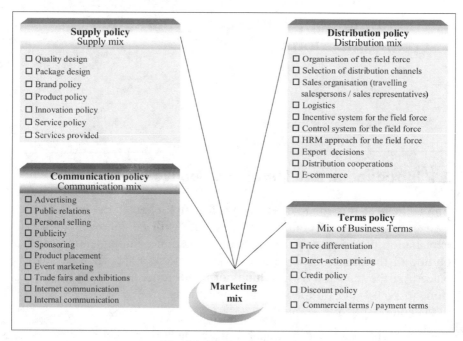

Fig. 2.1. The marketing mix

the product mix. Consequently, an organisation's complete communications mix consists of the tools presented in Fig. 2.1.

Seen from a realistic angle, communication policies can hardly ever be held directly responsible for purchasing behaviour. **Communications are to create attitudes**, which, on their part, are to **exert influence, generate change and to provide reasons for buyer wants and needs**. Moreover, they are designed to build up brand and product knowledge, to create brand and product preferences, and, maybe, even instil the desire to make a purchase.

However, although these factors are – without exception – psychological variables, they are, nonetheless, indispensable when it comes to generating actual purchasing behaviour.

The desire to purchase is further affected by the price and the package of a product, the placement of the latter in the sales outlets, the feeling of having purchased a quality product (which might lead to repeat purchases) and the measures taken by the competitors and the representatives of commerce. The combination of these factors is the prerequisite for the psychological effects to be achieved, i. e. for the communication message to be perceived and for the emotional excitement and appeal it may provoke. This result, however, presupposes that marketing communications have

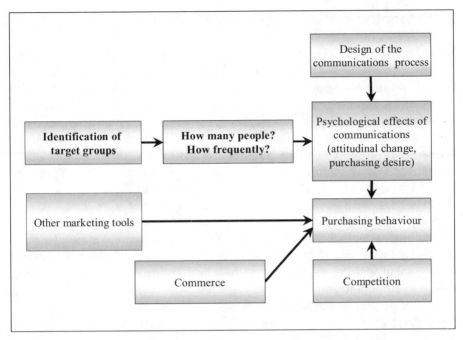

Fig. 2.2. Marketing and purchasing behaviour

reached the right group of persons in the first place, i. e. their target group or their targeted market segments.

It is the task of media planning to ensure that the above goals are met in a cost-efficient and result-oriented way. This involves decisions on the selection of the media class (e. g. television, magazines or papers) and on the media vehicles (e. g. *VOX, TV Times*). In addition, media planning devises the schedule of the planned insertions, determines the duration of the TV commercials (20 or 30 seconds) and the advertising space required in magazines (one full or 1/2 page). In all the above cases, these detailed communications objectives need to be embedded in the overall marketing goals.

Media planning warrants that target groups are reached and thus represents one of the pillars on which successful marketing is founded. By means of a systematic media analysis, media planning aims at conveying the messages of marketing communications to its selected target audiences.

Effective marketing communications depend on the media vehicles chosen, on the level of exposure that can be achieved by advertising and on the development of the individual tools of the communications mix. In addition, synergy effects may occur between the various advertising measures and between the other communication instruments employed (cf. Fig. 2.2).

2.3 Planning marketing communications

Management in practice does not always impress by the rationality of its actions. One reason for this may lie in the fact that managerial decisions are at times neither integrated nor well co-ordinated. Efficient marketing communications planning should pursue the route charted in Fig. 2.3. a route which essentially includes four stages, namely **analysis, planning, motivation** and **control.** This decisional process not only charts the **chronological sequence** of communications planning, but provides, in addition to that, a feedback system (similar to a closed control loop) elucidates the essential inter-correlated effects achieved in this vital area of marketing, that is to say, analysis, setting of goals, determination of strategies, budgets and measures as well as co-ordination and/or organisation and control.

The process, which is similar to the one pursued by marketing planning in total, also highlights the tasks/areas of responsibility of communications management and the steps taken as to who is to make the decisions with regard to communication policies.

Analysing the marketing opportunities of a business organisation has a sustained impact on the design and implementation of all its marketing measures. This also applies to marketing communications. This is the reason

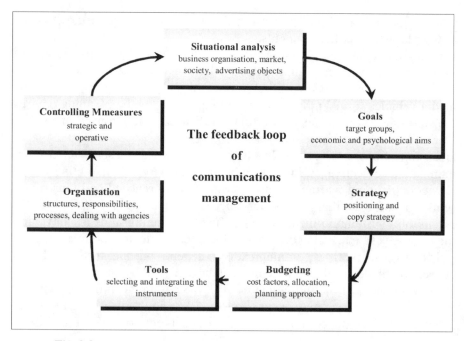

Fig. 2.3. Mapping the planning process in marketing communications

why companies should conduct a **situational analysis** not only of the external opportunities and risks that are relevant to their communications approach but also of their internal strengths and weaknesses (Stage 1). Methodologically, this analysis should be founded on the analyses of consumer behaviour, strengths and weaknesses, product life cycles, portfolios, positioning, competitive stance and critical success factors (CSFs). In addition, it should be based on environmental sustainability and random surveys as well as on scenario techniques. On the basis of the overall marketing goals and of the above situational analysis, the **communication goals** should be formulated (Stage 2). As a matter of principle, the economic objectives and the psychological, i.e. the communications aims, are formulated at this stage. The latter include the perception of specific messages, the former, for instance the revenues achieved from sales. As economic objectives are difficult to allocate to the individual marketing tools, they are of minor importance. Subsequently, the relevant target groups need to be identified and specified. Stage 3 concerns itself with the formulation of the **communication strategies** themselves. With a view to a company's competitive profile, they include the positioning it is to achieve as a result of the communication efforts, in other words, they seek the answer to the question as to how the potential customer is to perceive the business organisation in question (e.g. as "innovative" or "in"). Subsequently, in stage 4, the **communications budget** is determined and allocated to the individual communication tools involved. This comprises all financial resources which are available to marketing communications or which are an indispensable element thereof. Stage 5 is devoted to the design of the **communications mix**, that is to say, of the pool of the most effective and efficient marketing tools, including their appropriate step by step implementation. Stage 6 tackles the issue of **organisational implementation**, especially against the background of the integration and adjustment measures required. Assigning product management to a managerial level which supplements the system of corporate management functions is another essential feature of product-oriented marketing or business functions. The planning process is completed by applying **fundamental control measures** to marketing communications (stage 7), namely strategic and operative controlling. Strategic controlling assesses the strengths and weaknesses of the communication policies employed; operative controlling examines the impact of advertising campaigns.

2.4 Communications and the organisation of the marketing function

It could be argued that all organisational communication instruments, with the exception perhaps of Public relations (PR), should be assigned to a company's **marketing department.** In the area of consumer goods marketing, product managers usually assume responsibility for marketing communications. They are mostly in charge of marketing one specific product area in a company and their duties generally include communications. Public relations aim at representing the corporation as a whole in public as well as serving corporate interests in society. It therefore stands to reason that the communications function should be performed by the senior corporate management.

In most corporations, media planning relies on the support of **advertising and communications agencies**. The latter are service providers which advise the corporate marketing departments on all areas of communications. Their tasks comprise: consulting on communications in general, design proposals for first drafts, the production of advertising means and monitoring the genesis thereof, arranging the communication measures with the media,

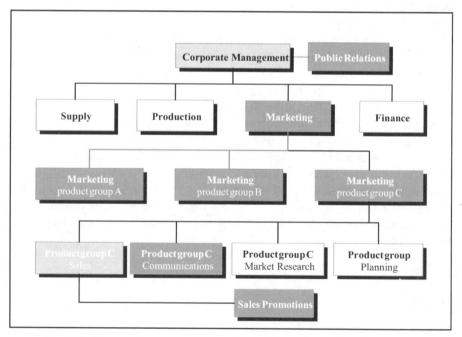

Fig. 2.4. Communications and the organisation of the marketing function

consulting on how to monitor the effectiveness of communications (e. g. by researching the advertising impact).

Some "**à la carte**" or "**specialist agencies**" focus on specific areas of marketing communications, e. g. advertising, sales promotions. The same applies to PR agencies (i. e. agencies for public relations) and media agencies which exclusively handle the booking of the advertising space and the commercials in the media. By contrast, there are **full-service agencies** that seek to cover the complete range of marketing communications including market research. As it may be cumbersome and costly to supervise a number of specialist agencies, companies increasingly tend to resort to these "down-the-line" service providers that either incorporated expert departments or collaborate with their subsidiaries in order to tackle the more specific tasks in marketing communications. In the wake of the internationalisation of the marketing function and, hence, of marketing communications, an increasing number of **internationally operating agencies** has come into existence.

Advertising agencies are usually managed by account executives who are in charge of serving individual clients and of administering the communications accounts of the latter. They are assisted by customer contact managers who, on the one hand, continually nurture the links forged with the marketing departments of the agency's clients and who assume control over the specialists within their agency such as the creative teams and market research groups.

Sales promotions represent a specific issue in marketing communications as, in practice, the sales function usually comes under the control of the head of sales for its close association with marketing. As this may impede the co-ordination of this task with the other communications tools, a closer alignment of sales with marketing and other communication tools is likely to be advantageous. On devising its promotional measures, the marketing department should, in return, take into account the specific needs of the sales department.

2.5 Multiple choice questions

Question 2/1: Which factors do successful marketing communications depend on?

(a)	the usage of commercials
(b)	the employment of all communications tools
(c)	the employment of all marketing tools
(d)	personal selling

Question 2/2: What do communications aim at?

(a)	a change in attitudes
(b)	offering reasons for certain needs
(c)	building up brand knowledge
(d)	a direct change in purchasing behaviour

Question 2/3: Which aspects are charted in the communications planning process?

(a)	feedback
(b)	integration
(c)	chronological order
(d)	purchasing behaviour

Question 2/4: What does the impact of marketing communications depend on?

(a)	the choice of media vehicles
(b)	the design of individual products
(c)	synergy effects between the various communication measures
(d)	the organisational structure

Question 2/5: Which are the tasks assigned to communications agencies?

(a)	sales consulting in general
(b)	producing the advertising means
(c)	arranging the communication measures with the media
(d)	monitoring the impact of communication measures

2.6 Case study

Medibeda Ltd. is a nationwide wholesaler who supplies medical materials and appliances to general practitioners to its domestic market.

Assignment

"Professionalize" communications for the above corporation. How can *Medibeda Ltd.* systematically plan its communications policy in future?

Solution

Medibeda Ltd. could pursue the following planning process in future:

By means of a **situational analysis,** *Medibeda Ltd.* should start by examining the external opportunities and risks which are relevant to its market communications. It should then subject its internal strengths and weaknesses to a thorough analysis. This SWOT analysis would give the company an understanding of its central communication problems such as tackling the consequences of the reform of the health system, which is currently being implemented by the German government, for its target groups.

Based on the analysis of its communication situation and in line with its marketing goals, the company will determine **communication goals**. In addition to the psychological aims (e. g. increasing the level of awareness of the company's name, building up a positive image), the company ought to formulate economic objectives with regard to its sales revenues and a higher percentage of business customers, for instance. In view of the increasing technological sophistication of the services offered by *Medibeda Ltd.*, its competitive advantage should be based on its positioning as consultation-oriented wholesaler. Target group planning should include identifying relevant professionals, such as general practitioners and hospitals. These groups

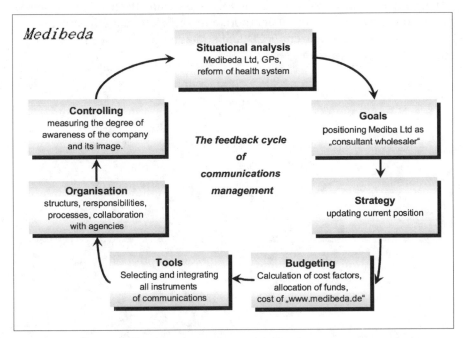

Fig. 2.5. Suggested solution: managing communications at *Medibeda Ltd.*

should be defined in terms of their size and their response to different pricing strategies.

The process of goal setting is followed by that the formulation of the **communications strategy**, that is to say that a communications focus will be developed for the company. Among other things, it is planned to update the corporate position of *Medibeda Ltd.* by adding a number of medical appliances to its current range medical items, most of which are disposables. This is to increase market awareness for the company's name and to create a positive image in the eyes of its target groups.

In line with the communications strategy, a **communications budget** will then be determined and allocated to the individual communication instruments. This budget will comprise all financial resources that are available to or required by marketing communications. Moreover, it will place special emphasis on improving and updating the company's Internet presence.

Planning the employment of the individual communication tools represents a focal area of the **communication mix.** The fact that these tools will have to be aligned with each other over an extended period of time (integrated marketing communications) will represent a special challenge. It will also be necessary, not least of all for financial reasons that *Medibeda Ltd.* should seek to benefit in this area from synergy effects with its marketing function.

Communications planning will be completed by **evaluating the success of marketing communications.** This involves assessing the level of awareness of the company's name and its corporate image. Potential adjustments that are to be made to the current goals and strategies and the measures undertaken will be result from this analysis.

3 The fundamental aspects of communications science

3.1 Introduction and expected learning outcomes

This chapter deals with the fundamental psychological aspects of communication insofar as these are relevant not only for the people employed in communications management but also for future senior executives.

On completing this chapter,

1. you will have learned how certain design features may affect communication processes,
2. you will understand how you and people other than yourself receive and process information and this might make your own behaviour a little more rational;
3. you will observe, in yourself and in other people, how learning can change behaviour in the long term,
4. and you will be in a position to understand by what means people can be and have been influenced.
5. In future, you might like to reserve your judgment when you observe other people's behaviour. Subsequently, this will enable you to respond to the behaviour of others in a more appropriate way.

3.2 Psychological structures

3.2.1 Perspectives, values and images

Human beings judge their environment on the grounds of their own multiple **expectations**, which, for their part, affect a person's response to his or her environment. The perception of the stimuli provided by the environment and the way in which these stimuli are processed, is greatly influenced by such human expectations. If the latter form part of the perception process, they are referred to as **perspectives** or **views.** People are never unbiased when determining their own angle on the world as their expectations impact on the point of view they will choose.

Perspectives affect human **perception**. On the other hand, there is always a chance that, over time a person's perception may change his or her expectations which express the sum total of this person's **affection** or disaffection towards a certain object.

A concept closely related to perception is that of "attitude", a term which, in specialist parlance, is (unfortunately) used synonymously with "perspective". However, whereas our perspectives only pertain to one specific part of human behaviour, i. e. to human perception or − more accurately − to the fallacies and snags involved therein, **attitudes** comprise the totality of human behaviour, e. g. a person's attitude towards health and consumption. In other words, the concept of "attitude" is more comprehensive than that of "perspective".

Attitudes include three components:

- a **cognitive** or "thinking" component which includes all human perspectives. **Cognitions** are all those knowledge items which human beings can mentally acquire; and **cognising**, therefore, signifies "the process of becoming mentally aware".
- an **evaluative** or "affective" component which not only includes objectively conceivable aspects but also those emotional aspects that guide human response to external stimuli.
- a **conative** or "doing" component which motivates our disposition for action; this component has close affinities with motivational psychology.

As human beings develop, they acquire their attitudes by learning. The more positive they expect the outcomes of their behaviour to be, the more quickly they perceive environmental signals, evaluate them positively and become willing to respond to them. The following chart outlines the major elements of the **attitude model** as it prevails in organisational theory.

The above model proposes a number of methods that are assumed to be able to **measure the individual components** of "attitude". Unfortunately, none of them are unproblematic as they rely on verbal statements in order to survey the partially emotional judgements made on stimuli. This approach requires, for instance, verbal **survey techniques,** such as questionnaires or interviews, whose subject often remains **hazy** to the interviewees who, to add insult to injury, never seem to be informed about the conclusions drawn from their statements. In a similar fashion, this applies to the surveys conducted on the nature of perception. Researchers who examine the impact of advertisements, for instance, will monitor the looks cast in a certain direction (monitoring the eye movements) and will measure the electric resistance of the skin. The disposition to take action cannot be surveyed verbally at all as people cannot make reliable statements on "what they would do if...". Notwithstanding certain reservations, one might nonetheless be able

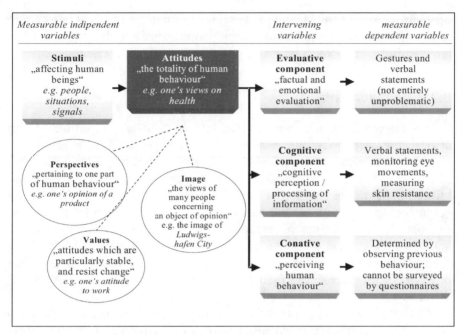

Fig. 3.1. The components of attitude

to conclude on a person's future disposition to take action by surveying current and past behaviours. The objections in this respect arise from the fact that we do not know to what extent future situations will be comparable to those which triggered off certain behaviours in the past.

In the last few years, the term "changing values", and, hence, "value" per se, have been traded in marketing theory – and practice – with increasing frequency. What are values? A person's cognitive system or system of attitudes is formed by a great number of inter-related attitudes. It consists of manifold knowledge items and the relationship that exists between them.

Some attitudes hold a highly focal position thereby exerting an influence on a large number of behaviours and knowledge components. Consequently, they are interrelated with many other attitudes and, as a result, may affect an entire area of a person's life. These central attitudes are defined as **values:** in other words values represent attitudes that are particularly sound and resist change. Cases in point are the personal relationships one develops with one's family, work or possibly one's natural environment. Values and attitudes can only be differentiated by their varying degree of intensity.

Another concept, namely that of "**image**", is also linked with that of perception. This term refers to the views many persons hold on one **object of**

opinion. The image of Mannheim City, for example, in the eyes of a certain group of persons, simply reflects these people's view of this town. Images are, therefore, viewpoints based on basic social entities.

3.2.2 Involvement

In social psychology, involvement translates as **"self-participation"**. It can also be considered to be one of the cognitive perceptions of human beings. It consists of two dimensions: **value-significance** and **value-utility**. Value-significance indicates the importance of a certain value for a person, value-utility the degree of usefulness that different objects may have in meeting certain value expectations. Based on this division, marketers tend to divide products into two distinctive categories, namely high involvement products and low involvement products. This is, however, a gross simplification as there are many nuances between the two extremes. Presumably, there is just one type of involvement in marketing practice whose level is more or less distinctive.

When it comes to high involvement products, consumers are prepared to engage in an **intensive intentional search for product or brand information,** whereas this demand for information declines substantially in the case of low involvement. In the latter instance, **learning** seems to occur accidentally as it depends on the attention aroused by strong stimuli.

The **brand loyalty** occasioned by a high level of involvement manifests itself more distinctly owing to the relatively stable perspective on which it is founded. In the case of low involvement, consumers automatically choose the brand they are used to. This behaviour, however, does not translate as loyalty.

Consumer relationships with a product are of essential importance for the overall level of buyer involvement. In addition, consumers experience different degrees of involvement with the various quality dimensions of a product and, as a result, need to be motivated in different ways. There are hardly any products whose quality dimensions are of no relevance at all to their users – who, in such a case, could be referred to as genuinely "low involved". Mineral water, for instance, might be considered to be a low-involvement product. However, there might exist market segments that are particularly highly involved with regard to the water's sodium bicarbonate content.

This is why the varying degrees of involvement on the part of certain consumer groups provide us with different approaches to **market segmentation** and, consequently, with different approaches when addressing consumers by means of marketing communications.

Behavioural dimensions	High involvement conditions	Low involvement conditions
Search for information	Consumers engage in an intentional search for product and brand information	Consumers restrict their search for product and brand information to a limited boundary.
Cognitive reactions	Consumenrs resist contradictory information and develop counter arguments	Consumers unintentionally absorb information that contradicts their views and hardly question it.
Information processing	Consumers process information in line with the model illustrating the „hierarchy of effects" model (awareness, attractiveness, attitude, trial purchase).	Consumers integrate information into a simplified perception and trial purchase sequence.
Change in attitude	Shifts in attitude are difficult to achieve.	Shifts in attitude occur more frequently but are not sustained.
Repetition of messages	In order to achieve the intended persuasion, the frequency of the advertising message alone is of less importance than the contents of the message.	The number of advertising messages may be entirely sufficient to cause persuasion.
Brand preference	Brand loyalty goes hand in hand with brand preference.	Routine behaviour is quite common; but this should not be mistaken for loyalty
Cognitive dissonance	Cognitive dissonance manifests itself more distinctly and is felt more strongly.	Cognitive dissonance is less often experienced and is easily dissolved.
Personal influence	Personal influence plays a major part. Other people are consulted as information providers.	Other people play hardly any part in the process of persuasion.

Fig 3.2. Different behaviours under high involvement and low involvement conditions

In this context, the following **persuasion processes** are conceivable. They are summed up, in a simplified manner, in the table below.

In the case of **low consumer involvement,** attractive TV commercials that are visually or acoustically appealing and have particularly benefited from a high number of insertions often result in high levels of brand or product awareness and, subsequently, in trial purchases. If these purchases are repeated, positive attitudes are gradually built up but this occurs due to force of habit rather than to actual conviction.

If consumers show **high involvement**, convictions and viewpoints are formed after the communication measures directed at them have been absorbed and processed by them. This occurs before the first purchase is actually made and may possibly have occasioned this purchase. In other words, in the case of high involvement persuasion may lead to a purchase, whereas in the case of low involvement persuasion results from the repeated purchases made.

The implementation of marketing strategies that are formed with a view to low consumer involvement therefore requires substantial advertising budgets as well as a reinforced emotional appeal that is strongly supported by visual images.

3.3 Psychological processes

3.3.1 Motivation

Motivation is understood as the internal energy that propels people to action. This drive is activated by a state of **tensions** that are **experienced as disagreeable** as they result from **unsatisfied needs.** Everyone has needs and each behaviour is result-oriented insofar as it aims at satisfying them. Motivation is a mental and hypothetical construct which is used to explain the relationship between current situations, the characteristic qualities of the persons involved and their ensuing actions.

The specialist literature in this field lists various types of motives whose high number seems to be somewhat arbitrary.

Cohen (1981: 201–210) offers a systematic model of possible motives:

First and foremost, **enrichment** and **ego-defence** are propagated as energizing motivational factors. The wish for ego-defence is engendered by the need to feel safe and secure, the wish for enrichment is caused by our striving for stimulation and satisfaction.

Secondly, *Cohen* contrasts rational with subconscious motives. **Rational motives** correspond with processes that can be mentally grasped, whereas **subliminal motives** cannot be described by the persons who experience them. One might therefore be tempted to dismiss them as irrational, although the label of "irrationality" would be highly dubious itself. Even behaviour which is not obvious to uninvolved outsiders may, nonetheless, seem rational to those that are directly concerned. Ego-defence motives, for instance, also play a role as a research issue in the theory of psychological reactance which focuses on the fact that people will always seek to defend their assumed or factually perceived freedom against imposed restrictions.

Thirdly, there are the postulates of **social motives** and **consistent motives;** the latter reflecting the quest for compliance and harmony. People's value systems need to be in harmony with their actions. The attempt to create such consistence between values and actions is elucidated, for instance, by the theory of cognitive dissonance.

Motives cannot be identified by observing behaviour, nor can they be measured directly. All one can do is draw conclusions as to possible behaviour from the current recognisable behaviour.

Motivation presupposes energy and excitement. These may be aimed at known pay-offs, e. g. if a product is purchased for its good price. The means chosen to reach this aim may vary as is the case when a certain brand or design is selected. We can conclude from this that target groups are often characterised by their specific **motivational structure** which, consequently, suggests a specific approach. Marketing measures exert an influence on the concrete determination of existing motives and/or needs. Buyers of jam, for instance, might be distinguished by the extent to which they would subscribe to purchasing motives such as Price

- Price and quality
- Consumption and taste
- Nature and health
- Refreshment
- No dominant orientation.

If this is so, advertising message and product packaging should make an appeal to one of these motives or to the complete set of motives. Moreover, the motivation behind the entire product and communication policy should be given due consideration. The above factors can also be employed to carry out a motivation-based (i. e. user-based) **market segmentation**.

Motives direct a person's **attention** towards different environmental stimuli. External stimuli (e. g. advertising messages) which appeal to already existing motives or motivations have a better chance of being perceived and processed than other stimuli.

Hawkins, Best und Coney (1992:304) distinguish between **overt** (i. e. manifest) and **covert** (i. e. latent or hidden) motives. The people concerned are fully aware of their **overt motives** and they would, therefore, not hesitate to make statements about them in interviews. **Covert motives** are often

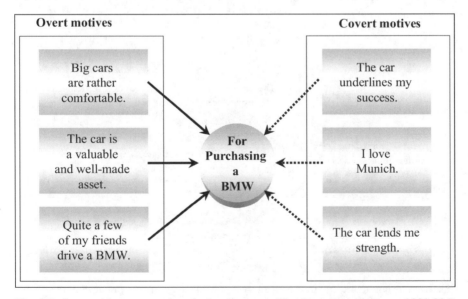

Fig. 3.3. Overt and covert motives for buying a car *(Hawkins, Best & Coney,* 1992:304)

concealed and even the persons involved cannot make clear statements on them in interviews. Nonetheless, it is of crucial importance that marketing communications should seek to address the latter motives in order to affect buying behaviour. Targeting latent motives can even be more effective than tackling overt ones. This is particularly true, if, by addressing these latent motives, independent product positioning becomes possible.

3.3.2 Emotions

Hardly any psychological concept has been so extensively covered as that of "emotions". According to *Scherer* (1990), emotions consist of five components which all perform independent functions (which are indicated in brackets).

- cognitive component (evaluation of stimuli)
- neuro-physiological component (systems control)
- motivational component (engendering the disposition to act)
- expressive component (communication)
- emotional component (reflection and control)

Characteristic features of emotions Examples

Inner excitement activation	„Joy" can possess the same degree of intensity as the more (complex) feeling of „cosiness". This signifies that both emotions are equally strong.
Direction taken, e. g. „likes" and dislikes" agreeable or disagreeable	The direction taken by both emotions is the same: They are both experienced as positive and agreeable.
Quality **Perception** of one's own emotional arousal: a cognitive process which is - more or less - apparent	*It is their quality that distinguishes the two emotions:* **joy** is associated with happiness, brightness, laughter **cosiness** is associated with safety, warmth, closeness
Awareness occurs at a more or less conscious Level. There may be visualisation but no verbal awareness.	**Verbal methods** assess the linguistic statements people make regarding their emotions. **Non-verbal methods** record spontaneous emotional impressions, e. g. during the presentation of advertisements.

Fig. 3.4. The landmarks of emotional analysis (abridged from *Kroeber-Riel & Weinberg*, 2003:105)

The **cognitive component** performs the positive or negative evaluation of external stimuli. The processing of information, as well as of associations, plays a major part in this context. The **neuro-physiological component** concerns itself with the excitement provoked by external stimuli, an excitement which for its part determines emotional states. The activation concept which has been frequently documented in marketing theory (e. g. *Kroeber-Riel & Weinberg,* 2003:58–100) also falls into this category. Emotional states often provoke a **disposition to act**. This explains the close relationship between motivation and emotions. The **expressive component**, which surveys reactions that can be observed externally, is of paramount importance. Many emotional reactions can be "read" by closely observing **facial expressions**. In some way, there is always a reference to **sensations** when emotions come into play. The principles for the classification of sensations were first suggested by *Wundt* (1905) who put forth the following five dimensions: desire/reluctance, arousal/satisfaction as well as tension/release. This, however, raises the question to what extent sensations are an independent component of human behaviour, as these emotional dimensions can also be explained by using exclusively cognitive criteria.

Izard (1994) by-passes the problem of having to define emotions against other areas of human behaviour by labelling certain **behavioural categories** as emotions, namely:

- interest
- joy
- surprise, shock
- sorrow, pain, grievance and depression
- fury, revulsion, disdain
- fear and other forms of anxiety
- shame and timidity
- the pangs of guilt, of conscience and moral convictions

Emotions such as joy, interest and surprise that are experienced as positive and agreeable are of general relevance to marketing.

Interest might be the most common of positive emotions: An object that evokes our interest catches and holds our eye. "As long as an interested person's eyes rest on an object, this person is captivated and fascinated by it." (*Izard,* 1994: 245). Moreover, eye fixation can trigger off sensations on a **neurological level**, that is to say it can increase the activity of the central nervous system.

In this case, stimuli are transmitted by activating the chains in the neural circuit. Stimuli are carried forward from neuron to neuron by impulses. From a neurological perspective, interest can be described as an increase in the frequency of excitatory impulses per unit of time; in other words neurons stimulate themselves more frequently and more intensively. This signifies that, if a person observes an object of genuine interest over a period of time, the visual stimulus conveyed to the brain is more frequent than that of a person who is only slightly interested in the same object over the same period of time. The more intensive the perception, the better the performance that can be expected in the areas of memory and learning.

Interest can be aroused by affective stimuli and by factual pieces of information, such as personal involvement, that are considered essential. But in many areas of consumption, **factual** and **functional information** is either of little relevance or does not permit independent communication. This is why it is more important to cast the act of consumption in the role of an affective experience. This is especially vital where products are technologically interchangeable. Such **experiential appeal** is appreciated even more if it is reinforced by humour, eroticism, pictures and music. The important role of emotional design is a now a conventional wisdom in the marketing of consumer goods. However, the fact that emotionally-designed marketing measures are of equal importance to the capital goods market (which is now more frequently referred to as "business to business market") has not been accepted to the same extent (*Raab & Unger*, 2005:236).

3.3.3 Social perception

The theory of social learning is founded on the concept of "attitude". Its central message is that there are no passive recipients of information who merely receive messages and respond to them. **Whatever human beings perceive is selected and evaluated.** Moreover, there is no "perception per se" as each perception is a product of a series of prevailing **assumptions on reality,** e. g. on one's co-workers, one's superiors or one's competitors. This is to say that perception is founded on the hypothesis of the percipient. On the one hand, the resulting perception derives from these assumptions and the signals emitted out from a person's environment. This turns the existing cognitive structure of individuals into an essential factor which impacts on their perception. However, this does not signify that the prevailing assumptions and hypotheses are necessarily more important than the information that is being received. Both factors influence each other. We speak of **"social cognition"**, as it is guided to a high degree by our relationships with other people. This not only refers to physical items but also to the relationships amongst people. Beliefs engender perception and perceptions generate beliefs (*Irle*, 1975:85).

At its core, the theory of social cognition centres on the following three statements made by *Lilli* and *Frey* (1993:56).

1. "The stronger our assumptions, the more likely they are to be activated". This signifies that human beings tend to (mis)take their most likely occurrences, their strongest assumptions and their most ardent beliefs for something they have actually perceived.
2. "The stronger our assumptions, the less frequently they need to be stimulated by the type of supportive information necessary to confirm them". This indicates that people require only little information in order to perceive what they believe in fervently, what they strongly suppose will happen and what they feel is most likely to happen.
3. "The stronger our assumptions, the more often they need to be activated by the kind of contradictory information which is necessary to prove them wrong." This third hypothesis is the counterpart of the second one. It contends that people actually need strong assumptions to contradict a previously received piece of information in order to be able to accept that they were wrong in strongly believing what they did or what they thought was bound to happen.

The third hypothesis is diametrically opposed to the second one. It maintains that any piece of information which contradicts people's assumptions needs to be very strong if it is to succeed in convincing them otherwise.

Only a few pieces of information suffice if we seek approval for our behaviour. However, relatively speaking, quite a few more are needed to enable us to admit to an error. **We tend to perceive of the world in a way which justifies our actions.**

But what exactly causes a hypothesis to be "strong"? What makes us believe something intensively, make serious assumptions about it or think it likely to happen? A strong hypothesis is produced under four conditions which complement each other:

The more often we believe to have experienced confirmation of it in the past, the stronger our hypothesis will be. The more frequently people believe that they have experienced a phenomenon, the more likely they are to believe that it is true. This is not altogether implausible. The snag is that the first perception may already have been fallacious and may have influenced the following ones. We may have been started from a single perspective (albeit an inappropriate one) and we may repeatedly have succumbed to the same **perceptual error**. Facing the facts, we have to concede that even a frequently repeated (seeming) confirmation of a hypothesis cannot assert its correctness. The fewer **alternative options** we have, the stronger the hypothesis. If a small number of people can see only one solution to a problem, all pieces of information that confirm this

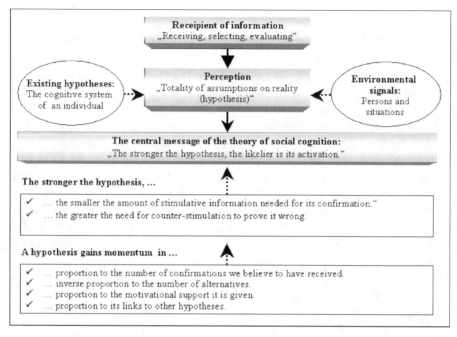

Fig. 3.5. The theory of social perception and its fundamental statements

solution will weigh more heavily than others that might put /call this (one possible) solution into question. This mechanism in itself should be a reason for us to consider as many options as possible when tackling a problem – if these options are economically viable.

The more emotional support a hypothesis receives, the more it gains momentum. In a nutshell, the more people desire something and the more other people support this, the more strongly it will be believed.

The more a hypothesis interacts with other hypotheses, the stronger it is. A person's *weltbild* can be described as a hypothetical system (i. e. of assumptions made on reality). The individual elements of this system (here: the hypotheses) expose a great number of relationships that differ in intensity. **We conclude from this that the more a hypothesis interacts with others, the stronger it is.** Consequently, if one realises that an error has been committed, one might have to adjust some features of one's *weltbild*. This signifies that, in particular, this part of our life that is of such importance to us is dominated by the mechanisms dealt with by the very hypotheses elucidated by the theory of social cognition.

It is difficult to escape from the mechanisms described in the above theory. However, **we can learn to beware of our own perceptions, to continuously investigate our fallacies** and to always presuppose that things could be different from what we seem to have observed at first sight. Senior executives, who subscribe to this, are sensitised to their environment. He who believes that he has to be power coercive, or – even worse – that he hardly ever errs, is simply naive. It is much more realistic to concede that human beings are capable of committing errors. We should even admit that as our decisions can never be perfect but always makeshift, the best we can achieve is to make as few mistakes as possible.

3.3.4 Cognitive dissonance

The theory of **cognitive dissonance** (Festinger, 1957; Irle, 1991, Frey & Gaska, 1993) investigates the way in which people handle the contradictions they perceive. It elucidates, in particular, how, after experiencing cognitive dissonance, they seek to re-establish a state of cognitive balance.

According to Festinger's original publication in 1957, which is still of the highest significance today, cognitive dissonance occurs when people receive **statements** that seem to **contradict** their previously performed actions. On realising that their actions also imply negative aspects, these people may easily experience a feeling of regret shortly after the action (which might have been a purchase). This feeling is referred to by *Festinger* as "post-decisional regret". In order to justify their action with hindsight and to avoid any information that might cast doubts on it, they intensify their search for additional information. Against this background, the perception of information might well be distorted in order to fit the purpose of post-decisional justification.

We can therefore roughly assume that the procurement and the adoption of information are geared towards **justifying** a person's previously committed actions **with hindsight**.

Irle (1975:310–346; 1991) extends the meaning of this term to include pre-decisional situations. People **select and distort information** not only to indulge in post-decisional justifications, they perceive, seek and interpret information from a "conditioned" viewpoint which seems to replace their "neutral" perception as soon as the decision has been announced or mentally conceived. According to *Irle*, the intensity of cognitive dissonance, and, hence, of the motivation to reduce it, depends on the degree of certainty that was experienced by the persons involved before they were exposed to dissonant information that challenged their assumptions.

Will the persons in question subsequently change their original assumptions (i. e. decisions) or will they reject information that risks entailing further dissonance? Will any new information they receive be distorted, inappropriately interpreted or ignored altogether? Will it be played down as

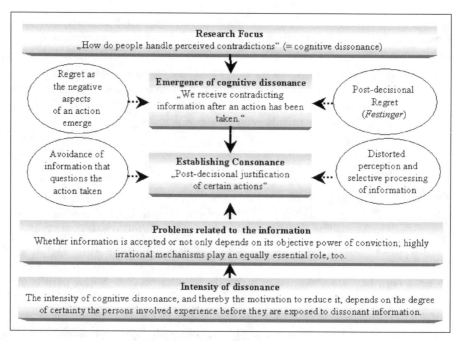

Fig. 3.6. The theory of cognitive dissonance

irrelevant? All these possibilities depend on the level of resistance of the cognitions at play in this context (e. g. original assumption, new information and/or the implied relation between the former and the latter).

We may safely assume – although this may not amount to a profound scientific analysis – which people tend to opt for the most convenient alternative. Can they admit to their errors without losing face? Can the most recent piece of information be considered reliable, or is it unfounded or even flawed? Is it easy to deny the link between the previous and the current situation ("We are facing a completely different situation here."). According to the research conducted on cognitive dissonance, it is important for marketers to realise that – in the above cognitive processes – the objectivity of a perceived piece of information may be (far) less accountable for the adoption of information than highly irrational mechanisms.

People who work in the medical profession can probably easily imagine a situation in which an expert has diagnosed an illness, which

1. expresses exclusively his or her own conviction,
2. is meant to be a statement made with regard to a number of other experts who might be more or less competent, or
3. is a follow-up diagnosis based on previous measures taken that have either had no consequences or severe consequences for the patient.

How will a person react to information which clearly contradicts his or her own diagnosis?

Moreover, we ought to consider that this information could be offered by other experts – who might be more or less competent – and that it might apply – or may not apply – to the case in question.

Let us further suppose that employees judge a member of staff's pay cheque and performance from the point of view of cognitive dissonance. A salary level which is thought to be too high, compared to the perceived low level of performance, would cause stress without automatically improving the person's performance. An income which is too low, would – according to the same theory – cause the level of performance to be corrected downwards to match the respective income bracket. This would cause **consonance** while reducing dissonance.

3.3.5 Psychological reactance

People are clearly intent on retaining and defending the behavioural manoeuvring space they regard as their own (i. e. their freedom) and which they feel is their due. And they will seek to reconquer it, if need be. Each factual, assumed or expected restriction of this subjectively enjoyed freedom – each threat to it – will provoke internal tensions and will motivate people to **reduce these tensions** and to re-establish their freedom by defending or reconquer it. This phenomenon is known as **psychological reactance** (*Brehm*, 1966). The underlying theory is founded on the threat to personal freedom or the elimination thereof. This theory proposes three possible threats to freedom or ways to eliminate it:

- Social influence, i. e. each form of communication: Behaviour can be suppressed, restricted, marginalized, ordained or recommended in a more or less strict fashion. Even unduly strong recommendations or unduly harsh orders with regard to a certain type of behaviour would be seen as a restriction of personal freedom as they would simultaneously exclude alternative options.
- Environmental forces: certain types of behaviour are ruled out or impeded by the physical environment. A high price, be it monetary or non-monetary, for instance, that has to be paid, could be seen as an attempt at restricting freedom.
- A person's own behaviour, i. e. an individual decision in favour of or against other alternatives: Each decision, even if it is we who have taken it, entails a restriction of our decisional leeway. This is why decisional prevarications can be explained, to a certain extent, in terms of anticipated reactance.

It appears to be an obvious conclusion that exerting active leadership on one's staff can cause reactance, especially in terms of social influence. However, what exactly determines the degree of resistance shown, i. e. the extents to which people are motivated to regain their freedom? We can therefore assume that reactance can be occasioned by a great number of communication measures employed in marketing, i. e. by all statements which may be perceived as restrictive in terms of personal freedom.

For reactance to occur, it is evidently indispensable that the persons involved need to feel that they enjoy decisional discretion. If this is the case, the **degree of reactance** can be measured in terms of the three following conditions:

- the importance of the freedom at risk for the person concerned
- the discretional power that the same person believes to possess. If people are uncertain about their decisions, they are unlikely to experience reactance when confronted with certain alternatives. On the contrary, they are likely to appreciate coercive influences as decisional guidelines.
- the perceived similarity of what is seen as an alternative. This depends in many ways on each person's competence. People who rate themselves as highly competent will be more inclined to spot (imagined) differences between existing alternatives than those who are aware of their deficiencies in this area. If the alternatives are believed to be similar, any attempt at influencing the decision to be taken will be welcomed as a supportive expedient rather than as an attempt to curtail one's personal freedom.

What kind of **reactions** on the part of the persons concerned may result from their perceived restriction of freedom and from psychological reactance?

1. Re-establishing personal freedom by taking action that seems appropriate In this case, people behave in the way they originally intended in spite of the risks this may involve. This is without any doubt, the most efficient way of re-establishing their jeopardized or eliminated freedom. However, the question arises as to whether the authority that reduces freedom within an organisation has the power to punish behaviour and to what extent it is allowed to exert this power. If administrative rules and regulations restrict an employee's freedom in an office by extending an employee's working hours, for instance, he might make up for this by increasing the number of his smokes thereby boosting the level of his individual inactivity (while meeting the company's requirement of being physically present). Moreover, people might seek to transfer their reduced freedom to other areas, e. g. by performing domestic tasks at their place of work.

2. Changes in attitude which counteract those forces that entail reactance
   Managers whose leadership style restricts the freedom experienced by
   their staff, for instance, will encounter problems on implementing programmes that require a higher level of identification with the organisation, more personal initiative etc. In the same way, product-related attitudes can be turned into their exact opposite.
3. Aggression, as an extreme form of changes in attitude and attractiveness.

It seems obvious that people should be inclined to respond to an authority that is curtailing their freedom in a hostile manner.

However, it should be pointed out that reactance effects have nothing to
do with the fact as to whether the measures restricting freedom are seen as
legitimate or illegitimate. Even restrictive measures that are felt to be legitimate may entail reactance.

Evidently, this has consequences for **human resource policies**: people
management, which goes hand in hand with perceived freedom restrictions,
is bound to be less successful than a management approach that can do
without these restrictions. This is not only caused by the fact that a **leadership style** which is accompanied by a high degree of freedom restriction
devalues and incapacitates the employees' personality. Those who restrict

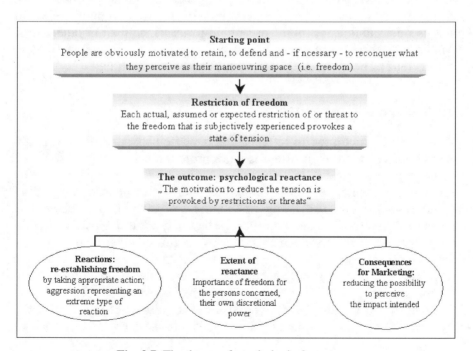

Fig. 3.7. The theory of psychological reactance

freedom are confronted by more than the effects of reactance as they re-quire **resources to carry out these freedom restrictions**. Restrictions of freedom that are inevitable can be justified and are – as a result – usually accepted. Such factual constraints may occur in the service sector but it also applies to the supply of goods. Empirical evidence has repeatedly been found for the fact that if an intention to exert influence manifests itself **directly**, each attempt to do so entails reactance. With regard to the **effect produced by advertisements** one may therefore assume that the more strongly such intentions make themselves felt, the more quickly they will meet with reactance.

This is why, on designing advertisements, it is advisable to ensure that the perceived intention to influence the target audience should be concealed as much as possible. This can be achieved by emotionally appealing images and by giving due consideration to the phenomenon of reactance when composing and phrasing the message of the copy. However, gambling argumentatively with the discretional powers of the consumers may turn out to be a double-edged sword: hinting at the buyers' decisional leeway may sensitise them for the intentions revealed in the advertisement and, consequently, and trigger off some reactance.

However, in the case of advertisements, consumers have become used to the more or less manifest intention to influence them and have learned to accept this to a grater or lesser extent. Influence exerted in public relations and product publicity is more susceptible to reactance than in other areas. And indeed, there is empirical evidence for the fact that in such cases consumers tend to be more motivated to display reactance effects.

3.3.6 Cognitive response

If messages, which seek to influence targeted persons, are intensively absorbed on reception, their effect is more profound and sustains itself over a longer period of time. In this process, a major part is often played by spontaneous mental reactions which are, more often than not, **unstructured responses**. In psychology, the latter are referred to as "cognitive responses" (Petty & Cacioppo, 1986). They may be thoughts that are directly related to the message that has just been perceived and they may provoke positive as well as negative reactions. On the other hand, cognitive responses can be thoughts that possess no logical factual relation at all to the message received but will still influence its impact.

All in all, it is the **multi-facetted nature of cognitive activities** which determines the effect of communications. The more these cognitive responses are felt to be agreeable and affirmative when perceived, the more positive their effect. The more intensively the recipients focus on the message while it is being communicated, the longer and deeper will be its impact on them.

However, communication effects do not only result from absorbing the stimuli being offered but also from calling up information stored in the memory. **Sustainable and stable communication effects** can only be achieved by active and intensive information processing. If this does not occur, only short-term results can be produced, such as change in a person's momentary perspective.

The first path leading to this goal is referred to as the **central route to persuasion;** the second one, which is typical of marketing communications and especially of communications in advertising, is known as the **peripheral route to persuasion.** This raises the question as to which factors are responsible for either route, a question which *Petty & Cacioppo* (1986) seek to answer by proposing the "Elaboration Likelihood Model" (ELM) outlined in the following:

Active and intensive processing of information presupposes that the percipient of the messages is **capable of processing information and motivated to do so**. As far as individual capability is concerned, we can justly assume that most people are mentally capable of absorbing advertised messages. Some advertising vehicles, however, risk sidetracking the viewers' attention during the presentation of the advertisements. In addition, there is no possibility to immediately repeat the message to the recipients and, for them, no possibility to focus on the message in great detail. This applies essentially to radio and TV broadcasts, in other words, to consumer markets. By contrast, the users of print(ed) media can decide for themselves when and how long they deal with the contents of the message. Motivation is largely guided by the significance which the message communicated has for its percipients. However, even if the latter take a profound interest in the product presented, one **cannot** assume that they are equally interested in the advertising message. This level of interest seems to be constantly **overstated** by advertising practitioners. Empirical communications research indicates that even if the percipients are perfectly interested, they may only glance briefly at the advertisements, may prefer pictorial elements to verbal statements and emotionally appealing pictures to matter-of-fact ones. Moreover, they may take in the contents of the copy in a cursory fashion.

This elucidates the first stage of "ELM". In other words, it seeks to explain under which conditions active and intensive processing of information is possible. Only on concluding this stage is a genuine and sustainable attitudinal change possible. If these conditions cannot be met, shifts in attitude and desire can nonetheless be affected. However, they are short-lived and only last as long as the percipients can remember the advertising message or are aware of it in any other way. This necessitates that targeted groups should be permanently exposed to communicative measures. As advertising effects are short-lived and unstable by their very nature, a competitor's advertisements could be quick to suppress one's own advertising message or interfere with its effects. If influence is exerted peripherally, follow-up communication messages need to be delivered speedily enough for the first message to still be remembered, i. e. subsequent messages back up previous ones. If the first message has ceased to be mentally available, influence cannot be exerted any longer; the second message might therefore have "to start from scratch".

The second stage of ELM focuses on the quality of information processing, that is to say, it tackles the "cognitive responses" which are triggered off during the influencing phase of the communication process. At this stage, it is important that percipients should actively produce thoughts or partially reproduce these from their memory. Effects always result from the impressions currently acting on the percipients and from what their current level of awareness. This state of affairs is further influenced by the fact that the recipients of communication messages tend to recall, first and foremost, those items of information from their memory which they consider to be related to the particular issue at hand. The totality of multitudinous reactions that can

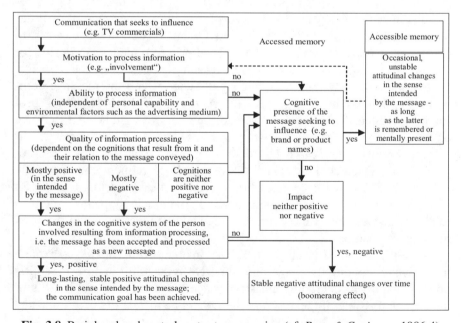

Fig. 3.8. Peripheral and central routes to persuasion (cf. *Petty & Cacioppo*, 1986:4)

occur in the wake of spontaneous impacts or as an act of remembrance accounts for the **intensity of the communication impact.** In this context, even associations that are neither logically nor rationally related to the object of influence are of relevance. The **direction taken by persuasion** is determined by the emotional and cognitive values attributed to the sensations experienced during perception. If neutral sensations prevail on the whole or if sensations, which are appreciated as positive, set off those rated as negative, the attitude change achieved will be an unstable one that has been brought about by peripheral means.

However, if **positive** sensations (in the sense intended by the message) prevail during the impact of the communication message, an enduring shift in attitude is possible as it is in line with the message conveyed. If negative thoughts predominate, an enduring shift in attitude may occur which not only goes against what was originally intended but actually moves in the opposite direction. This is known as **"boomerang effect" or "negative attitude change"**.

Whether an impact is actually made as a result of the prevailing intensive and positive "cognitive responses" depends on the **entire cognitive system** of the targeted person. This phenomenon links up the above context with the previously discussed theory of cognitive dissonance which, in principle, maintains that human beings absorb items of information and process them accordingly if these items happen to match their self-perception and square with the image they have formed of themselves. We all tend to deny, reinterpret or even perceive inaccurately those pieces of information that do not fit in with this concept. For this reason it is possible that people are unwilling to change their attitudes in accordance with a message received as the latter does to match their concept of self-perception. This signifies that, in spite of the influence we intend our communication measures to exert, we should always take into account the existing values, goals and prejudgments of the recipients of our message as well as their biased views and prejudices.

Let us now sum up ELM: There are two routes to persuasion, a central one and a peripheral one. Under certain circumstances, the central route will bring about a sustained and sound change in a person's attitude whereas the peripheral one will cause no more than an unstable attitude change provided that the message perceived is still fresh in this person's mind. Certain essential factors of persuasion may be media-specific or depend on the focus audiences but the most important prerequisites concerning the central route to persuasion are the capability to process information and the motivation to perform this process actively and intensively. The next stage constitutes the positive, negative or neutral mental processing of the information during its presentation. When negative and neutral responses are equally intensive or when neutral responses predominate, changes in attitude are short-lived and remain unstable.

When positive or negative "cognitive responses" dominate, enduring attitude changes can be achieved if the persons concerned are prepared to allow this to happen. The more they consider the newly acquired attitude as part of their self and their mental universe, the more they are willing to change their attitudes as a result of the impact created by the message they received.

The cognitive response chart shows that the peripheral route to persuasion continually risks having no or no lasting impact. By contrast, the central route may provoke boomerang effects which can virtually not occur in the case of peripheral persuasion as there is no readiness to focus intensively on the argumentation of the message.

A sustained and enduring communication effect is only possible if all the above conditions are met, namely, motivation, capability and a clear predominance of positive sensations during the act of perception which are supported (shortly after) by a person's willingness to change his or her attitude.

Let us now consider some of the consequences this may have for **marketing communications**. We have already explained that, faced with assumedly unreceptive audiences in the area of marketing communications, a series of short-term communication activities is more likely to achieve a long-term persuasive impact. This also applies to the classic type of advertisements placed in specialist magazines. When marketing capital goods, there is the additional opportunity of using personal selling methods in order to achieve a more intensive and hence more long-term persuasion impact. This attempt will be met with success if the personal selling approach has been aligned with the design and the contents of other forms of marketing communications.

If sales negotiations are associated with previous product experiences or advertising messages, the persuasion impact can be either enhanced or impeded. And if sales negotiations are designed accordingly, they can succeed in increasing the associations made on the grounds of the message received from advertisements even if these were only perused in a cursory fashion before the sales talks.

The cognitive response concept highlights the necessity to create **sustainable long-term communication** concepts. If the design of the advertisements is subject to frequent changes, especially with a view to the communication tools employed, the percipients will find it hard, if not impossible, to produce the above-mentioned associations, i. e. the cognitive links that are formed between the various messages. This raises the question as to whether a constant repetition of messages will not cause redundancy no matter what communication tool is used. This risk is of particular relevance

The impact of communication

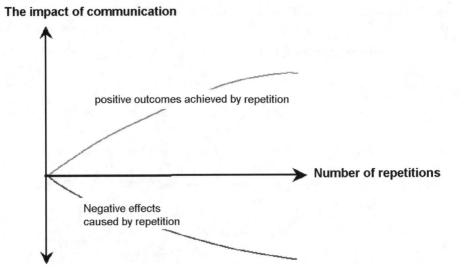

Fig. 3.9. Positive (cf. *Zajonc*, 1968:1pp) and negative learning outcomes (cf. *Berlyne*, 1970:279pp) resulting from repetition

if the design of the messages frequently refers back to previous examples. However, we know that we absorb items well-known to us more quickly than new or unknown ones and the design of communication strategies ought to take this into account. This also would constitute a plausible justification of long-term strategic planning.

As early as 1968, *Zajonc* was able to prove such a **positive learning effect** in his experiments. The more frequently the stimuli are presented, the more favourable is their perception. The related learning curve is charted in Fig. 3.9.

However, one cannot deny that constant repetition will entail negative outcomes, such as redundancy and boredom. This, too, was proved by *Berlyne* (1970) in his communications experiments (cf. Fig. 3.10).

It is interesting to note that there is empirical evidence for both effects even though they are diametrically opposed. This has led *Berlyne* to develop his "two-factor theory of communications" which contends that the impact of communication strategies is influenced by positive learning outcomes and by negative redundancy effects, the bottom line of this being that communication strategies sum up the net effect of both postulates.

If this is the case, it is important that one should benefit from the positive learning effect while avoiding the negative one in order to edge as closely to the upper learning curve as possible.

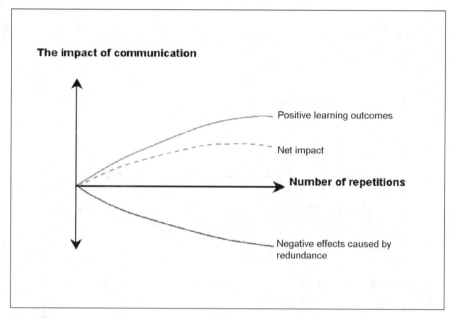

Fig. 3.10. Communication outcomes seen as the net effect between learning and redundancy.

This goal can be reached by retaining the same strategy for a longer period of time while constantly varying its details. As with a genuinely good jazz number, the fine art of marketing communications thrives on this combination of the recurring **variations** of one **consistent theme** which, subsequently, continues to arouse the audience's interest. These variations can be performed with all individual communication tools. We therefore require strong elements that are sustainable over time but allow the variations of their particular details. The best-known and most consistent concept in the sense outlined above can be found in the sector of consumer goods, more precisely in the communication strategy of "Marlboro" cigarettes. This brand has been communicated uniformly over thirty years and has in the course of time gained market leadership. Similar phenomena have been observed with a large variety of other consumer brands. Especially in the capital goods sector, where communication budgets tend to be limited than this would be the case with consumer goods, it is vital that all communication tools be aligned before being employed as this will create synergy effects on a large scale. Viewed from a holistic psychological perspective, this translates as: "The total amounts to more than the sum of its parts".

3.4 Multiple choice questions

Question 3/1: Which of the following statements on "attitudes" are correct?

(a)	"Cognition" refers to everything that human beings can mentally perceive.
(b)	Measuring attitude is unproblematic.
(c)	Values reflect change resistant attitudes.
(d)	Attitudes represent "the views held by a number of people" on one particular issue.

Question 3/2: Which are the features that characterise the condition of "high involvement"?

(a)	Consumers actively seek information on products and brands.
b)	Consumers react to information which conflicts with their own views in a passive way.
(c)	It is difficult to achieve changes in one's perceived opinion.
(d)	The number of advertising messages itself is enough to have an impact on the consumer.

Question 3/3: Which of the following statements on "motivation" are correct.

(a)	Motives are observable behaviour. They can be identified and measured.
(b)	Motives of which a person is fully aware are referred to as "overt motives".
(c)	In marketing communications it is less important to stimulate a person's covert motives.
(d)	Advertising statements which stimulate existing motives are more likely to be actively perceived and processed than other stimuli.

Question 3/4: What exactly is meant by the term "strong hypothesis"?

(a)	an assumption which has often been taken as confirmed.
(b)	an assumption for which we have alternatives.
(c)	an assumption which receives intensive emotional support.
(d)	an assumption which has no connection to other hypotheses.

Question 3/5: Which statements derive from the theory of cognitive dissonance?

(a)	Accepting the negative aspects of their actions, people experience a feeling of regret shortly before taking action.
(b)	In a post-decisional situation, human beings process information in a distorted and selective fashion in order to justify the decisions taken.
(c)	The strength of cognitive dissonance depends on the degree of assertion experienced by the person in question.
(d)	Information acceptance depends on its objective strength of conviction.

3.5 Case study

You are the Marketing Manager of *Cosmetics plc*, a corporation that produces toiletries and skin care articles. You have been requested to integrate the most essential research findings concerning the theory of "cognitive

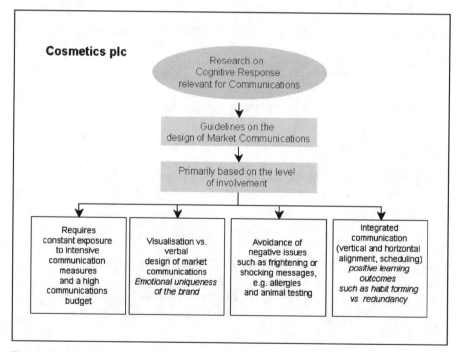

Fig. 3.11. Solution chart: Applying the research findings on cognitive response to *Cosmetics plc*.

response" into the design of your company's market communication scheme.

Solution

1. The research work conducted on "cognitive response" has provided us with the specific aspects of "low" and "high" consumer involvement and of its impact on the **design of market communication concepts** (*Raab & Unger*, 2005:102). These findings indicate that, under high involvement conditions, *Cosmetics plc* can achieve sound results provided that the associations created are sufficiently intensive. However, the company should bear in mind that the above conditions apply to a limited number a specific articles only, such as sun lotion.

2. In the case of "low involvement" it is vital for Cosmetics plc to constantly present themselves to their target groups at a high level of frequency. The enduring and intensive impact of communication measures represents a vital success factor. Discontinuation of the advertising measures is not advisable. This obviously signifies that "low involvement" requires a relatively high budget for marketing communications. On the other hand, a low level of consumer involvement implies a low degree of willingness to assess the contents of the advertisements in a critical fashion.

3. The research on cognitive response has confirmed that, in cases in which there is little willingness to process advertising messages, **pictorial representations** which produce an affective response promise to exert a higher degree of influence in market communication than any **verbal messages.** In our age of information overload, pictures seem to be received more readily than comprehensive verbal messages even though it is more difficult to predict how pictures are interpreted. With regard to *Cosmetics plc* one can therefore conclude that – in the case of low involvement – creating **emotional brand uniqueness** is more important than the communication of complex quality patterns.

4. The research on cognitive response has also proved that it is important to **avoid negative features** (e. g. frightening messages, shocking pictures) although this postulate is not unanimously shared by all marketing practitioners. This would signify that *Cosmetics plc* need to take a close look at issues such as allergies and animal testing. Product awareness and a favourable product attitude are important for the successful positioning of a brand. However, the popular marketing wisdom, which claims that "any news is good news" is not shared by those responsible for marketing communications at *Cosmetics plc*. In line with cognitive response research, the corporation holds that mental associations with brands and items of market communication need to be positive.

5. As the various target groups of *Cosmetics plc* might associate the products with emotions that cannot be directly derived from the message communicated, it is of utmost importance to develop an **"integrated marketing communications concept"** which sets out by **vertically** aligning the manifold and multi-layered measures used by organisations (i. e. by including all current communications measures taken) with the large variety of the messages they are intended to transmit to the customers. This is supplemented by an alignment over (a longer period of) **time** which forms the second pillar of integrated marketing communications. Consequently, *Cosmetics plc* is faced with two consequences: on the one hand, its long-term communications concepts aim at creating a **positive learning outcome** by forming a habit, on the other hand, the constant repetition of the statements made may cause a feeling of redundancy and thereby lead to a negative effect. For this reason *Cosmetics plc* will seek to maintain the central **design features** (such as emphasising a "modern life-style") and it will do this without introducing any changes whatsoever. Based on its overall corporate communications strategy, the business organisation will eventually admit to the necessary changes in an incremental fashion which will systematically build on the learning outcomes that are currently being established.

4 Information behaviour and socialisation

4.1 Introduction and expected learning outcomes

This chapter deals, first and foremost, with the dimensions of information behaviour. Moreover, it will elucidate which social and environmental factors influence purchasing behaviour.
On completing this chapter,

1. you will know what stages are typical of information behaviour and how these stages can be described;
2. you will realize which factors impact on the reception of information and the subjective need for information;
3. you will understand in which way the presentation of information needs to be adjusted to the techniques employed by buyers who process the information presented to them;
4. you will be able to identify the social institutions that are instrumental in forging individual behaviour;
5. you will know the consequences of information overload

4.2 Information behaviour

Human information behaviour may be divided into five stages:

1. the subjective need for information
2. the search for information
3. information processing
4. the storage of information
5. information dissemination and application

4.2.1 The subjective need for information

According to *Raffée & Silberer* (1975:37) the subjective need for information arises from a combination of three factors which all interact and influence each other.

Cognitive determinants

These may be a person's individual experience, value orientation, memory capacity, attitudes and/or the perceived complexity of the issue that is to be decided on.

Motivational determinants

These may include the desire to obtain complete clarity with regard to the decision to be taken and to achieve consistency in the decisional process. In addition, we may list personal interests, the wish for security and the desire to reduce the number of personal commitments and assignments.

Situational determinants

These may be personal deficiencies, the nature and the accessibility of a person's environment, the availability of information, time pressure, the necessity to justify one's decisions, the opportunity to emulate the behaviour and the decisions of others or to delegate one's own decisions.

In addition, there is a link between the need for information and the ensuing buying behaviour. Especially when **purchases are made spontaneously**, hardly any information is required. However, the longer a purchase has been planned or intended, the more information is necessary. *Kroeber-Riel & Weinberg* (2003:410) distinguish between affective, cognitive und reactive actions. One can assume that 10 to 20% of all purchases made are genuinely spontaneous (op.cit.:389). In addition, the intensity with which the need for information makes itself felt depends on the degree of the subjective post-purchase satisfaction which, for its part, correlates with each buyer's expectations.

To a certain degree, the need for information is influenced by the level of **buyer involvement** in each purchasing situation. It has already been pointed out that purchasing decisions based on high consumer involvement are guided by cognitive determinants to a much greater extent than low-involvement buying decisions. We can therefore maintain that intensive information processing goes hand in hand with a high level of buyer involvement and that straightforward or routine buying decisions are characterised by a low level of buyer involvement (*Kroeber-Riel & Weinberg,* 2003:372, 373).

The subjective need for information is further influenced by the subjective feeling of security on the part of the decision takers and by the importance they subjectively attribute to the decision to be taken.

The impact of the **risk** which buyers subjectively calculate is softened by their brand loyalty, their purchasing habits, the information they have gathered, their price considerations and/or by their emulating the purchasing behaviour of others. Last but not least, buyers can lower their own subjective expectations concerning the purchases to be made.

4.2.2 Searching for information

The way in which people seek and obtain information can be described by employing the dimensions of "internal / external" and "focused / coincidental". **Internal information gathering** relies on the memory and on data which are either intentionally or accidentally accessed, remembered and absorbed.

External information gathering reflects personal communication activities, such as receiving advertisements from the mass media or intentionally searching for information from potential manufacturers or suppliers. It is to be expected that the media reach will be extended by **interactive television programmes** which open up new avenues for the intentional provision of external information. In the US, TV-channels that are exclusively reserved for **informative advertising** and which address interested parties in search of specific information on product groups, have established themselves as a permanent feature of TV reality. In Europe, too, such channels are becoming more prominent.

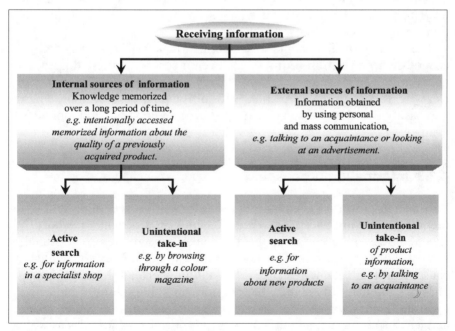

Fig. 4.1. The dimensions of information search (adapted from *Kroeber-Riel* & *Weinberg*, 2003:246)

Empirical research has offered some insight into how different **groups of people** devise strategies to obtain information in correlation with their subjective need for information. *Fritz* (1981*)* shows, for instance, that **senior citizens** – contrary to common sense and general expectations – maintain a low level of intensity in their search for information although they may well realize that flawed decisions could be highly risky and obtaining further information would be highly beneficial. The **reinforcing principles** that impact most on purchase behaviour can be explained by the theory of learning: "If the usage of a product constitutes a positive experience, it confirms the purchasing decision made and thereby determines the habitualisation of purchasing behaviour which equals brand loyalty." (*Fritz*, 1981: 129*)*. This indicates that the risk perceived in buying over-the-counter medication does not affect the intensity of the search for information but the choice of the information sources. In other words, the buyer might rely more strongly on personal rather than on medical information in future.

There is a positive correlation between the buyers' **level of education** and the **intensity with which they seek information.** This is of relevance, for instance, when young people purchase consumer durables. In addition, class-related differences come to bear on buying behaviour: "The higher the social class a person belongs to, the sounder his or her education, the more information on product quality becomes important". This trend inverses itself a proportion to the decreasing class status when aesthetical considerations gradually replace the relevance of quality.

The extent to which people seek information is further influenced by the **cost of the information required** but even if cost is incurred, this does not necessarily lead to a more extensive search for information. This is the reason why, if consumer information is to fulfil the purpose of improving the purchasing decisions of consumers, it should be unbiased and more easily available.

4.2.3 Information processing

Information processing is connected to **information reception** and to the **mental processing** and the **storing** of stimuli in a person's memory. We should, however, bear in mind that the human capacity to receive stimuli is limited. For consumers in the modern, industrialized Western world, this causes a problem, namely that of **information overload.** More information does not automatically signify better information but seems to indicate the opposite. This is why only a limited amount of information can be taken in and why its absorption additionally depends on existing attitudes as well as the current level of attentiveness and excitement. Consequently, simple

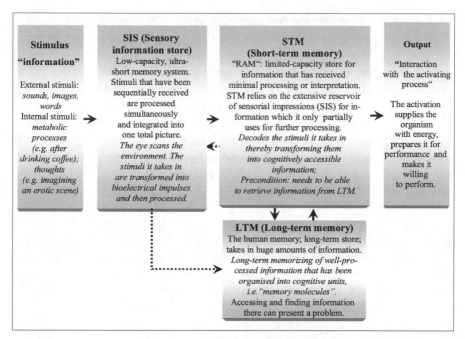

Fig. 4.2. Information processing (adapted from *Kroeber-Riel* & *Weinberg* 2003:226)

pictorial messages which directly address the needs of the target groups are gaining ground over complex "texty" messages. This leads to a **decrease in the cognitive elements impacting on purchasing decisions**, especially in FMCG markets. Furthermore, complex decisional issues may be reduced to a small number of tried and tested options and to a series of product collaterals that are taken for highly significant "key information". Such mechanisms have also increasingly made an appearance in the marketing of capital goods. The **product adoption process** which moves from product awareness to product evaluation and purchase, has become more and more shackled by simplifying mechanisms such as the application of **repetitive thought patterns,** prejudice and stereotypes. Marketing needs to take this into account by adapting the presentation of product information to the information processing techniques that are contemporarily favoured by buyers.

The way in which messages influence human learning and the degree to which these messages are appreciated are determined by the manner in which they have been processed. This has become an axiom of consumer psychology. Moreover, the richer the **associations** conjured up by a message, the stronger its impact. A "snappy" message, the right choice of music and information that is felt to be relevant encourage that type of elaboration.

The current level of **involvement**, too, determines whether information processing is intensive or superficial, with the degree of intensity rising in line with a person's perceived level of involvement (op.cit.:134*).*

Tybout & Artz (1994) have shown **gender-specific differences** in information processing according to which female decision takers are more often guided by **factual orientation** and tend to rely on detailed information, whereas their male counterparts tend to focus on the message as a whole and on the impression it creates. However, the gender distinctions made here are relatively subtle and can also be explained in terms of the different requirements associated with the messages and the often dissimilar tasks performed members of each sex.

Gender, however, is an influencing factor on information processing in general and to consumer response to product messages in particular, insofar as buyers obviously prefer products whose presentation makes use of notions that correlate with their self-definition and self-perception and, thus, with their assumed femininity or masculinity (cf. *Tybout & Artz,* 1994: 136). However, this statement probably not only applies to the gender-specific dimension of the "self", but to all other dimensions of the latter as well.

As far as the storage of information is concerned, new electronic devices such as interactive television programmes that act as external memories will gain considerable momentum as a supplement to the internal memory.

4.2.4 Information dissemination

Information is passed on in groups and social relationships where it is subject to the **structure of the groups.** The size of the group, for instance, may determine the intensity of the contact between the individual group members. Information dissemination further depends on the **climate predominant in each group**. Thus, the wish for cohesion within the group, i. e. the wish for conformity with the other members of a group can be considerably affected by the predominant atmosphere. In addition, it is the **situation of the group** in general, e. g. the interests they share, which is relevant for the dissemination of information in this group. The importance of each member for the group is defined by the other group members in terms of credibility and assumed competencies. Such groups can be found in private life as well as in the areas of leisure, work and vocational training.

Information deficits on the part of the consumers can **genuinely impede market mechanisms.** They constitute an essential and powerful leverage that tips the balance in favour of the suppliers. This seems to make a mockery of claims to user-oriented production. If **consumer sovereignty** exists at all, it does so at a low level. Moreover, it is stunted by the formidable expert

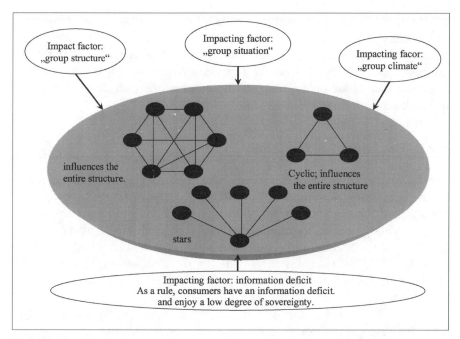

Fig. 4.3. Communication structures adopted for the consumer (adapted from *Zimbardo & Gerrig*, 1999:749)

power of suppliers who are in a position to use influencing mechanisms that the consumers are unable to fathom.

4.2.5 Social factors impacting on buyer behaviour

Buyer behaviour is guided by the measures adopted in business organisations and by the competitive, commercial, political and social environment of the latter. Companies seek to control buyer behaviour **directly** by a combination of communication policies and by employing specific distribution policies such as personal selling, special offers and product information. **Indirectly,** but in the long term possibly to a greater effect, they seek to alter buyer behaviour by product and pricing policies. Their efforts are countered by their competitive activity and by commerce as a whole where a set of identical tools is applied.

To the same extent, lobbies and associations such as the Board of Industry and environmental groups seek to convert the consumers to their particular views. Such phenomena may well be supportive of a company's own marketing strategy but they may also represent a hindrance. The social environment, which is a highly significant issue, will be dealt with in the following section.

Behaviour is forged by social institutions, such as family, community groups, class and social strata, culture, subculture and society as a whole. All these factors are responsible for the process of socialisation that leaves its mark on each member of a society.

4.2.6 The impact of the family

The family, a primary social nucleus, is the decisive factor for some essential aspects of consumption. It determines the social **origin of consumer groups** and thereby the consumption behaviour and the media usage patterns of young people. In particular, family life cycles, role patterns in the family and the weighting of purchase influences within the family have a hand in this. The role played by male family members in the purchase of everyday items is on the increase, as are communal decisions related to goods that are used or consumed on a daily basis.

The consumer behaviour of families is characterised by the respective stage they are going through, the most important ones being:

1. couples with children under 18,
2. couples with children over 18,
3. childless couples,
4. single parents,
5. single persons.

In the course of time, family structures follow the rhythm of life cycles, hence the term **family life cycle.** According to this model, families traditionally go through the five following stages (*Blackwell, Miniard & Engel, 2006*:492, 493):

Young singles: In absolute figures, the members of this group adhere to a low income bracket but their income is, relatively speaking, often freely disposable. They spend more money than the other groups on fashion items, clothes, beverages, restaurant and bar food, holidays, leisure and social activities.

Childless couples: These couples dispose of higher incomes, which are equally freely dispensable provided both partners are in employment. They spend relatively high amounts on furniture and household appliances, likewise on holidays and cars. They will eventually have built up financial reserves (e. g. building society contracts) for possible future family planning.

Young couples with children: (stage 1): To start with, these young couples with children face major financial commitments which they are obliged to meet with a decreasing income (measured in absolute figures). The requirements of their small children, the necessity to find housing, food and clothing dominate their consumption routines. More often than not, they are dissatisfied with their financial situation. These families are most likely to respond to special offers. As they are fairly inexperienced consumers, they tend to be somewhat uncertain about the quality of many everyday products.

Couples with children (Stage 2): This term refers to couples whose children have grown older and have reached school age. During this stage, the person who has run the household, often returns to working life. This tends to improve the financial situation of the family and to raise the expectation threshold regarding everyday products. In addition, products that characterise the couple's lifestyle are increasingly purchased: e. g. bikes, musical instruments, sports equipment, holidays, and further educational activities.

Couples with children (Stage 3): These are families whose children have become independent and often have their own jobs. The members of these families have been in regular employment and usually benefit from a relatively high income level which goes hand in hand with steadily increasing requirements and expectations. As a result of the changes affecting the family structure, housing and accommodation requirements change, too. The need for furniture and fitted kitchens, for instance, frequently determines the amount of expenses incurred. The housekeeper is a highly experienced consumer who increasingly desires value for money and makes comparisons. A major part of the family income is spent on the children's further education, e. g. on a university course.

During Stage 2 or 3, a house or an apartment may be purchased, which substantially reduces the freely available income, independent of the income expressed in absolute figures. This will decrease high-level consumption to a greater or lesser extent.

Couples whose grown-up children have left the family home: This stage, during which both partners still lead an active working life while their children have already flown the nest and have completed their education and/or training, is characterized by a distinct income surplus, which is used to finance the existing interests such as purchase of further property, consumption of luxury items, holidays or hobbies and leisure activities.

Senior couples who have retired from work: during the post-retirement stage, quite a few couples need to come to terms with a considerable income reduction. Others can resort to the substantial reserves put aside earlier in life or to other sources of income. Consumption behaviour is now increasingly guided by health concerns and a comfortable lifestyle; suitable leisure activities for senior citizens play a relatively important role, too. It became apparent in the 1990's that the consumption behaviour of contemporary senior citizens can hardly be compared to that of former generations. Active OAPs have become an interesting target group which has been unjustifiably neglected by professional marketers.

Widowed or single persons: This group can be categorized in terms of "working life" and "retirement". As long as the members of this group feature on a payroll, they tend to enjoy a relatively high income and to spend higher amounts on holidays, recreation und health products. They often become more interested in social activities, too. To a lesser extent, retired widows and widowers may show similar consumption patterns, which are due to their reduced incomes. In addition, these persons have special needs with regard to social recognition and security.

However, the **classic family life cycle** is becoming an increasingly inadequate model, as a large number of couples remain childless. This improves their chances of consuming more, provided both persons have a disposable income. Moreover, compared to the situation in the past few

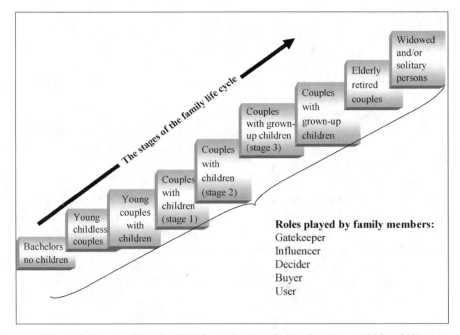

Fig. 4.4. Stages of the family life cycle (*Busch, Dögl & Unger,* 2001: 660)

decades, the number of single households is evidently growing. The classic model also falls short of reality in another respect: more and more married couples split up and/or dissolve their marriage. On the one hand, this may entail additional financial obligations and thus curtail consumption. On the other hand, this middle-aged group of persons may rekindle the demand for items (e. g. furniture) that had already been consumed at an earlier stage.

Family structures, too, may be more subject to changes owing to the following (*Williams,* 1982: 218): more opportunity to benefit from leisure time, increased formal education, growing number of working women, higher life expectancy. The size of the traditional family decreases as a result of the fact that women nowadays act as mothers for a relatively short period of time. This also affects gender-specific role behaviour.

Consumption behaviour is influenced by the **different roles** played by the individual members of the Decision Making Unit (DMU):

- Gatekeepers exert their influence on information processing in their families by determining the type and the amount of information made available.
- Influencers have a say in most consumption decisions even if they do not directly benefit from the articles purchased. They assist in providing technical information, if required, suggest alternative offerings and determine the brands which, in their eyes, can best satisfy the needs of their family.
- Deciders influence their family's final decision on the brands and product categories to be used. At this point, it becomes evident that one person can assume different roles; in many families gatekeepers and decision makers are the same person.
- Buyers carry out the final consumption decisions. They may deviate from the purchase decisions taken in their families, when they are exposed to situational factors at the place of purchase. When the consumption decision is made at the place of consumption itself, the purchaser takes on the role of the decision taker.
- Users or end consumers often initiate the purchasing process and consume the goods acquired. It stands to reason that each member of a household obviously becomes a user at some stage and that some products are consumed communally. The product experience gained and expressed by the users is relevant for all further purchase decisions.

The various roles played by different family members may give rise to contention when purchasing decisions are taken jointly. Such conflicts would be mainly due to differences in motivational beliefs and in differing appraisals of purchasing options. *Lackman & Lanasa* (1993) point out that men tend to appreciate products from an **functional**, i. e. a user's, perspective, whereas women seem to assess products from an aesthetic, i. e. **emotional,** angle. Such attitudes are, however, currently changing and may, subsequently, cause the above roles to be exchanged.

If **conflicts** are perceived as such, they can be resolved by a series of solution-oriented strategies which might involve using the expertise available within a family and jointly searching for a better solution. Moreover, a communal decision could be taken which satisfies as many wishes as possible. Alternatively, intra-familiar decision routines and mechanisms could be brought into play. Alternatively, a dominant family member might resort to authoritarian behaviour.

4.2.7 Cultural influences

Cultural influences are closely linked to group and societal differentiation. Especially the latter is seen as the formative element of culture. The term "culture" can also refer to continents, nations and social segments (subcultures).

Culture is generally defined as the sum total of learned – or otherwise socially acquired –, collectively structured and disseminated habits, lifestyles, ways of life, rules, symbols as well as the value and knowledge systems of individuals and entire populations. Cultural knowledge is handed down by learning, imitation or instruction and includes the ways in which human beings think, feel and act. Cultural factors provide an external framework to human behaviour, and thus to **market and consumer behaviour** within one cultural entity.

For marketing purposes, the distinction made between **affluent societies** (*Galbraith,* 1958) and **demand societies** might be of utmost importance as such cultural differences allow the differentiation of preferences, behavioural patterns and value systems of the individual members of one culture. Cultural anthropology and ethnology, in particular, have provided us with sound explanations of social value systems "which express themselves in inter-culturally highly differentiated lifestyles and behavioural patterns" (*Wiswede*, 1983: 194*)*.

One cannot assume that regions which enjoy equally high economic standards are culturally identical or that this results in cultural convergence. Differences in linguistic expression, value systems and moral attitudes, to name but a few, will always remain. Cultural factors that are relevant in terms of consumption are, above all, related to the goods consumed, to consumer needs and to market structures. As for the goods, there may be, for instance differing preferences with regard to "artificial" and "natural" products and

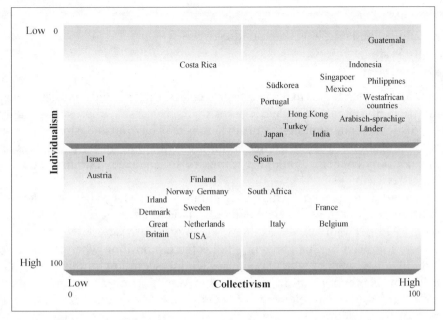

Fig. 4.5. Comparing cultural dimensions (*Hofstede*, 1994:54)

marginal aspects may suddenly gain importance. A case in point is animal testing which, in many Asian countries, is perceived as an absolute necessity to warrant the safety of cosmetics, whereas this issue is publicly and hotly contested in European countries. The more a society develops, the more its **needs** become **differentiated,** a phenomenon which is caused by the differentiation of the consumer products themselves. In addition, consumer markets are characterized by different forms of symbolism. Developed economies offer a broader scope for **lifestyle-related consumption**, as they increasingly accept the co-existence of differentiated subcultures. Moreover, there are culture-specific regulations concerning human interaction and market structures: Whereas in certain southern European and Asian cultures, sales talks may initially seem to have been transferred to the lesser scenes of action (small talk about the family and personal matters), German and US American interlocutors prefer to immediately come to the point of the negotiations to be conducted.

Even within one culture there is considerable differentiation, which is referred to as **subculture**. Subcultures emerge in:

- regionally defined areas that subscribe to certain traditions
- homogeneous populations,
- age groups (young people, senior citizens),

- ethnic groups,
- political and religious communities,
- professional groups,
- social strata.

Marketing strategies make use of such culture-specific differences in order to efficiently target individual market segments or subcultures. Especially linguistic misunderstandings and deviations may have an undesired effect on communication. *Kroeber-Riel & Weinberg* (2003:556) justly point out that this not only concerns "thoughts expressed in language" but also thoughts expressed in images.

According to the above chart, each culture can be placed between the two extreme poles of individualism and collectivism. Even in Europe, which is seen as rather individualistic, there are big differences. Great Britain – closely followed by Scandinavia – holds the top position when it comes to individualism whereas Asian countries tend to score low in this area. **Collectivism** is predominant in regions where groups, rather than individuals, are valued as the core elements of society. Individuals only exist as members of their group. They are forced to perform tasks for higher ranking group members and are offered protection in return (*Lasserre & Schütte*, 1996:102). This type of group orientation constitutes the foundation of networking. Collectivist features develop in communities in which, over the long-term, social cohesion and stability present optimal solutions to existing and arising problems or are absolutely vital for the community's survival. **Individualism** is closely associated with safeguarding personal dignity as it allows people to enjoy the feeling of being special. Personal opinions are freely expressed and those who refrain from doing so are perceived as weak.

International marketing strategies therefore need to tackle the question as to whether cultural regions can or ought to be approached differently. In other words, are there enough common cultural features to justify a global approach of ones target group.

4.2.8 Information overload

A fair number of Western and Central European countries, the USA, Canada, Australia and Japan are currently being transformed into information societies. This stage is characterized by the growing contribution of the IT sector to a country's gross domestic product (GDP) which in the Western world has already reached the 50% threshold. In the above regions, this will cause the information volume to grow even further. On the other hand, the genetically determined human capacity for information processing remains unchanged as it cannot be essentially enlarged by learning processes. This will result in the fact that an even a greater amount of the information being offered will remain untapped than was the case in the past.

At present, as little as 5 per cent of the inflowing information can be absorbed and processed. This indicates that the information overload which we have experienced since the 1980's will weigh even more heavily, and so will the consequences arising from this situation:

One can assume that stimuli that enjoy a higher degree of familiarity will be absorbed more quickly than unknown stimuli. In addition, well-known stimuli from a person's environment will be met with a greater degree of acceptance. **Familiar stimuli** serve as landmarks in a world which sends out more information than the recipients can cope with. They represent a much-needed anchor in "a sea of uncertainties". When it comes to consumption, well-known brands are able to function in a similar fashion. This signifies, however, that consumers must be able to associate these brand names with clear and unequivocal images. Marketers should rise to this challenge by providing continuous (long-term) advertising strategies. They should, more generally speaking, develop a communication strategy which comprises and harmonizes advertising, public relations, sales promotion and packaging. Brands require a clear and unmistakable **image profile**, which needs to be put into place by appropriate communication policies and by pursuing an unequivocal product policy which should be completely in line with the image communicated. New products should be given particular attention in compliance with these policies and should be completely aligned with the image profile intended. This obviously imposes severe impediments on the technological innovation potential of business organisations as marketing aspects need to be given an even higher priority over technological opportunities than before. Especially in saturated markets, in which products become more and more exchangeable from a technological perspective, image factors will be decisive in the market success of a product. Mistakes in this area will make themselves sorely felt.

4.2.9 Some consequences for marketing

In information societies, the number of possible **media vehicles** is steadily on the increase. This has long since been the case with printed media such as illustrated magazines and, more recently, with the electronic media used in mass communication. At the same time, privately registered radio- and television programmes have **decreased the media reach of established providers**. Furthermore, more and more users are in a position to benefit from **foreign programmes** via satellite and cable TV. If an approximate 80% of households use cable TV and if no less than 70% of these household make active use of this facility, one can assume that households using cable TV, including the satellite systems, can receive up to 70 TV programmes. As a result, an unchanged marketing budget – that also needs to be price-adjusted – will achieve **less and less advertising impact**. This has manifold consequences. The **cost** of establishing new brands or newly branded products by means of advertising **will continually rise,** whereas the advertising impact will decrease if budget spend remains constant. For this reason, **"line extension"** i. e. the more intensive usage of existing brands when launching new ones, seems to be advisable without, however, jeopardizing or watering down the image or the competencies of the brands used for this purpose.

As cross-border TV programmes will become more frequent and an increasing number of people will tune in to them, **European branding and advertising strategies** ought to be devised. A further reason for this lies in the fact that a high number of citizens have adopted an increasingly international focus in their lives.

As TV users can comfortably **"zap"** the advertisements during commercial breaks, the design of TV commercials needs to be hold a sensory, experiential appeal that allows the viewer to enjoy the message advertised without lessening its impact. However, it should also be stated that at least 20% of TV viewers switch to other programmes during commercial breaks, which further diminishes the impact of advertising. Further changes might be in the pipeline, as pay-TV might achieve a breakthrough in the very near future.

The reduced reach of TV broadcasts can only be countered by placing additional advertisements in other programmes or by using different media vehicles (radio, magazines etc.). The additional cost can, to some extent, be compensated for by shortening the broadcasting time (20-second commercials instead of 30-second ones), but this approach is risky and represents a limitation in itself, diminishing as it does, the effect of TV insertions. Raising the marketing budget, therefore, seems the inevitable solution. This is the price to pay for the additional advertising opportunities which some operators in the advertising sector have repeatedly demanded!

4.3 Multiple choice questions

Question 4/1: Where does the customers' need for information result from?

(a)	Their value system
(b)	Their wish for security
(c)	Their need to justify a purchasing decision
(d)	the complexity of the object to be purchased

Question 4/2: Which of the following statements are correct?

(a)	Internally, information is provided through personal communication.
(b)	There is a negative correlation between the level of education and the intensity with which information is obtained.
(c)	The degree of involvement determines whether information processing is intensive or superficial.
(d)	The richer the associations which are activated by the message, the weaker its impact.

Question 4/3: Which of the following statements are correct?

(a)	The genetically determined human capacity to process information increases over time.
(b)	Well-known or otherwise familiar stimuli are perceived more quickly than unknown ones.
(c)	In information societies, the number of possible advertising vehicles is experiencing an increase.
(d)	The establishment of new brands by means of advertising will be increasingly costly.

Question 4/4: Where do subcultures spring from?

(a)	From regionally defined areas that subscribe to distinct traditions.
(b)	From homogeneous population groups
(c)	From age groups
(d)	from professional groups

Question 4/5: Which aspects exert an influence on information dissemination?

(a)	the time at which a group comes into existence
(b)	the group structure
(c)	the group atmosphere
(d)	the group situation

4.4 Case study

You are the Marketing Manager of "Cosmetics plc", a producer of skin care and toiletries. You have been asked to apply the specific findings of the "information processing theory" to the design of your corporation's market communications.

Solution

1. The information aimed at the recipients of the market communication measures of Cosmetics plc is stored in the sensory information memory (SIM). This storage takes no longer than a split second (0.1 to 1.0 seconds) but it nonetheless decides on the nature of the different monitoring processes and whether information is passed on or not. The short-term memory (STM) then resorts to the comprehensive reservoir of sensorial impressions which exist in the ultra short-term memory. This second storage takes about one minute. On the other hand, the short-term memory, for its part, draws from the existing information in the long-term memory thereby occupying an intermediate position between the two storage systems. Only a small part of the information stored in the short-term memory is "admitted" to the long-term memory which disposes of a nearly unlimited storage capacity and can therefore be considered as the human memory per se. The success of *Cosmetics plc* will be decided upon by the company's customers who continuously select

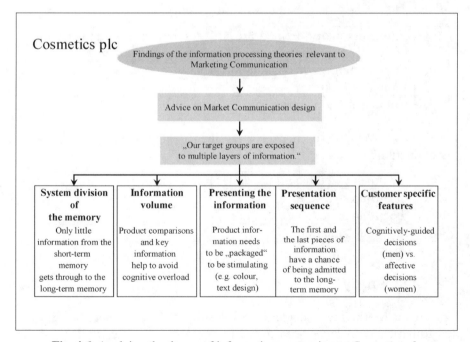

Fig. 4.6. Applying the theory of information processing to *Cosmetics plc*

information that is important for them, store it and recall it if need be. The people responsible for marketing communication face the task of **providing appropriate information that is tailored to their specific customers** and which enables them to influence the decision behaviour of these customers in line with the intentions of *Cosmetics plc*. As a rule, one should bear in mind that customers are mostly guided by information which attracts their attention and which stimulates them to a certain extent. The key elements in this process are the design and the presentation of advertising means (*Raab & Unger*, 2005:109).

2. During the purchase decision process, the customers of *Cosmetics plc* are exposed to a **great amount of information.** Processing the entire amount would cognitively overburden the consumer. As a result, not all information can be received and processed. The customers of the above business will therefore seek to maximise the success of their decisions by minimizing their decision efforts. This is achieved, on the one hand, by **comparing** similar products and by deciding in favour of the product that offers most advantages, and by relying on **key information** such as brand name, price, components and product quality.

3. When decisions are taken, the information available is usually not modified but directly absorbed. Research into information processing, however, tends to underestimate the influence of the **external appearance** of the information provided. In order to trigger off and to activate the attention of one's customers, thereby creating the grounds for an efficient reception, processing, and storing of product information, *Cosmetics plc* ought to "package" it in a stimulating fashion. Design features such as colour, text design, images and the placement of the advertisements play an important role in this. One can assume, for instance, that coloured ads are more favourably accepted and are remembered longer than black and white ones. As to copy writing, *Cosmetics plc* is convinced that the willingness of the targeted groups to pay detailed attention to the information offered can be raised if the copy uses contrast and is agreeable to the eye and if the size of the letters warrants easy readability. For the same reasons, the images chosen should be clearly and logically arranged. **Cognitive response research** confirms the findings summed up above: If there is no or only very little motivation to process information, **image messages** that engender affective reactions promise to produce a more effective advertising impact than market communication whose design relies on verbal arguments. Furthermore, corporate management prefers to place advertisements on the right hand side of the advertising medium rather than on the left.

4. Information, such as the commercials inserted during the TV breaks, is usually perceived as a **sequence** and is not absorbed simultaneously. Communications management at *Cosmetics plc* benefits from the fact that if information is presented as a sequence, the first and the last information items primarily enjoy an advantageous position. This is referred to as the "primary recency effect" The first pieces of information encounter an empty memory which offers them a relatively good chance of making it to the long-term memory. The more information is added, the more pressure is applied to the memory and the individual pieces of information might be confused. One could mention the similarly designed spots for certain product types as a case in point. The interested party memorises three spots which might merge into two or one and the user will later only remember the latter which will then proceed to the memory without further hindrance as the information supply to the latter has ceased. Information that has already been admitted can then be processed in peace and quiet.

5. Communications management at *Cosmetics plc* is based on the assumption that information processing often depends on a great number of **specific user criteria**. As for gender orientation, men tend to take buying decisions on a cognitive basis whereas women emphasise primarily the affective aspects. Moreover, women focus more intensely on the contents of the advertising message thereby developing greater sensitivity for the message details whereas men perceive the message as an entity thus neglecting some of its details. These findings are of particular relevance for *Cosmetics plc* as the company is planning to launch its new series "cosmetics for men" in the near future.

5 Analysing the communication situation

5.1 Expected learning outcomes

This chapter will investigate how business organisations can obtain information about the persons who use media and media vehicles and when and to what degree of intensity these media are made use of. This will be followed up by a discussion of the essential research issues concerning the impact of advertising. The chapter will be concluded by taking a close look at the appropriate methods that can be adopted to analyse long-term external developments that are of relevance to the communication process as well as their respective internal resources.

On completing this chapter,

1. you will have learned what kind of media analyses explain media behaviour as well as buyer behaviour,
2. you will understand which factors influence the impact of advertising,
3. you will know how to identify the core elements of the communication model,
4. you will be able to draw conclusions about the environmental developments that are relevant to market communications and to categorise them as opportunities or threats, and
5. you will be in a position to conduct an appropriate analysis of a company's internal communication resources, e. g. by assessing its strengths and weaknesses.

5.2 Media analysis

In order to meet the objectives of media planning, marketers need to know exactly **who uses media or media vehicles and when or how intensively these media are used.** Media analysts provide answers to these questions by thoroughly researching which target groups can be reached by which media and what other elements play a role when the various media vehicles are used. There are several analytical methods which can be divided into two groups:

- pure media analyses which focus only on media user behaviour,
- market-media analyses which additionally investigate buyer behaviour

The best-known typical media surveys in Germany are *Media-Analyse (MA,* i. e. "Media Analysis"), which is commissioned annually by a group of professional media analysts (aka *Arbeitsgemeinschaft Media-Analyse; AGMA),* and *Allensbacher Werbeträger-Analyse* (AWA, i. e. "Allensbach Media Vehicle Analysis"), which is likewise performed once a year.

5.2.1 Media analysis and TV usage research

Media Analysis (www.agma-mmc.de) investigates the **media usage behaviour** of the German population by multiple random sampling.

One of the random investigations, which explore **the usage of radio programmes,** involves a sample of approximately **20,000 persons**. Further surveys sampling the same number of people explore the usage of magazines and related print media. Both investigations additionally collect data on the usage of daily newspapers and cinema visits.

TV usage is researched on the basis of electronically-aided data collection and analysed by the *Gesellschaft für Konsumforschung (GfK,* i. e. "Society for Consumption Research" whose English logo is "Growth from Knowledge"). Whereas *Media Analysis* conducts interviews with persons who are randomly selected each year, TV usage research is carried out with a nationwide household panel that samples 6,000 respondent households or roughly 15,000 persons in the following way: A digitalised meter provided by *GfK* (www.gfk.com) is attached to the TV set of the selected households. This computer, which is the size of a radio alarm clock, monitors all imaginable activities that require a TV screen. It only takes seconds to record which TV programmes are being watched, which TV games are being played, whether teletexts or video texts have been read and which feature films have been recorded on video. If viewers briefly switch over to other programmes during commercial breaks, this is also instantly tracked.. The data obtained is transferred via telephone directly to the *GfK* computer where it is electronically analysed.

5.2.2 The people meter

Although it is interesting to know which households have switched on their TV sets and what type of activity occurs on them, what researchers really want to find out is who exactly uses the TV programmes that are under observation. For this reason the *GfK* researchers have created what they refer to as a "people meter". This appliance enables the individual members of the selected households to register as TV users by means of an infrared remote control. It records in seconds which persons are present, when they have switched the TV set on or off or when and how often they have switched over to another programme.

A critical comment

Theoretically, the "people meter" can show who is in the room when the TV set is switched on and who can, consequently, be reached by the commercials that are being broadcast. But there are sound reasons to query these findings. Even if an individual person makes a conscientious effort to register his or her presence and absence when watching television on their own or with others, it cannot be taken for granted that they apply the same care to the area that is of interest to commercial advertising. Will a person, who briefly leaves the room when the commercials start, always conscientiously indicate his or her absence? What exactly is the percentage of those who briefly leave the room? What is the percentage of those that fail to communicate their (brief) absence? Will these problems produce flawed results? Would the percentage of those whose movements cannot be precisely recorded be the same for all population and target groups? Would it be possible to correct and recalculate this percentage at a later stage on the basis of more reliable estimates? Do different groups of persons (housewives, men, children) show differences in their TV behaviour? These questions have so far not been sufficiently explored. However, some surveys indicate (*Danaher & Beed*, 1993) that "people meters" are used correctly.

5.2.3 Data merging

After completing the random sampling of media audience behaviour, the data collected is amalgamated and interlinked for analytical purposes. For instance, groups of persons who show a high number of similar demographic characteristics with regard to their usage of media are merged into one virtual consumer. If a group of persons who share the socioeconomic structure X, for instance, can easily be reached while watching the early-evening soaps (e. g. *Coronation Street*, *Neighbours*) and if a print media survey incidentally suggests that persons showing the same characteristics can also be easily reached via women's magazines (e. g. *Women's Weekly*), one can assume that this group represents a demographic segment that can be targeted twice, namely via the afore-mentioned magazines and TV programmes.

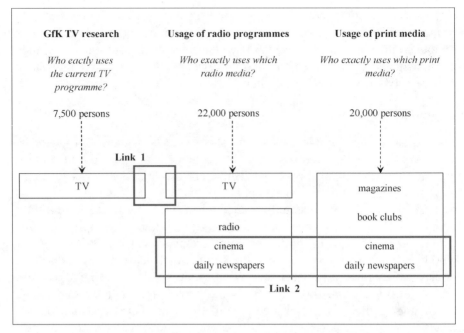

Fig. 5.1. Amalgamating the data provided by *Media Analysis*

Data merging is carried out step by step. First, the TV data is amalgamated with the radio data and this set of data is then merged with the print media data. If the usage of daily newspapers and of cinemas is surveyed simultaneously, a definite link can be established between the two sets of data.

5.2.4 AWA and Media Analysis: a comparison

A further prominent survey is *Allensbacher Werbeträger-Analyse (AWA;* www.ifd-allensbach.de)**,** i. e. *Allensbach Media Vehicle Analysis*, which covers consumer magazines, newspapers, newspaper supplements, radio, TV and cinema. Its research is based on interviews conducted with about 20,000 people who constitute a representative sample of the total population of German people over 13 years of age. Compared to *Media Analysis*, *AWA* is hampered by a disadvantage, including, as it does, all media types in the interview questions that are put to the randomly selected participants. This places a considerable strain on interviewers and respondents. Just like *Media Analysis* which relies on interviews to research radio usage rather than conducting an electronic investigation, *AWA* arrives at its findings in the same way. In addition to the data gathered about the media activities of the respondents, which are assessed in a purely quantitative manner, *AWA*, to a greater extent than is the case with *Media Analysis*, breaks this data down further into psychographic lifestyle categories such as ownership and consumption patterns.

Compared to *AWA* which is performed by one single institute *(i. e. Allensbach), Media Analysis* is methodologically sounder as it is carried out by five different institutes. However, one should not overlook that there are often significant variances in the data produced by the five media surveys, in spite of the fact that all participating institutes use the same data collection methods. It is true that these variances tend to disappear as soon as the data conglomerate is aggregated but, nonetheless, certain reservations remain as to the quality of this method of data collecting. On the other hand, it seems justifiable to hope that the above variances will balance one another out when they are distributed amongst all participating institutes.

The media analyses summed up above are essentially founded on socio-demographic stratification, whose features are listed in the breakdown below.

Additional information is available, for instance on which daily news-papers or magazines the interviewed persons subscribe to. Ownership fea-tures include telephones, TV sets, video recorders, PCs, cable TV, house-hold appliances such as washing machines, ironing and sewing machines,

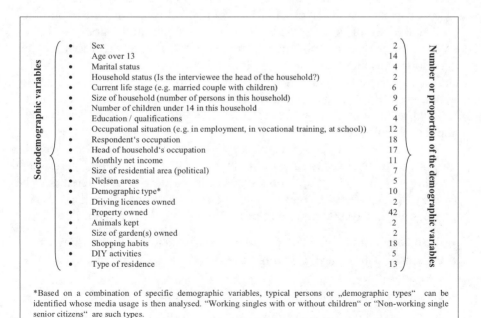

Sociodemographic variables		Number or proportion of the demographic variables
• Sex	2	
• Age over 13	14	
• Marital status	4	
• Household status (Is the interviewee the head of the household?)	2	
• Current life stage (e.g. married couple with children)	6	
• Size of household (number of persons in this household)	9	
• Number of children under 14 in this household	6	
• Education / qualifications	4	
• Occupational situation (e.g. in employment, in vocational training, at school))	12	
• Respondent's occupation	18	
• Head of household's occupation	17	
• Monthly net income	11	
• Size of residential area (political)	7	
• Nielsen areas	5	
• Demographic type*	10	
• Driving licences owned	2	
• Property owned	42	
• Animals kept	2	
• Size of garden(s) owned	2	
• Shopping habits	18	
• DIY activities	5	
• Type of residence	13	

*Based on a combination of specific demographic variables, typical persons or „demographic types" can be identified whose media usage is then analysed. "Working singles with or without children" or "Non-working single senior citizens" are such types.

Fig. 5.2. Overview of the data collected by *Media Analysis* (excerpt)

bathroom scales, camcorders and cameras, blood pressure testers etc. Moreover, the interview includes questions on leisure and shopping habits as well as political inclinations.

Like market research in general, the above analyses face a **timing problem.** When their results are published, the information they are founded on refers to a past research period, whereas advertising measures are usually planned for the years ahead. Current changes in media structure may therefore cause planning problems. For this reason, omnibus surveys or continuous surveys whose data are released on a regular basis is advisable for media planning. A comprehensive annual analysis would (ideally) be composed of ad-hoc rolling samples, taken and evaluated on a monthly basis, as such a progressive analysis would allow the researcher to identify changes at an early stage. This is why the data provided by the *GfK* analysts is now made available within a short period of time.

5.2.5 Further surveys

Apart from these two rival analyses, there are a number of surveys which are published more or less regularly and which focus on specific target groups such as children, young people or public decision takers. Important economic sectors, such as the pharmaceutical industry, are also catered for.

As pharmaceutical advertising has been steadily gaining in importance and, as this sector is in a position to benefit from a large variety of industry-specific periodic publications, a reader survey of medical journals has been indispensable (stratified sampling). Such a survey is *LA-Med*" (which stands for "Reader Analysis of Medical Periodicals") which was set up with a view to investigating the reading behaviour of medical practitioners. *LA-Pharm,* a related study, samples the reading activities of pharmacists and their employees.

Furthermore, there are several surveys that are commissioned by the **major publishing companies**. One that should be mentioned here is the *Typology of Wishes* (www.sinus-milieus.de) which is conducted for the *Hubert Burda Media* Group. It uses personal interviewing methods and samples around 10,000 people. It provides information on the following:

- the readership of some 85 consumer magazines and TV programmes,
- consumer behaviour (including buyers and users) in roughly 20 areas of consumption,
- specific psychographic characteristics of the interviewees.

Provided that the survey has been properly executed, the results regarding the reading and viewing activities of magazine readers and TV audiences should be comparable to those produced by *Media Analysis* and *Allensbach Media Vehicle Analysis*. The advantage of the *Typology of Wishes* lies in the fact that it also includes consumer behaviour and psychographic readership features on a larger scale.

A related competitor of the *Typology of Wishes* is *Consumer Analysis (Verbraucheranalyse, VA)* that has been commissioned by the publishing groups of *Springer* and *Bauer*. Apart from covering important media such as magazines, newspapers radio and television, data is provided on consumer behaviour, ownership of specific items, leisure interests, the product information buyers are interested in, consumer attitudes, brand awareness and price sensitivity. In addition to the product areas under investigation, data is supplied on individual brands. Based on the analysis of 300 product areas and over 1,000 brands, *Consumer Analysis* relies on demographic variables that are analogous to those researched by *Media Analysis*. It supplies information on roughly 30 leisure and product areas.

Further stratified surveys worth mentioning are *Kinder-Lese-Analyse (Kinder-LA)* that researches children's reading activities and *Jugend-Media-Analyse (Jugend-MA)* that investigates the media usage of young people. In addition, there are surveys that focus on religious groups *(Konpres; Konfessionsgebundene Medien)*, decision takers *(Lese-Analyse Entscheidungsträger; LAE)* and communication in general, such as *Kommunikationsanalyse (KA)* that is commissioned by the *Gruner & Jahr*.

5.2.6 Evaluation

Surveys conducted for the major publishing companies are particularly prone to arrive at the results desired by the commissioning organisations. This also applies to the research which *GfK* performs for the major broadcasting corporations. Surveys of this nature are likely to produce **flawed** results that are in line with the interests of those who have commissioned the surveys.

The following questions and the criteria they deal with should facilitate the task of critically evaluating the large number of existing surveys:

• Who is the commissioning party and which media have been researched?

The commissioning company and the media surveyed are often interlinked. Radio broadcasters, for instance, may wish to know more about the reach of their programmes, and publishers might be interested in finding out how well their magazines are performing. However, this would suggest that the data supplied should be met with a fair amount of scepticism. Commissioned survey research may be biased towards the expectations of the commissioning party.

- What is influence that the interested parties (e. g. publishers or radio corporations) may potential exert on the results submitted to them?
- Is there a discernible systematic bias in the evaluation of the data provided?
- Which institutions have conducted the survey?
- The answer to this question allows conclusions as to the dependability of the data.
- At what time was the survey conducted? When were its results published?
- These two items show whether the data supplied is recent enough to be relevant for the planning process.
- What were the size and the composition of the random sampling?
- The decisive question in this context is whether one's own target group is well represented by the sample investigated. The absolute size of the sample is of no relevance.
- Are the survey results appropriate?
- Is media usage the sole research object or does the survey contain information on consumer behaviour and the psychological characteristics of the interviewees?

In media studies, the *IVW* (*Informationsgemeinschaft zur Feststellung der Verbreitung von Werbeträgern e.V.*; www.ivw.de) holds a special position in Germany. This association was founded as far back as 1949 at the initiative of the *ZAW (Zentralausschuss der Werbewirtschaft*; www.zaw.de), the central national committee of the advertising sector. Its major responsibility is the supervision of publications and of the circulation reports provided by all the media corporations that are associated with it. Membership is optional but by becoming an *IVW* subscriber, media corporations signal to the advertising sector that they comply with the committee's supervisory standards.

Despite the weaknesses of the currently existing surveys, one can assume that they provide a sufficient amount of reasonably accurate estimates about what kind of persons (who are demographically stratified) use which types of media, when these media are used and to what degree of intensity, so that these groups can subsequently be reached by advertising measures.

5.3 Advertising research

In advertising practice, two questions are continually raised. One is concerned with "the ultimate" **advertising impact**, the other with "the most appropriate" method of researching this impact. Neither of these questions is quite apposite. They should focus instead on the complex system of "response elements" which bring about the advertising impact. This, however, would require specific measuring techniques. Compare the following passage to *Unger & Durante* (2000) for further in-depth information which also includes research details on the impact of advertising.

5.3.1 The communication model

The following section will structure the multiple dimensions of the advertising impact by applying *Irle's* model (1975:30) which elucidates, *inter alia*, the following components:

- sender and stimulus,
- (pure) perception,
- the act of memorizing,
- preconscious perception,
- mental processing of the contents communicated (cognition),
- personal cognitive structures,
- intended actions,
- observable behaviour.

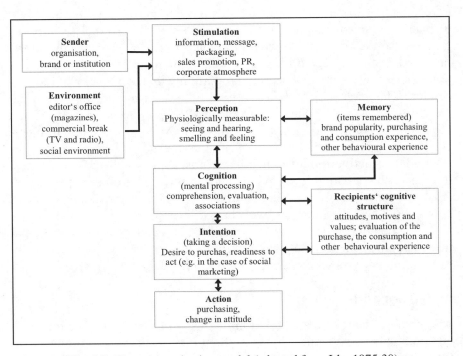

Fig. 5.3. The communication model (adapted from Irle, 1975:30)

Then the feedback between the individual elements and their social environment will be dealt with.

The communication model of relevance here is shown in the following exhibit. The arrows indicate the influence each element exerts on the others. Double arrows retrace the feedback process.

5.3.2 The dimensions of the advertising impact

(1) Stimulation

The complex phenomenon of the "stimulus" is at the start of all possible influences. Recipients do not only perceive advertisements as single stimuli but take in each advertising message together with other stimuli issuing from the media environment. Which part of a message (e. g. of an advertisement) is actually perceived never depends on the design of this particular message alone but also on that of other messages. This is why the **effects achieved by placing** an advertisement efficiently in the sequence of the commercials evidently play a major part, too.

(2) Perception

Perception *per se* can be described – in a physiologically grossly simplified manner – as *the stimulation of the nerve cells* of the external sensory organs. These external cells forward the signals to the "neuron chains" of the brain. All items perceived are thus stored in the memory whose capability to memorize over time increases in proportion with the intensity of the perception. This intensity can be quantified by measuring the changes in the electrical resistance of the skin (*Kroeber-Riel & Weinberg*, 2003:33pp., 63pp. 68 and 192). The capability of the memory to process stimuli intensively and to learn, which derives from the intensity of the perception, is referred to as **activation level**. In other words, the lower the skin resistance, the higher the attention level. As changes in this "electro-dermal reaction" (EDR) occur at precise moments in time, it is possible to make exact statements about how the attention level changes over time.

The perception process, however, cannot be elucidated by queries and investigation and researchers have therefore tried to analyse it mechanically by recording **eye movements** (cf. *Schub von Bossiazky*, 1992:51–59).

(3) Memory interaction

All perceived messages are stored in the memory where they interact with other ongoing perceptions. Moreover, the former may exert an influence on the latter. This is process is indicated by the double arrows in Fig. 5.3.

A **neo-behaviourist** assumption should be mentioned here, according to which the constant stimulation of cells leads to the phenomenon of **"facilitation"**. In other words, a stimulus which is repeatedly perceived, can be absorbed more easily and more quickly over time. Stimuli, which occur simultaneously, too, can be associated with each other increasingly quickly (*Lefrancois*, 1994:70–87).

If respondents are aware of the stimulus material and identify it as an advertising message, for instance, this is referred to as "recognition", if they actively recollect this message, the term "recall" is used.

Recalls can be prompted or unaided. A high recall rate can be occasioned by two factors, namely by the design of the message itself and by what has already been learned about the brand advertised. It is manifestly evident that advertisements for well-known brands achieve a higher recollection rate than advertisements for unknown brands even though the latter may have been designed with an identical degree of intensity.

(4) Cognition

Cognitive or mental processing occurs subsequent to perception. During this phase a mechanism that is known as the reduction of cognitive dissonances (*Festinger*, 1957; *Irle*, 1978) plays a decisive role. It includes

1. resistance to influences that are experienced as constraints (theory of psychological reactance (*Brehm*, 1966),
2. all kinds of associations, i.e. the mental connection between the advertisements observed and personal experience, product appreciation etc.
3. attributions, i.e. people make an inference, for instance, about the underlying purpose of the constraints imposed (*Hewstone*, 1983).

Most mechanisms are not exclusively determined by the external stimulus that is to be processed but, to a large extent, by stored contents and existing opinions.

The emotional processing of communication also takes place in this context. Mental processing influences current perception retrospectively. If a person's interest is aroused, perception intensifies. Disagreeable thoughts and contaminant information (referred to as "noise) that cause dissonance can inhibit and distort perception. People tend to adjust messages to their self-image and to discard those that do not match this image. This explains why **human perception is selective**.

Mental effects can be recorded by **face-to face interviews** and other **polling techniques**; these might include the measuring of associations, a method that was developed by cognitive response research (*Petty & Cacioppo*, 1986). The number of associations that can be ascertained allows us to draw conclusions as to the intensity of the related mental activities and the quality of the inferences about the direction of the potential impact. This type of measurement is based on the premise that stimulus processing can be expressed in words. Visual impressions can be recorded by means of picture scales. In this case, the testing panel does not need to verbalise their experience.

(5) Interaction between perception and cognition

Human beings cannot completely perceive visual stimuli. They take in more and more of their elements, one by one, with increasing intensity. Thus, perception is no spontaneous act but a more or less structured process. Perception is initiated by some emotional and cognitive orientation responses which are perfectly diffuse. However, this initial impression comes to bear on the ensuing perception process. The **first impression,** which is also known as **preconscious perception** (*Steffenhagen*, 1984) is created within seconds when the first contact is made with the stimulus. This highlights the fact that we are dealing with the effects of **subliminal perception**. The biggest problem with subliminal perception is the fact that some people still believe in it (*Rogers & Smith*, 1993).

The type of perception we are looking at consists of pictorial impressions that are so short they cannot be verbalised by human beings. Although it is true that this first impression has an influence on the ensuing perception and processing of stimuli, it cannot be consciously mentally captured. This is why classic research methods fail to elucidate the effects of communication.

The **tachistoscope,** however, is in a position to project pictorial material such as advertisements or package enclosures onto a canvas or a screen. The projection can be executed in an extremely short period of time, i. e. in one thousandth of a second. In addition, there are procedures that briefly expose the pictorial items to spotlights. The projection is so brief that the members of the test panel are unable to identify what exactly they have just seen and undergo a fairly diffuse and predominantly sensory experience.

By conducting an interview after the projection, one can establish the direction which this impression is likely to take. However, the processing of the stimuli is not only influenced by the stimuli that are being offered but also by existing cognitive structures of the recipients.

(6) The influence of cognitive structures

Each *weltbild* is composed of manifold wants, needs, opinions, convictions, perspectives and attitudes, and it is one of the essential communication goals to have a sustained effect on these cognitive structures.

A change in cognitive structures may progress through the following stages:

1. overcoming psychological purchase barriers,
2. improving the social acceptance of products,
3. creating an interest in a product,
4. influencing the perceived significance of different quality features,
5. improving a more favourable product attitude,
6. creating product preferences,
7. arousing usage expectations

One ought to bear in mind that changes in cognitive structures do not usually occur as a result of a message one has perceived. This can be a problem when it comes to **pre-testing the advertising media**, a technique which often relies on only one presentation. Media pre-testing is therefore not necessarily the best expedient to influence cognitive structures. Moreover, opinions and attitudes are not only impacted on by advertising measures but also by product awareness, consumption experiences and a large number of other communication measures and by the competitors in commerce and the media.

For this reason, it seems problematic to claim that changes in cognitive structures, such as image changes, can be clearly attributed to one concrete advertising measure, i. e. one's own advertising campaign.

Bauer, Huber & Hägele (1998) show that the **conjoint analysis** is able to track changes in brand or product preferences after only one single contact with the advertising media – this usually is the case in test situations. This, however, necessitates two (i. e. conjoint) interviews about market preferences:

1. with a control panel that has had no contact with advertising media, and
2. with a comparable test panel after contact with the advertising medium has been established.

If the only distinguishing feature between the two groups is the contact with the advertising medium, the preference differences recorded can probably be subscribed to this contact (*Bauer, Huber & Hägele*, 1998:180 – 194).

(7) Generating a desire to act

The intention to act results from the way in which the stimuli received have been processed, from the existing cognitive structures and from the cognitive structures that have already been changed in the wake of stimuli processing. However, there is very little certainty as to whether the interpretation of the attitudes measured are really meaningful for future behaviour and it seems problematic **to question** consumers about their purchase intentions **directly** after an advertising or communication test, although in advertising practice this is quite common. Researchers who investigate advertising effects are very likely to ask in their questionnaires "Would you be prepared to test this product?" or "Would you buy this product at least once?" But it would be difficult to draw concrete conclusions on the basis of buyer behaviour that has actually occurred.

The double arrows in Fig. 5.2. illustrate the fact that the emerging purchase intention retroactively impacts on existing cognitive structures. This can be seen as a mechanism which reduces cognitive dissonance. In the same way, the actual stimuli processing is influenced by the arising purchase intention Moreover, the intention to take a casual interest in the product which is being presented in a commercial intensifies the processing of stimuli as well as perception.

(8) The impact of advertising on purchasing behaviour

It was outlined above that intended behaviour, which derives from stimuli as well as from other sources, finally leads to observable actions, such as purchasing behaviour. These actions are, on the one hand, the ultimate goal of each and every marketing activity. On the other hand, they are the worst possible quality indicators concerning communication measures, as they can be influenced, more than anything else, by **additional factors**. Apart from personality factors, these are: the social environment, competing marketing measures, consumption activities in completely different areas (which nonetheless tie up purchasing power) and, last but not least, the commercial marketing in general.

The more we move in the communication model from the actual perception towards observable behaviour, the more difficult it is to draw conclusions about the quality of market communication.

By using modern **test market research designs**, the percentage of purchasing behaviour evoked by advertising has become measurable. The test markets are chosen on the basis of the EAN (i. e. European Article Numbering) bar code and a directly connected panel of households, whose purchasing behaviour is recorded when buyers present their store cards at the checkout. In addition, they are linked up with TV research so that their TV usage can be completely monitored as well. Last but not least, their attitude towards print adverts, poster advertising and mail shots is also included in this research.

By introducing novel communication technologies, it has become feasible to test several advertising strategies in one local test market. On the basis of the data that is now available on purchasing behaviour, and on the socio-demographic features of the household panels, structurally identical test groups can be formed. The cable TV programmes of the latter are fed different commercials about a product by using blending techniques. Subsequently, different purchasing reactions of the household panels can be recorded.

5.4 Future developments

The future of media research will belong to the **single source data surveys** that have become increasingly popular since the 1990's. "With this technique, individuals' behaviour is tracked from television sets to the checkout counter." (*Dibb* et al., 2001:504) This sophisticated approach which investigates media usage as well as consumption patterns has been generally favoured by the publishing companies (e. g. *Typology of Wishes* and *Consumer Analysis*) and has now been syndicated to areas other than publishing. **Scanning technology** – in collaboration with household panels – is now offering novel research opportunities that do not necessitate any interviews. A panel of currently 9,000 households (an extension to 12,000 household is under review) forms the empirical foundation for *A.C. Nielsen*'s research. His audits monitor all purchases of consumer goods, the purchase of magazines and newspapers (as well as regular subscriptions to them) and TV usage (*Milde*, 1993:27) in 1,000 households, where TV meters have been installed for this purpose. This research design is comparable to the afore-mentioned *GfK* survey. Participants monitor each purchase made by a hand-held scanner. This is possible as EAN bar codes can now be found on nearly all product types. The purchase of print media is also registered by means of bar codes.

"TV usage is measured by a micro computer which is mounted on the TV set, aka TV meter. This device checks at 2 second intervals which TV channel has been selected and stores the channel number together with information on which members of the household are in the process of watching TV. These persons indicate this by pressing a button on a specific remote control device" (op. cit.). The data retrieved is transmitted via modems and the telephone lines to a central collection point.

The data banks thus created provide information about purchase behaviour, exposure to marketing measures, media usage and other pieces of information culled from additional investigations.

Whereas, in the past, media planning was founded on demographically stratified target audiences, single source research now permits planning on the basis of buyer households.

According to *Assael & Poltrack* (1991, 1993, 1994 and 1996), advertising plans relying directly on measured buyer behaviour produce more efficient media plans than conventional designs based on socio-demographically stratified target groups.

Several studies have shown that, *summa summarum*, media selection founded on single source surveys, which simultaneously record consumption behaviour and media usage, have an edge over traditional designs. In future, it will probably be necessary to define target groups not only in terms of socio-demographic stratification but also according to their purchasing behaviour. This presupposes sufficiently large samples that will need to considerably exceed the current number of 1,000 households. Only area samples that cover large areas whose commercial structure and households are equally representative will suffice in terms of efficient media planning.

5.5 Selected methods of strategic analysis

Permanently auditing the marketing environment is of considerable importance for the planning of marketing measures and their implementation. Globally changing value orientation, fashions and styles may influence the contents of communication messages. The social acceptance of certain consumption areas may change und thus suddenly represent a new chance (e. g. the social acceptance of environmentally friendly fuels) or threat (e. g. outlawing of environmentally hazardous sources of energy) for marketing, especially the marketing of newly developed products.

For this reason, there will be, in the following sections, an emphasis on some selected methods which can be employed to analyse long-term external developments as well as internal resources.

5.5.1 Analysing opportunities and threats

In our day and age, corporations distinguish themselves by their increasing dynamics and complexity. Changes in their macro-environment considerably affect the management of marketing communications. These changes in the marketing environment create new opportunities for marketing communications (e. g. by a greater differentiation of the media system), but they also hold new threats (e. g. increased information overload of the targeted persons). Consequently, communications management needs to keep an eye on the most important developments, which, however, will not be discussed in great detail in this publication. Executives, therefore, employ a specific

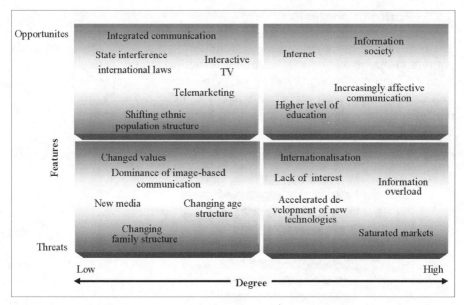

Fig. 5.4. Communications-oriented auditing of environmental developments (an example)

opportunity and risk analysis in order to identify the relevant external environmental forces which are of significance for their corporation.

5.5.2 Analysing strengths and weaknesses

The decisions taken with regard to market communications are considerably affected by the competitive situation which companies are facing. They need to take into account the activities of their rivals, especially when they decide on positioning and the way in which this is communicated but also when they start their media planning process and design their advertising messages (*Unger & Fuchs*, 2005:79).

Analysing a company's strengths and weaknesses, i. e. its competitive stance, requires qualitative as well as quantitative data. **Qualitative data** tackle, first and foremost, the contents of the messages issued by a company's major competitors. Some of the questions to be answered here are: How have these competitors positioned themselves in the market? How do they design their messages? **Quantitative data** particularly deal with the total amount spent on communication by the competitors and by this entire economic sector, the tools and the media employed and the advertising time allocated.

5.5.3 Portfolio analysis

The portfolio analysis ensures that a corporation is always considered as an entity and that its philosophy is future as well as strategy oriented. Market communication can only be reasonably planned and implemented if it is imbedded in an overall corporate strategy (*Unger & Fuchs*, 2005:64). The portfolio analysis determines, above all, **budget** requirements.

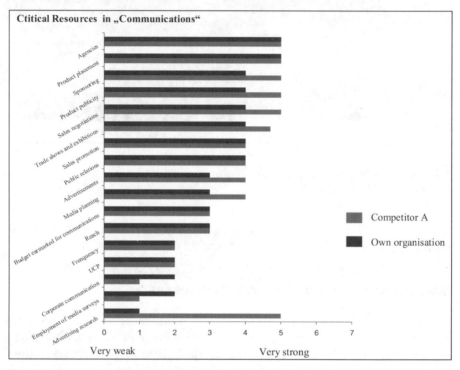

Fig. 5.5. Communication-oriented analysis of strengths and weaknesses (an example)

5.5.4 Positioning analysis

The positioning of their business units and the product and service they offers is a vital decision area for corporate management. It encompasses the central idea that captures the corporation's or brand's meaning and their distinctiveness and thus represents the starting point of each and every communication concept. This applies even though it is the **market of opinions** and not the **product market** which is the central issue of communications management. Subsequently, it is the psychological factors,

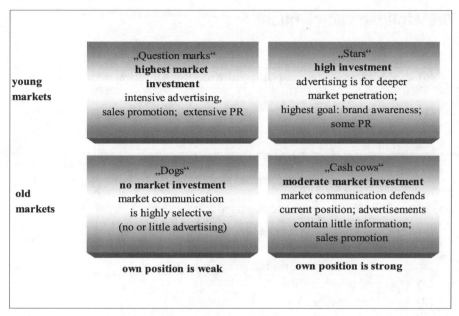

Fig. 5.6. Portfolio analysis based on communication strategies (*Unger & Fuchs*, 2005:65).

i. e. the affective benefits (which are added benefits) that are instrumental to positioning (*Unger & Fuchs*, 2005:65).

On positioning their products, and on communicating this position to their customers, companies ought to avoid the following mistakes (*Kotler & Bliemel*, 2001: 497):

- **Underpositioning** occurs when there is a perceived lack of differentiation, i. e. the target groups cannot identify any special features about a company or its offers which are considered to be one of many.
- **Overpositioning** results from the fact that a company and its offer are perceived as too specific or too narrow by the target group. This causes certain demand potentials to be restricted or even excluded.
- **Confused positioning** arises due to an uncertain or diffuse image in the minds of customers due to contradictory positioning attempts, multiple utility claims or frequent repositioning.
- **Doubtful positioning,** i. e. the target group has strong reservations about the company or brand and accredits it with little credibility.

5.6 Multiple choice questions

Question 5/1: Which of these statements on "media analysis" are correct?

(a)	Media analyses capture information on how many persons spend how much time to what avail?
(b)	Typical media analyses simply elucidate purchasing behaviour.
(c)	Market media analyses include media and purchasing behaviour.
(d)	Media analysis uses different random sampling designs to investigate media usage behaviour.

Question 5/2: What criteria can be used to assess media analyses?

(a)	the commissioning company and the media researched
(b)	the potential influence the commissioning publishers, TV corporations or institutions can exert on the results
(c)	cost of investigation
(d)	size and composition of the sample

Question 5/3: Which of the statements below on the "communication model" are correct?

(a)	Recipients perceive advertisements as a single stimulus.
(b)	"Facilitation" means that repeated stimuli are processed at an increasingly slower pace.
(c)	Market communications aim at exerting a sustainable influence on cognitive structures.
(d)	It will be more and more cost-intensive to achieve a good market penetration with new products.

Question 5/4: What mistakes can be made when products are positioned?

(a)	Underpositioning
(b)	adequate positioning
(c)	Overpositioning
(d)	ambiguous positioning

Question 5/5: Which "critical resources" are aimed at in a communication-oriented strengths and weaknesses analysis?

(a)	quality of sales intermediaries
(b)	quality of advertising
(c)	quality of media planning
(d)	quality of service

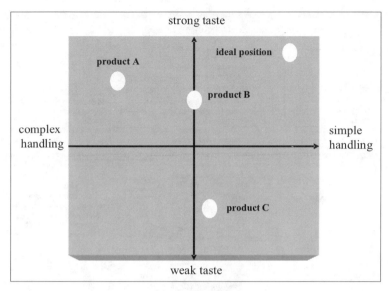

Fig. 5.7. Two-dimensional positioning model (*Unger & Fuchs*, 2005:71)

5.7 Case study

You are the Marketing Manager of *Cosmetics plc*, a producer of skin care products, and you have been requested to systematically tackle the question as to whether the **impact of your advertising measures on buyer behaviour** can be measured.
Solution

1. The communication model shows the part of market research that is the object of the above assignment (see Figure below and item 4.3.1).
2. It stands to reason that the data provided by conventional panel research (e. g. a panel of selected households, the commercial Nielsen panel or the GfK panel) can never be an instrument of systematic communications research for companies such as *Cosmetics plc* (*Unger & Fuchs*, 2005:607). **These panels always measure the success of the marketing mix as a whole** and the results produced include additional factors such as competitive behaviour, the current business cycle and commercial influences. This research therefore does not reflect the success of advertising measures (as opposed to the impact of "communication measures") but simply the marketing success as such.

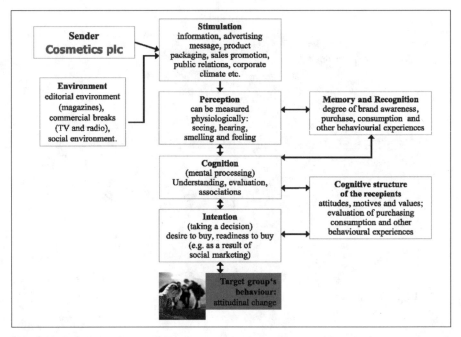

Fig. 5.8. The dimensions of the communication effects achieved at *Cosmetics plc* (adapted from *Irle*, 1975:30).

3. However, *Cosmetics plc* can now resort to the opportunities provided by **electronic panel research,** which is currently offered in Germany by *GfK* and A.C. Nielsen (i. e. the *GfK* behaviour scan and ERIM panel respectively), Nielsen-Telerim) if they really wish to measure the share advertising has in the marketing success (i. e. the "advertising success" itself).

4. In 1977, 13 European countries introduced EAN coding (see: www.ean-int.org) in order to save the cost of price labelling and to simplify checkout procedures. These codes are used at Electronic Points of Sale (EPOS) to record the number of all FMCGs (Fast Moving Consumer Goods) sold and thereby the relationship between the sales and the totality of purchasers. Additionally, they can supply data on:
a) the price of the item purchased;
b) the number of similar or identical items sold (including those supplied by the competitors);
c) competing pricing at the same sales outlet;
d) number of buyers, who acquired a certain article within a certain period of time;

e) ther items that were acquired with the item in question and how often the former were purchased;

f) purchase during a specific promotional measure or shortly after an intercom announcement in the sales outlet;

g) purchases that can be associated, under certain circumstances, with specific households and their media behaviour provided that electronically aided combined household and commercial panels have been created for these households,

h) classic consumer advertising measures directed via TV or test advertisements to certain households,

The information mentioned under f), g) and h) can be obtained by *Cosmetics plc* if the conventional EAN-based household code is connected with a novel type of household panel. Such a panel would provide all participating households with scanner-readable identity cards which are presented at each purchase. Sales outlets that are equipped with check-out scanners can then record relevant purchase data as well as the **media behaviour** of these households.

The media behaviour of the customers of *Cosmetics plc* will be captured by the *Gfk* **TV research** which supplies the participating households with "people meters" for their TV set which precisely records all types of TV usage and transfers this data to a central data base.

1. Moreover, the households (of potential and existing) customers of *Cosmetics plc* may be supplied with free magazines in which **test ads** have been placed. This would enable the company to additionally measure the impact of print commercials or of a media mix including TV as well as the print media.

2. The afore-mentioned novel communication technologies will enable companies to check the efficiency of **a combination of advertising strategies** in a given local test market. Consequently, they would put *Cosmetics plc* in a position to establish structurally identical test groups in each of their intended test markets on the basis of the data that has so far been obtained on the purchasing behaviour of the households concerned. As these test groups would be exclusively set up by using electronically collected data (and without employing any polling techniques whatsoever) and as the purchase behaviour of these test groups would be captured in the same way, the **effects of testing** could be reduced to a bare minimum. However, companies need to consider that this approach would only provide exact information about how many households had potentially established contact with TV commercials or magazines: A switched-on TV set does not necessarily mean that this contact automatically includes watching the commercials.

3. Last but not least, it is cable TV that makes it possible for *Cosmetics plc* to test **a combination of TV commercials in a local test market** with a view to the purchasing impact they have achieved. This would again require the formation of test and control groups which are completely comparable in terms of their socio-demographic features and the purchasing behaviour they have shown in the past. Via cable TV, these test groups will be exposed to different commercials of one specific product: Group 1, for instance, will receive commercial A and Group II will be fed commercial B whereas the control group will not be exposed to any commercials of the same product at all but to a completely different commercial. This combination can also be used for two different motives in newspaper advertisements with one part of the test households receiving motive A and another part being offered motive B.

4. By way of conclusion, we can state that, by employing the approach outlined above, *Cosmetics plc* will gain information about the **buyer behaviour** that finally occurred, but it will, nonetheless, remain in complete ignorance about the underlying **cognitive and affective processes** that motivate its target groups. Knowing these processes is, however, a prerequisite for systematically optimised advertising. This signifies that if *Cosmetics plc* were to discard these processes and to reduce its market research to scanner-based techniques, it would take a step backwards towards a methodological research approach which sees human beings as **"black boxes",** which bar all internal processes from view.

6 The goals of communication policies

6.1 Expected learning outcomes

This chapter will address the significance of precisely-defined target groups and will discuss the categories generally used to provide such definitions. Subsequently, there will be a focus on the importance of creating a certain corporate image, internally as well as externally, and on the contribution made to this image by what is referred to as "corporate identity". This will be followed by elucidating the idea of a Unique Communication Proposition (UCP) and the economic and operative aims that underlie a company's communication policies. The formulation of media aims and objectives will conclude this chapter.

On completing this chapter,

1. you will know how target groups can be analysed,
2. you will be able to explain what constitutes a company's "corporate identity mix" ,
3. you will have learned to distinguish between USP and UCP,
4. you will be in a position to explain the operational and economic goals of communications,
5. you will be able to distinguish between media aims such as "frequent exposure" and "media reach".

6.2 Profiling the target audience

Consumer behaviour in most populations is becoming more and more diverse. For this reason, an accurate identification of a company's target audience (i. e. viewers, readers, listeners) in combination with appropriate market segmentation studies have become indispensable for the success of marketing communications.

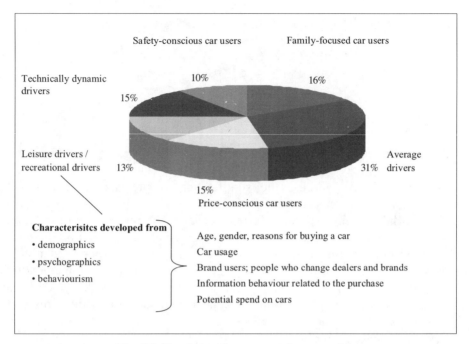

Fig. 6.1. Typology of consumers (an example)

Target audiences need to be identified for essentially two reasons:

- Marketing seeks to meet the needs of target groups as best as it can. We can safely assume that the impact of advertising messages can be substantially improved if they have been designed in harmony with the attitudinal make-up of the target audiences they are directed at. A precise definition of these groups can therefore assist in optimising the design of suitable advertisements.
- If a company knows which customers to target and if media surveys have revealed which media these persons use, an appropriately defined target audience warrants a commercially sensible choice of media classes and vehicles. If such a definition is to be relevant for media planning, it must make sure that the target audiences have been determined by employing the same characteristics as the most commonly applied media surveys.

Target groups can be determined by the following characteristics:

- demographics such as age, sex, income, occupation;
- psychographics such as interests, values or attitudes;

- economic features such as ownership of estates, household appliances (e. g. deep freezers) or computers owned
- observable consumer behaviour as it is known from the data provided by household panel research

There are various institutes that provide a number of surveys which offer information on certain quantitative characteristics of the target groups (e. g. male persons aged from 21 to 39). Such surveys are *inter alia*:

- Media Analysis (MA) provided by AG.MA (in German: Arbeitsgemeinschaft Media-Analyse),
- the Allensbach media vehicle analysis (in German: Allensbacher Werbeträgeranalyse or AWA),
- the GfK TV panel,
- end-user survey (in German: Verbraucher-Analyse or VA),
- the Typology of Wishes (German acronym: TdW; provided by TdW Intermedia),
- the consumer audits provided by Nielsen and GfK .

These studies permit a large variety of quantitative assessments such as:

- composition of target groups and their percentage of the population total,

How does target groups interrelate with other socio-demographic characteristics?
How many women aged 35 to 55, for instance, dispose of what yearly income?
How many people who dispose of a certain personal income are male?

- extrapolations

How big is the target group described by a certain combination of features?
What is the percentage of buyers in this group?
How many readers of a specific magazine belong to this target group?

- buyer behaviour

How many group members who purchased item A, also bought item B within the same period of time?
How many persons who previously bought product A, followed this up by (how many) repeat purchases in the subsequent test period?
How many persons have changed to product B or have acquired neither of these products?

- choice of the sales point

How many group members have bought which products in what kind of sales outlet?

How many items have they bought and at what price?

- media usage

As companies also know which persons use which media, the choice of media can thus be simultaneously optimised on the basis of the above and other pieces of information.

For reasons of practicality, it could be more advantageous to conduct this type of survey by using a **questionnaire** which contains a checklist of questions such as the following (adapted from *Huth & Pflaum*, 2005: 253 pp.):

Can the target group in question be typified demographically in terms of age, gender, income bracket, marital status, size of family, children?

Can this target group be structured psycho-graphically on the basis of the following or of similar underlying questions?

- Which type of need is of essential importance to this target audience?
- Which activating techniques can be applied to improve the learning outcome expected from the advertising measure to be taken?
- What kind of positive reinforcement can be employed to strengthen the learning effects?
- How can the target group's opinions and product expectations be confirmed?
- Which perceptual capabilities can be activated or stimulated to enhance memorisation?
- Do the target group and the product in question necessitate the avoidance or the provocation of "cognitive dissonances" during or after the purchase?
- How can the target group's thoughts, feelings etc. be characterised?
- Can one create favourable product attitudes in a specific target group?

Which sociological features are seen as characteristic for this target group? This question could be underpinned by the following:
- Are there groups with typical members and how can they be described?
- Which norms can be perceived in this group of typical members?
- Is there a role differentiation within this group?
- Are there opinion leaders?
- Are there marginalized subgroups and how can they be depicted?
- Are there reference groups?

- Does this group dispose of the consumer goods that are relevant for our advertising issues?
  - Are there observable typical consumer attitudes that could be of interest in terms of the advertising assignment that we are confronted with?
  - Who is the purchase "decider"? Who are the buyers and the users of the product in question? Are these the same or different persons?
  - What kind of relationship is there between the wants and the needs of the target group? How is the product positioned with regard to the preferences expressed within the target group?
  - Is there an observable brand awareness or brand loyalty in the target group?
  Which is the role played by rational purchasing decisions such as:
  - price
  - maintenance, service, customer services
  - quality
  - packaging, safety etc.

- When is the purchase made? Purchasing habits and their fluctuations.
- Where is the purchase made? Is there a sales-related geographical pattern?
- Which strong or weak areas have been identified on selling similar products in the same market?
- Are there discernible reasons for the existence of these areas? Were the success areas built up intentionally in the past? Were there other intentional factors?
- What are the consequences resulting from this place and time-related analysis? Would it be more advantageous to carry out advertising measures (related to the afore-mentioned places and purchasing times) in the areas of success or would it be advisable to step up advertising in the weak areas by way of compensation.

6.3 Targeting methods

The analogy method

Marketing often focuses on the identification of groups whose members could be potential consumers, i.e. on target markets, whereas media planning is, first and foremost, concerned with finding out which target group members can be reached by what media as efficiently as possible.

The analogy method is based on the assumption that the same demographic characteristics impact on consumer attitudes and on consumer media usage in the same way. This assumption is based on consumer research such as the *GfK* **end user survey.** Moreover, there are surveys on **media usage** such as the TV audience research and the data provided by *Media Analysis*. Researchers investigate whether market segments can best be distinguished by their level of consumption in general, by the number of the purchases made or by the intensity of the consumption. Moreover, they are interested in finding out which characteristics determine these segments most clearly: demographics or psychographics? Last but not least, they seek to trial the question as to whether the groups covered by media surveys also show the same typical habits when it comes to their usage of media. Having taken the cost of airtime into account, the intensity of media usage within these groups is, *inter alia*, an important criterion of media selection.

This approach, however, is only appropriate, if consumer surveys as well as media surveys use the same characteristics to define consumers and media users.

Amalgamated surveys

If the assumptions that underpin the above analogies are largely accepted, the data provided by several surveys can be merged. Currently, this approach is the most widely used one.

It permits, for instance, to merge **readership and print media surveys** print media surveys with **TV broadcasting surveys** and consumer behaviour studies with media usage analyses, again assuming that all surveys have applied identical description methods and sampling patterns. Shared characteristics are especially suitable in the above context, if there is a definite correlation between them. The merges studies are subsequently presented as one single study. However, the above premises are not always strictly complied with. It may therefore occur that the samples are arrived at by differing methods. As the result of these "mergers", flawed approaches which hide the deficiencies of one survey behind the other, frequently fail to manifest themselves.

If there is an extremely strong correlation and a nearly identical structural pattern between the two surveys to be merged, they virtually simulate a "single source study". And indeed, it is the single source method that holds the most potential for the future.

The single source method

Let's sum up the snags involved in the analogy and the amalgamation approaches once more: Currently, the majority of surveys (that are provided by panels) are ad hoc investigations into either buying behaviour or media behaviour. If marketers are able to identify a certain group of the population, e. g. male persons aged from 29 to 49, who tend to consume substantial amounts of red wine, they will look for the following information in media surveys: Which media are intensively favoured and used more often than by the average reader or viewer in this male age group. The answer might be the favourite magazine of German hobby chefs and gourmets. From this marketers would develop the hypothesis that red wine lovers aged 29 to 40 tend to read *"Der Gourmet"*.

Such an assumption would cumulate the potentially possible methodological errors of two surveys. The same problem occurs when the results of two surveys are added up arithmetically.

The single source method offers a solution to this dilemma as it integrates both **media and consumer behaviour** in one survey. However, the results of these global surveys which investigate media and the consumer behaviour in large markets, are still too unspecific to meet the requirements of media planning regarding a specific product or business organisation. The experience of US researchers suggests that, in future, single source methods will definitely win the day as they bypass the errors that have hampered the analogy method. Furthermore, they appear to be sounder and more meaningful.

Why has the single source method only recently seemed plausible and possible? Although the problems arising from the analogy and amalgamation methods have long since been known, the single source method was unsuccessful as it was cumbersome and required a considerable amount of data. The individual members of a typical household panel, for instance, were compelled to log their entire consumption activities in "purchase diaries" and this was followed up by face-to face interviews in which the same group of persons provided data about approximately 100 magazines and newspapers, all radio and TV broadcasters, all other media they used and the cinemas they went to. However, such intensive interviewing is methodologically unviable and risks distorting the overall perspective of the interviewee in the long term. This is also known as the **panel effect**.

Nowadays, the situation is such that all **TV viewing activities** can be electronically recorded without requiring any effort on the part of the panel members. This does not necessitate the somewhat controversial "people meters" which are – in the eyes of the authors of this module – dispensable. Consumer behaviour in its entirety does not need to be recorded in

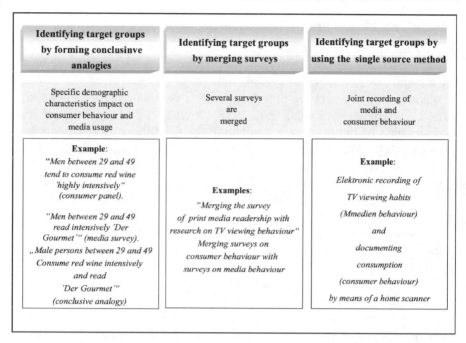

Fig. 6.2. Methods to identify target consumers

writing any more as this task can now be carried out by **home scanners**.
Even magazine purchases can thus be monitored although this does not
apply to the reader's personal usage of the magazines purchased. This has
reduced the interview effort and technologically paved the way for the
single source method.

6.4 Corporate identity

6.4.1 Defining corporate identity

The term *corporate identity* signifies the communal feeling of identity
within an organisation to which all employees subscribe. The identity of an
organisation depicts its **characteristic properties** which – ideally – are
exclusively associated with this organisation. This implies that each organisation enjoys an intentional **uniqueness**. If a corporation is unmistakable this translates as a distinctive competitive edge in market communications. A company's identity should be reflected in the way in which it
communicates and determines it's "character", and how it practises its
philosophy. The specific hallmark of corporate identity is its **focus on** an

organisation's **inner assets**, i. e. its people, a focus that also stretches to the suppliers, the labour market and other external environmental sectors. The copy strategy, by contrast, exclusively makes reference to a company's sales market.

It should be pointed out in the above context that the semantic construct of "corporate identity" is founded on the idea that organisations generally behave like people. This interpretation seems highly problematic. However, the psychology of human perception looking into how human beings perceive and are perceived cannot simply be conferred to abstract objects such as businesses and other organisations. This is why the transferred epithet of "personal identity" should be seen as no more than a **metaphor** for business organisations, and the limitations of this approach should always be borne in mind (metaphors focus on one essential similarity between two items but tend to neglect their multi-faceted differences). The authors who first propagated this concept did nonetheless believe in its transferability; business studies in general tend to "borrow" their metaphors and similes from biology with a further point in case being the concepts of the "market life cycle" and the "technology life cycle" or the general likening of organisations to living organisms. Metaphors of this nature are adequate if they generate creative or innovative ideas but one should always be sceptical if biological processes are used as direct similes for the socio-technological phenomena that occur in corporations.

Corporate identity aims at forging an unambiguous and unmistakable relationship between the image, the actions and the communications of each organisation.

Alluding to the concept of the marketing mix, the founding fathers (*Birkigt, Stadler & Funk*, 1995:23) of "corporate identity" present the following outline of their concept, which they referred to as "identity mix":

A corporation's personality, which refers to the interrelation between human beings and the company and which continually develops and evolves, lies at the core of corporate identity. However, the authors of this module do not believe in this assumed interrelation between people and corporations. It is not the enterprises and organisations – let alone the nations – that take action but the people who form those social systems. For this reason, corporate identity is employed as an expedient to **coordinate** the behaviour of as many people as possible who constitute a business. This aspect underlies the importance of internal marketing and of internal communications. Compared to the copy strategy and its exclusive emphasis on the sales markets, corporate identity enjoys a much greater scope. Internal measures aim at persuading everybody who is involved and to bring their behaviour in line with corporate identity.

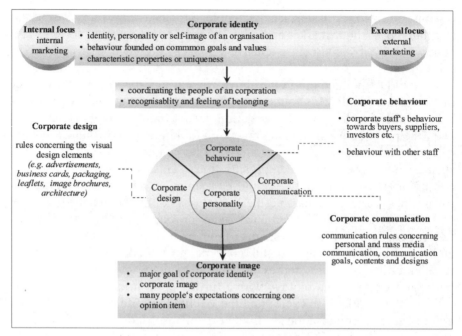

Fig. 6.3. Charting corporate identity (adapted from *Birkigt, Stadler, Funk*, 1995:23)

6.4.2 Corporate behaviour

It is now received knowledge (*Birkigt, Stadler & Funk*, 1995:23 pp.) that the "corporate personality" expresses the **self-concept** of a corporation. This is integrated in this organisation's philosophy and thereby becomes the behavioural guideline for all measures taken to promote the feeling of corporate identity. At this point we should emphasise again that social systems such as business organisations cannot experience any degree of self-reflection. Only people are capable of that; and this situation is rendered even more complex by the fact that the ethical standards that govern families, religious communities, governments and the cultural background of those involved in organisational life also may exert a strong external influence on everyone concerned. However, this is exactly where corporate identity come + s into play which is to be **driving force that ensures that corporate behaviour is guided by the organisation's common goals and values** under precisely such complex conditions.

Thus, corporate identity become the expedient that influences the behaviour of all members of an enterprise. this applies, in the one hand, the behaviour of corporate staff concerning competitors, buyers, suppliers, investors and other institutions. On the other hand, it comprises the **behaviour**

amongst members of staff such as the superiors' leadership styles and peer behaviour.

6.4.3 Corporate communication

Communication rules need to be laid down not only with a view to the **communication with the mass media** but also for direct **personal communication** in sales negotiations and individual statements of the members of the management. They ought to guide the contents as well as the style of communications.

In addition, corporate communication is responsible for the formulation of the communication goals which can be broken down into quantifiable objectives that are measurable economically (such as a corporation's market share or simply its sales targets) or aims that can be assessed psychologically such as image, favourable attitudes, level of awareness or the competence to tailor specific orders.

Corporate communication goals are strategic and therefore take a long-term view. They provide the framework for the short-term focus of the operational aims which they integrate into the overall communications strategy.

6.4.4 Corporate design

The term "corporate design" refers to the **formal aspects of communications**. It embraces all visual design elements employed in an enterprise, i.e. the design of advertisements, company letter heads and layouts and business cards. In particular, it includes a company's packaging and colour schemes, its symbols as well as its interior design and architecture, and this might, if need be, extended to dress codes and the type of company cars. Moreover, corporate design plays a powerful part in the conception of product and service catalogues, in-house newsletters, image brochures and other corporate literature.

Continuity, which warrants that the advertising measures undertaken are recognised, is of utmost importance to corporate identity. At times of information overload it is particularly essential that all messages should be quickly and unmistakably associated with one's own corporation. Ideally, this will also create **synergy effects** between all communication measures.

Compared to the other elements of corporate identity, marketing practitioners tend **to overestimate** the significance of corporate design and to focus too heavily on a corporation's compliance with the formal design rules, occasionally at the expense of the communicated **contents.** Be that as it may, formal design which makes use of a whole series of visual features remains the starting point of each and every communication approach. Owing to their importance, it seems appropriate to deal with the most significant elements of corporate design, which are graphic illustrations, architecture, product and packaging design, in much greater detail:

1. Graphic design

Graphic design is considered to be the fundament on which corporate design is built. It provides the framework in which all graphic design components are integrated.

Symbols or icons

Symbols or icons are associated with attributed meanings and are capable of communicating complex semantic issues. They are indicators of a person's association with manifold social systems such as clubs, cooperations and other organisations and, over time, they can become synonymous with these systems. The term "brand name", for instance, was borrowed from the cattle branding of former times, where the burned-in mark or "brand" emphasized ownership claims. Nowadays, the brand name stands for the origin of a product. Finally, symbols can show how certain objects are used or suggest advisable actions (sign posts, road signs, etc.).

As a rule, corporate symbols can be seen as the most essential component of design. They may represent the purpose of an enterprise and may indicate which products, people and trade marks belong to it. As symbols are often determined and retained over time, they are associated to a large extent with the continuity of corporate communications and possibly with corporate management. In organisational literature, "symbols" are also termed "logos" (which is short for "logotypes"), "company emblems", "trademarks" or "brand marks". All these expressions are semantically closely related or even synonymous. Logos often include pictures or nonverbal symbols, but they may consist of letters or words that show a corporation's name inscribed in its own characteristic lettering.

In a nutshell: Corporate symbols are the most outstanding components of graphic design, which, for its part, constitutes the centre piece of corporate design which represents core area of corporate identity. For this reason, it is, without any doubt, the most important task of marketing communications to develop a corporate logo that stands for the organisation as a whole.

We would like to highlight four different types of symbols:

Pictorial trademarks

Branded products in particular tend to employ pictures in their logos, the most famous being the "apple", i. e. the corporate symbol the well-known IT company, or the "Red Cross", the emblem of the international humanitarian organisation. The *Deutsche Bank* logo also falls into this category as do the Vauxhall (*Opel* or *Holden*) symbol and the "radio tower", the symbol of the major Southern German radio broadcaster which constitutes a fairly direct pictorial replica. Whether the "dotted S", the trademark of the German savings banks, is actually a picture or a letter symbol is a moot point.

Signatures

Scripts, i. e. ornately written trade names, are the counterparts of picture symbols. The distinctive white *Coca Cola* brand name on red background is a case in point. No matter in which alphabet (Arabic, Latin, Chinese) this signature is rendered, it is immediately recognised. Further well-known script signatures are, to name but a few, are *Walt Disney* (e. g. films and publications), the Camel (shoes, cigarettes), *Bahlsen* (biscuits), *ecco* (shoes), *Vox* and *n tv* (German TV programmes) and *Toto Lotto* (the German national lottery).

Acronyms and letters

Brand names may be too long and may therefore need to be reduced to their acronyms or to single letters. There are numerous examples such as *DB* (German Railways), *ICE* (Intercity Express), *ADAC* (the leading German Automobile club), *n tv* (the news channel), *RTL* (the Luxembourg radio and TV broadcasters) to name but a few. The letters and acronyms too, are set in a distinctive type (face).

Combined symbols

Pictorial symbols may seem to be advantageous in communications as they transmit the advertising message very intensively. However, images may be interpreted incorrectly. Typographical symbols, by contrast, may be hampered by a weaker communication impact but, in exchange, they are much less ambiguous. Single letters and acronyms do not enjoy any of these advantages; a combination of pictorial and typographical elements therefore seems to be advisable.

The following examples represent well-received combinations of such combinations: *Lufthansa* (the major German air carrier), *John Deere* (a full-line provider of agricultural machines), *Wella* (hair care products), the car producers *Citroen, Renault, Peugeot, Toyota, Mitsubishi, Apolli-naris* (table water), *TUI* (travel agents and tour organisers) and, last but not least, *Wüstenrot,* a German building society.

BMW (motor vehicles), *MAN* (trucks, coaches and articulated vehicles) and the ISP (Internet service provider) AOL represent successful combinations of acronyms and pictures.

It goes without saying that the above statements do not refer to popular organisations such as the *ADAC* (and to the acronym of its trade name) or to extremely strong trademarks such as *Coca Cola.* Over the years, this brand has been so extensively (and intensively) promoted that ordinary design directives do not apply any longer. *Coca Cola* definitely plays in a league of is own.

Layouts

Set layouts focus on the formal aspects of the design such as the physical arrangement of the copy (i. e. headlines, sub-headings, body copy and signature) and of the illustrations. It also includes line spacing, column widths, the structure and size of charts, graphs and diagrams as well as the size of the copy and the illustrations. Like all other design elements, set layouts are responsible for the consistency of the advertisements and thereby warrant the continuity and recognition of the communication measures implemented.

Typefaces and typography

On choosing a typeface, designers should not only be guided by the distinctive characteristics of the chosen typeface but even more so by its readability. As a rule, marketing communications ought to restrict the number of types used in all their tasks to a few.

Typography refers to the structure of the entire text: the paragraphs, the lines, the highlighting of certain text elements. In all these cases, the major aims should be to attract the readers' attention and to ensure the user-friendliness of the text design while avoiding graphic(al) overload.

Colours

People identify with an object, first and foremost, via its colour which may conjure up for them the feeling of recognition and provoke refusal or acceptance. In different cultures, however, colours may symbolise specific emotions. Moreover, selected colour combinations may create uniqueness. *Toom*, a supermarket chain, for instance, uses a distinctive combination of red and yellow in their corporate colour scheme. The *MakroMarkt* (yellow) and *MediaMarkt* (red) chains (durables and electronic equipment) exclusively use colour to differentiate their own commercials from others.

2. Architecture

Business and other organisation can support their distinguishing qualities by developing their own characteristic type of architecture. *Heidelberger Druckmaschinen AG*, who are global producers of printing presses, for instance, Fig. items that are directly related to printing technology at their headquarters and the BMW office building in Munich integrates architectural features that imitate engine and motor components.

A further case in point is the US department store chain "Best & Co." This company seeks to achieve publicity by decorating the walls of its outlets with "surprise" elements that are to incite perceptual curiosity in the eyes of the(ir) beholders. The "Best & Co." stores hold the promise of the unexpected and controversial, of rich, albeit conflicting, visual experiences. Moreover, they communicate their own angle on the marketing of consumer goods: emotional, extraordinary, independent. Similar attempts are those shopping centres whose walls show a fake damage on one side or whose façade displays the protruding rear of a Cadillac.

However, architecture should be more than just the outside appearance of a building. Its ought to include graphic design as well as interior design elements such decorative materials and colour schemes in the inside rooms and the design of the offices as these features all reflect corporate policy and philosophy as well as the marketing approach chosen.

3. Product design and packaging

Product design and product packaging constitute the core area marketing, i. e. the sales policies directed at the outside. Moreover, they are the most salient indicators of what a company has to offer to its marketplace. The offer thus is the centre piece of marketing per se and represents the starting point of all activities regarding corporate identity.

Squaring product and quality expectations with corporate identity and buyer expectations represents the greatest challenge to marketing. High value items, for instance, require a classy design of the advertising copy.

Originally, packaging used to serve the traditional purposes of transportation, protection, warehousing. However, with the self-service facilities on the increase, packaging, like the brand name, has evolved into a tool of marketing communication, which does not always occur verbally. Package design, too, can become an image and advertising vehicle and communicate certain product properties. In addition, user-friendly packaging, for instance, can be instrumental in conveying the idea of product quality. This area is also of relevance to corporate design.

The marketing of consumer goods makes particular use of product packaging as this is where buyers most frequently encounter design elements such as the corporate logo.

Thus, corporate design is an instrument which, if appropriately employed, is apt to enhance a company's image and to instil the will to purchases in potential buyers. This also works for capital goods where the design can communicate the quality standards.

Design manuals sum up all applicable design rules and directives. They lay down which and to what extent symbols and colour schemes are permitted and which layouts may be used in corporate correspondence and in advertising.

Exceptions to the above fundamental rules and alternative guidelines can also be regulated in the design manual. What should the designer do, for example, if he is requested to place a red logo before a red background?

6.4.5 Corporate image

Corporate behaviour, corporate communication and corporate design are the essential elements of each and every concept of corporate identity. They all contribute to the creation of a certain corporate image which should be fairly consistent for all business units of an organisation. For marketing purposes, it is always advantageous if the different image components have been aligned with each other as this enhances the consistency and persuasiveness of the meaning which is to be conveyed. The corporate image therefore represents the aim of corporate identity; it is not a communication instrument in itself.

According to *Birkigt, Stadler und Funk* (1995:28), the term "corporate identity" refers to the image an organisation has formed of itself whereas "corporate image" refers to the outside perception of this organisation. The socio-psychological image concept (*Lilli*, 1983) offers an explanation for this. Expectations which human beings form on virtually all objects and phenomena of their environment are attitudes which influence our perception. Images are created when a large number of people associate such **perceptual attitudes** with a certain issue. Consequently, a brand image would consist of the amount of expectations that many people have expressed with regard to this brand. However, it needs to be specified which people exactly are involved in this process and what exactly their expectations are focused on. The "image" which is defined by the common usage of this term, is virtually non-existent. This is why questions such as the following need to be asked: What are the expectations that female consumers aged 29 to 49, whose monthly income exceeds € 3,000 and spend more than the average amount on cosmetics concerning the brand name "beauty"? Do they look for natural ingredients, protection from skin irritations, effective skin care, or do they wish to buy a prestigious product? Integrated market communications therefore focus on the co-ordination of communication tools and on the projection a target image that can be conferred to predefined buyers and strongly fixed in their minds. The **corporate image thus created** is to lay the foundations for credibility, acceptance, trust and customer satisfaction.

This definition of "image" does not necessitate any further discussions concerning the differences between self-perception and outside perception can be discarded. Self-perception creates an image too, but it is an image that has been projected by all or some members of staff of an organisation.

6.5 Unique Communication Proposition (UCP)

Generally speaking, the Unique Communication Proposition (UCP) **communicates a unique** (or otherwise unmistakable) **product promise** (or proposition) to potential buyers and/or **positions a product** in their minds. It is intended to "convey" the Unique Selling Proposition (USP) of this a product to the target groups, i. e. its unique (or unmistakable) utilities (*Meffert*, 2000:711; *Unger & Fuchs*, 2005:169).

In many markets, a **USP** which merely states the **basic utility** of a sales item is of no or of little relevance to the target customers given the similarity of many offers. In other words, marketing is facing the challenge of having to successfully advertise products that have no genuine USP. As a result, business organisations seek to enhance their product profiles by **adding psychological utilities.** Such additional differential benefits can be the promise of prestige (Cartier), of a desired lifestyle (e. g. Coca Cola's Harley Davidson's association with the American Way of Life) or of a seemingly extra-dimensional experience (e. g. the Marlboro portrait of freedom and adventure).

On principle, product positioning should be communicated in a manner which ensures that the offer always appears **attractive** in the eyes of the targeted buyers and that it can be **clearly differentiated** from competing offers. The specific appeal it exerts on the target groups stems more from the **added product utilities** and from the **possible solutions** it can offer to the buyers than from the actual product qualities. For this reason, the UCP should be developed with a medium or long-term perspective in mind. A great number of suppliers still retain their strong focus on product qualities where it might be more advisable to look for social or psychological positioning opportunities rather than for technological ones. Moreover, positioning is always effected **in relation to** a company's **existing competitors**. As to the necessity of competitive differentiation, one can justifiably assume that communications management tends to neglect this important aspect of positioning – especially when it comes to advertising. Consequently, the form as well as the contents of communicative statements become interchangeable.

If the **formal aspects** of an advertisement are **exchangeable**, this indicates that the design of two or more communication messages relies too much on similar physical features, as is the case with the ubiquitous motif of young and dynamic people, so that the recipients experience difficulty in associating this image with one particular brand or company. Such stereotype presentations resort to popular verbal and non-verbal clichés and, as a result, the statements to be communicated lose part of their salience and become more difficult to remember.

The **contents** of an advertisement become **interchangeable** when competing companies send out identical information or emotional messages to their target groups with the effect that potential buyers cannot identify the "emitting" organisation without problems.

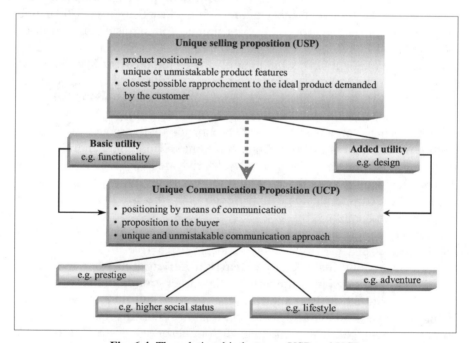

Fig. 6.4. The relationship between USP and UCP

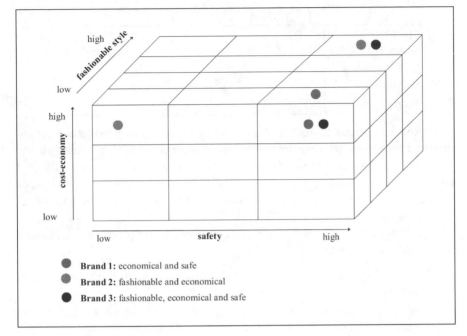

Fig. 6.5. Possible positioning of three competing products

In a nutshell, positioning signifies creating buyer attitudes with regard to a company's offer and in relation to competing offers. Attitudes are expectations that are formed on any object. They are influenced by the preconceived ideas that have already been associated with these objects. Whatever people perceive is thus controlled by what they expect in accordance with this pre-perception. There is, therefore, no unbiased perception. Positioning means anchoring such new product expectations in a person's perception.

Let us assume that the product supplied to a market is assessed in terms of the following criteria:

1. cost-effectiveness
2. safety
3. fashionable style

Accordingly, the positioning of three competing brands might occur as shown in the three-dimensional diagram below.

If positioning exceeds three dimensions, it can be explained by exploring its semantic differential which is outlined below:

The brand is seen as:

	1	2	3	4	5	6	7	8	9	
sporting										unsporting
economical										uneconomical
fashiobale										dated
heavy										light
sound										unsound

Positioning needs to address all essential aspects of a product whose individual variables are determined by its market. Positioning should, however, not involve too many dimensions as these would blur its different facets. As the factual properties of many sales items tend to be alike, successful positioning frequently resorts to largely **picture-based** and affective presentations.

Positioning should seek to meet the following **perceptual requirements** (cf. *Tomczak, & Roosdorp*, 1993:34).

- Compatibility: the degree to which the different positioning dimensions are perceived to be consistent with each other;
- Communicability or observability: the degree to which all statements concerning the positioning of a product or brand are apparent and transmittable to potential buyers; all associations evoked by these statements should be unequivocal.
- Credibility: the degree to which positioning efforts are experienced as plausible and (emotionally) persuasive;
- Independence: the degree to which a product is perceived as meaningfully different from competing brands;
- Need orientation: the degree to which positioning promises the fulfilment of individual needs. Successful positioning is founded on currently experienced needs and adapts to changing needs. Ideally its impact is powerful enough to change existing needs.
- Topicality: the degree to which positioning caters for current trends, consumption styles, value orientations etc.

As to its **message**, the following questions should be raised (*Kotler & Bliemel* (2001:934 pp.):

- What is meant to be said? – Message contents (also: title or theme, USP, pretensions);
- How is customer supposed to be addressed? – Message appeal (e. g. by using rational, affective, ethical motives);
- How can the message be made convincing and conclusive? Message structure, e. g. the order in which its arguments are put forth;

- How can the message be made articulate and expressive? – Mode of expression chosen, e. g. the choice of words and the voice quality (speed and rhythm of speech, voice pitch, pronunciation) of a radio announcer / newscaster;
- Who is to convey the message? – Message bearer, e. g. employing celebrities who convincingly embody the contents of the message.

6.6 Economic objectives and communication goals

It makes sense to break down the general goals of market communications into economic objectives and communication aims. **Economic objectives** are forecast targets such as turnover, market share and profit. Using economic communication aims can be problematic in as far as these are subject to the impact of all marketing instruments (such as the products themselves as well as their pricing, distribution and promotion). Moreover, these aims are influenced by external factors such as current trends or the actions taken by competitors. In addition, the time lag which occurs between the implementation of communication measures and the effects they eventually produce (also known as "time lag effect") usually makes it difficult to allocate the results achieved to the specific advertising efforts undertaken within certain periods of time, as the above effects tend to exceed their scheduled time frame.

Advertising aims are always communication goals, which are psychological aims derived from the marketing goals.

Advertising aims can be divided into cognitive aims that are concerned with thinking and the acquisition of knowledge and other mental processes, affective aims (emotion-driven and related to feeling) and conative (i. e. action-related) aims (*Bruhn*, 2003 a:236).

Cognitive advertising aims:

- creating awareness for one's own message or the perception of messages in general; attracting attention to how the messages perceived are processed and memorised; also: changing, intensifying or stabilising the attitudes of a given number of persons within a certain period of time.

The perception of messages depends on whether they have received a sufficient amount of attention. Only if this condition is met, will further communication effects occur. Appropriate picture and text components can strengthen cognitive processing, which is intended to eventually influence buyer attitudes, motives and values, the latter being the most authentic goal of communications.

- creating brand perception and awareness
- increasing product and/or brand knowledge
- stimulating product- and/or brand evaluation

Affective advertising aims

- generating attitudes, motives, values and images which affect purchasing behaviour;
- influencing the expected product utility;
- arousing interest in special product offers;
- creating favourable brand attitudes;
- removing psychological purchase barriers;
- increasing the social acceptance of certain products;
- arousing an interest in one particular product or service;
- stabilising brand consciousness and creating product or brand convictions;
- influencing brand preferences;
- positioning one's own products against those of one's competitors, i. e. developing a clear and distinct product and brand profile
- This type of product positioning is generally considered to be of utmost importance.
- making an experiential appeal
- post-purchase confirmation of the buying decision

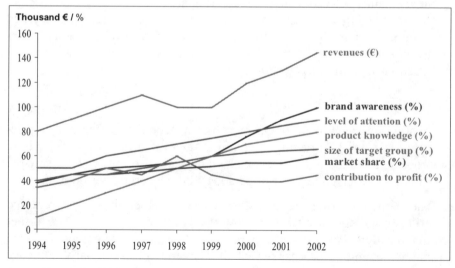

Fig. 6.6. Plotting the aims of communications management (an example)

Conative advertising aims

- influencing information behaviour;
- initiating the search for more detailed product information;
- provoking a purchase desire (initial orders and repeat orders);
- provoking a trial purchase;
- provoking repeat purchases and cross buying.

Communication aims should, as a rule, follow the commercially relevant academic postulates of clarity, feasibility and compatibility. The "goal trajectory" below, which plots the aims of communication management mentioned above, may be considered to be an appropriate "tool" to model systematically structured goal setting.

6.7 Formulating media objectives

In line with the overall marketing goals, precise media objectives are instrumental in tackling the issues of **media reach** (aka media coverage, media penetration) and **exposure frequency**.

- Media objectives typically specify the number of the members of a predetermined target audience to be reached in an aligned market segment. As these persons are meant to be exposed to the advertisements as often as possible, the task to be performed, in this context, is that of maximising exposure frequency in line with a specified media coverage and an allocated budget.

Example: A company has been allocated an advertising budget of € X million and wishes to reach Y million persons (marketing objective). It seeks to maximise its advertising impact accordingly.

This approach, however, has little to show for. From a market-psychological perspective, the company should at least have a rough idea what degree of penetration would make sense in their market.

- Media objectives also quantify the exposures to a message that are considered to be necessary. The exposure frequency derived from this should be aimed at as many people as possible. Full maximisation of exposure has been achieved if all the persons that can somehow be defined as members of a target audience have been exposed to a media message at the frequency level specified. The task to be completed here can be summed up as maximisation of the advertising reach in line with the specified exposure frequency and the allocated budget.

Example: A company has a disposable advertising budget of € X million and, relying on its knowledge of consumer psychology, it roughly works out what level of advertising impact would be sensible under the given circumstances. Subsequently, it seeks to maximise its advertising reach under these terms.

This is an acceptable solution if the budget has really been allocated in a top-down manner (which is perhaps not the most rational approach but one that occurs quite frequently) and if the advertising impact can be estimated, which might often be the case. Under these conditions, companies will obviously want to try out how many persons they can maximally reach. If the company also knows how much these persons are likely to consume, it can work out how much additional turnover can possibly be achieved with the allocated budget. This signifies that the projected turnover depends on the earmarked budget which is slightly unusual in terms of the traditional marketing theory but nonetheless justifiable.

The formulation of objectives as outlined above always starts from a given budget. Economically speaking, however, an alternative approach might be optimal:

The planned advertising message is directed at a predefined part of a targeted audience or at a specifically selected market segment (**media reach**, aka media coverage, media penetration). The **frequency** of media exposure, too, has been predetermined as has the **advertising impact** that is to be obtained. The quest is now for a communication budget that will cover all measures to be implemented. Media planning is therefore facing the challenge of minimising the communication budget in view of the media objectives to be met.

This presupposes, however, that a media format has been determined in advance for each of the selected media classes. Moreover, decisions need to be taken on how the total budget is to be shared out between the different types of media vehicles.

Whereas the formulation of the goals in the first two examples implies that the methods employed will produce the optimal (i. e. the most economical) results with the financial resources (the budget) available, in the latter case, the goals are set and the desired outcome is budget minimisation. This represents a classical application of the **economic principle**.

Bearing in mind that the marketing of consumer goods requires particularly huge budgets, it is surprising that this principle is not more often complied with.

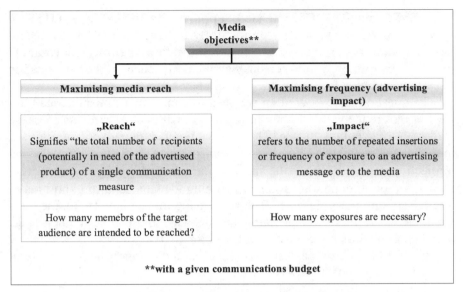

Fig. 6.6. Charting the contents of media objectives

Those that have attentively studied the above passages will have noticed that media coverage and the frequency of media exposure may principally be interpreted as **competing goals**. The reasons for this are the following:

In connection with the marketing goals and the sales targets the following issue needs to be discussed: How many prospective buyers need to be persuaded to make a purchase if the media objectives are to be met? This raises three further essential questions: Can new potential buyers be won over from the current group of non-users or from the company's competitors or should an increase in turnover be achieved with those users that already rank among this company's customers. What is the intended demand per user?

Finally, companies need to find out how many potential users should be exposed to advertising so that one part of them can be converted to buying. This requires that realistic estimates can actually be made. Alternatively, detailed information should be supplied by market research so that at least an adequately accurate estimate is possible.

The above questions contribute substantially to the principal definition of "media reach" (which is also referred to as media coverage or media penetration). This term signifies "the sum total of the recipients (potentially in need of the advertised product) of one communication measure".

A further central decision to be taken on the media issue is that concerning the **advertising impact**, i. e. determining the number of insertions that are necessary. This includes the question about which frequency of media exposure is required. The intended "**opportunity to see**" (i. e. OTS; for readers and viewers) and the "**opportunity to hear**" (i. e. OTH for listeners and viewers) or, generally speaking, the "**opportunity to contact**" (OTC), determines which persons should be reached by communication measures and how frequently they should be exposed.

The question as to how often we need to contact consumers actually refers to the frequency with they have contact with the advertising message and with the medium chosen. These items produce the advertising impact, not the media vehicle. For this reason, companies require hypothetical projections about whether the information on media vehicles contacts – which are quite common in media planning – really lead to exposures to the advertising message itself. The advertising impact is not only the most essential issue in media planning but also the most critical one. Thus, a reduced advertising exposure from eight to five insertions within six months for budgetary reasons might result in a disproportional decrease of the advertising impact.

This conflict may be illustrated by a fairly simple example:

Supposing there are 12 radio and TV magazines and the budget available stretches to three insertions in each. For reasons of simplicity we assume that all insertions cost the same. This would produce a maximal media penetration at an exposure frequency of three. We could, on the other hand, reduce our advertising efforts to six magazines only. Alternatively, one could buy 12 insertions in 3 magazines, or – carrying the idea to extremes – 36 insertions in a single one, although this would entail a minimal penetration at the highest possible frequency of 36.

This shows that the assumption that **media coverage** and **advertising impact** are conflicting issues is correct.

In a nutshell: Faced with a set budget, we can either buy a few insertions in a large number of media vehicles thereby maximising our media coverage, for instance by inserting the same amount of advertisements twice, or we can focus on one specific market segment (e. g. all the readers of the magazine Radio Times) and opt for the highest possible number of insertions, thereby maximising the advertising impact. All variations between these two positions are possible.

The question that evidently imposes itself is: "What is the optimal relation between advertising impact and media reach with regard to the implementation of our marketing aims and objectives?"

6.8 Multiple choice questions

Question 6/1: Which of the following statements on the definition of target audiences are correct?

(a)	If target audiences are identified by means of analogies, the assumption is that demographic features do not exert any influence on media usage.
(b)	Defining target audiences by survey amalgamation is the exception rather than the rule.
(c)	Identical features used in the description of consumers as well as media behaviour are suitable for data fusion if there is a strong positive correlation between them.
(d)	The single source method surveys media and consumer behaviour simultaneously.

Question 6/2: What is meant by "corporate identity"?

(a)	the characteristic features of a business organisation
(b)	the intended independence of such an organisation
(c)	functional directives concerning visual design elements
(d)	the perceived corporate image

Question 6/3: The "unique communication proposition" refers to …

(a)	unique or unmistakable product features
(b)	a communicated proposition
(c)	the interchangeability of the formal aspects of the communicated message
(d)	the closest possible rapprochement to the "ideal" product demanded by the customers

Question 6/4: Which perceptual requirements should positioning meet?

(a)	compatibility
(b)	differentiation
(c)	credibility
(d)	needs-orientation

Question 6/5: Which of these statements on advertising goals are correct?

(a)	Advertising goals are always economic goals.
(b)	Communication aims cannot be implemented.
(c)	Affective advertising goals aim at generating attitudes and motives.
(d)	Conative advertising goals seek to arouse attention for one's own message.

6.9 Case study

Renova plc are members of a franchising group that provides domestic services on a nationwide basis. The company specialises in renovating and fitting kitchens, doors and staircases for private households.

Their slogan promises that "*Renova* will satisfy all individual renovation needs of their customers".

They have recently moved into the areas of bathroom repairs and fitted furniture. In the next three years, they intend to expand their business activity to the entire German market, and this expansion is to be supported by a comprehensive advertising campaign. Advertising objectives have already been formulated: Aided by advertising, *Renova plc* intend to reach an awareness rate of 60% for their name with their targeted age group of 35 to 45.

You are the Marketing Manager of this company and have been requested to formulate their **advertising objectives**.

Solution

First and foremost, advertising aims serve the purpose of **monitoring** the success of advertising. Secondly, they form the basis for the **controlling**

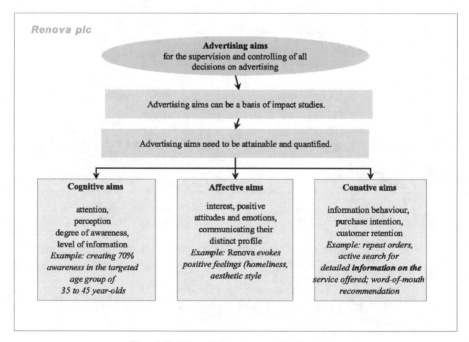

Fig. 6.7. Advertising aims and objectives

function, which ensures that all advertising decisions have been aligned with the advertising aims. As the economic impact of advertising (e. g. the increase in sales and revenues) cannot conclusively be associated with single advertising measures, advertising mainly emphasises the psychological product or service benefits. Advertising aims should be attainable and quantified so that their results can be re-used, for instance, in advertising impact studies.

Renova plc's advertising aims fall into the aforementioned three categories of cognitive, affective and conative goals (*Bruhn*, 2003 a:136). They are charted on the following page.

1. Cognitive aims

- Renova plc intend to reach a certain degree of attention to and perception of their TV commercials and advertisements. Moreover, they wish to create a 60% level of awareness for their slogan in their targeted age group. Their advertising success will be measured by interviews and questionnaires.
- A further possible objective is an advertisement-prompted 70% level of awareness of the *Renova* brand and of the company's general performance amongst their target group of 35 to 49 years of age.
- *Renova plc* also wish to extend customer information concerning the services they are offering including the additional differential benefits of their service (e. g. the high quality of their renovation work). Moreover, they need to communicate the fact that they are now expanding their offer (e. g. window repairs and fittings).

2. Affective aims

- *Renova plc* aims at arousing their existing and prospective customers' interest in their services on offer.
- Additionally, they seek to create positive attitudes in their target groups and to convey a positive image of their company to them.
- Concerning the positioning of the service they are offering, *Renova plc* intend to communicate the quality of their work and their dependability as a unique proposition (or differential advantage) to their target customers.
- A further aim is to ensure that customers associate the name *Renova* with positive emotions such as homeliness and aesthetic style.

3. Conative aims

- *Renova plc* intends to improve their target group's information behaviour (e. g. by inducing them to demand detailed information on the services currently on offer).
- They also consider inciting purchase desires (initial and repeat orders) in their relevant target groups.
- Furthermore, *Renova plc* are interested in strengthening customer retention (e. g. follow-up orders, cross buying, recommendation by word of mouth).

7 Communication strategies

7.1 Learning outcomes

This chapter will outline the possible directions communication policies can principally take such as adjusting to the company's already existing product-market matrix. Competitive positioning strategies which aim at distinguishing one's own communication message from that of commercial rivals will be given priority.

Subsequently, there will be a focus on the copy strategy which serves an exemplary purpose in communications. By way of conclusion, we will deal with the concept of integrated marketing communications which is founded on the idea that the success of market communications does not derive from optimising the individual components of the communications mix but from their coordinated application.

On completing this chapter,

1. you will know which fundamental position a company can adopt regarding communications;
2. you will have learned how market communications can assist companies in positioning themselves against their competitors;
3. you will be able to name the components of the copy strategy;
4. you will have understood the principal intentions of integrated marketing communications.

7.2 Positioning the product

Figure 7.1 which is shown below maps the principle directions communication policies can take.

Position enhancing is intended to strengthen the position of a product that is currently being offered. This also means building up the brand and maintaining its specific profile. Position updating refers to new products that can benefit from an existing position. Revised offers and new types of offers can assist in updating a product's current position. **"Repositioning"** signifies that an existing product is being relaunched into a new position. As the offer remains mostly unchanged, repositioning is mainly the result of

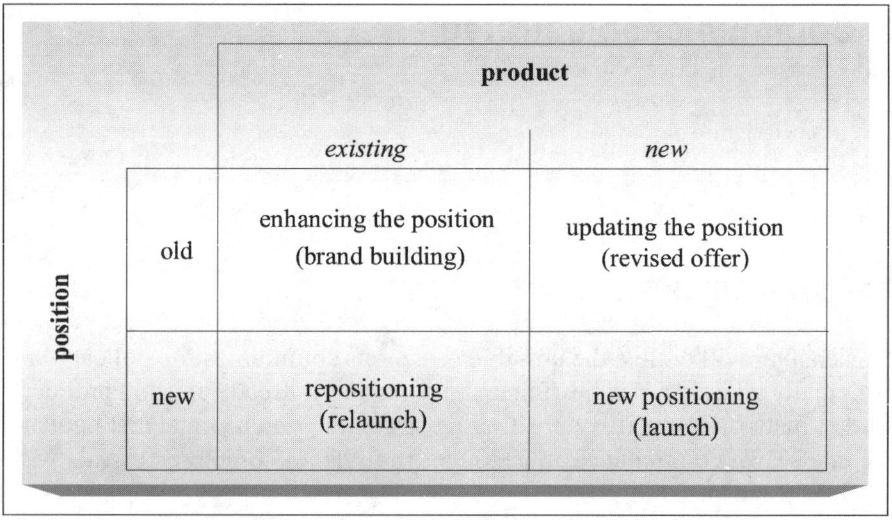

		product	
		existing	*new*
position	old	enhancing the position (brand building)	updating the position (revised offer)
	new	repositioning (relaunch)	new positioning (launch)

Fig. 7.1. The principal product positions (*Unger & Fuchs*, 2005: 138)

market communications which seek to sell the existing offer as an appealing experience. An example of a successful relaunch is the German liqueur *Jägermeister*. But "relaunch" can also mean that a new similar product has been substituted for an existing one in order to initiate a new product life cycle. In this case, a relaunch is only successful if consumers perceive the offer as a new one. This may require product alterations such as product upgrading, which are then communicated as new product benefits. **New positioning** which combines the advantages of a new launch with new positioning enjoys the broadest range of opportunities but the positioning effort requires careful planning as the errors that are committed in this context are difficult to rectify.

7.3 Positioning strategies

Generally speaking market communications has the two positioning options to choose from which are elucidated in Fig. 7.2, namely **differentiation strategies** and **me-too strategies**. The former aim at establishing a company's own advertising message in relation or against identified commercial rivals or competing products, the latter deliberately transmit similar or identical messages.

According to *Kroeber-Riel & Weinberg* (2003: 219 pp.) the following criteria are traditionally applied to identify the attributes that are suitable for the positioning of products and services:

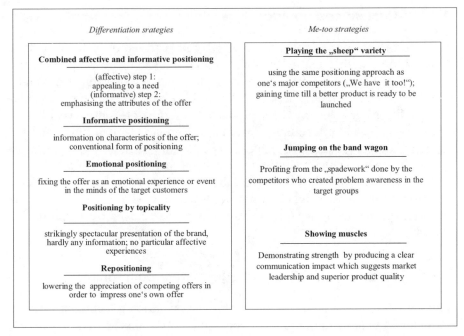

Differentiation srategies	*Me-too strategies*
Combined affective and informative positioning	**Playing the „sheep" variety**
(affective) step 1: appealing to a need (informative) step 2: emphasising the attributes of the offer	using the same positioning approach as one's major competitors („We have it too!"); gaining time till a better product is ready to be launched
Informative positioning	
information on characteristics of the offer; conventional form of positioning	
Emotional positioning	**Jumping on the band wagon**
fixing the offer as an emotional experience or event in the minds of the target customers	Profiting from the „spadework" done by the competitors who created problem awareness in the target groups
Positioning by topicality	
strikingly spectacular presentation of the brand, hardly any information; no particular affective experiences	**Showing muscles**
Repositioning	Demonstrating strength by producing a clear communication impact which suggests market leadership and superior product quality
lowering the appreciation of competing offers in order to impress one's own offer	

Fig. 7.2. Positioning strategies (adapted from *Fuchs & Unger*, 2005:139–143)

7.3.1 Informative positioning

Informative positioning can be considered to be the most conventional form of positioning. It signifies that marketers transmits information about the collaterals and characteristics of an offer that are perceived to be of particular suitability in terms of current need-fulfilment. This type of communication seems less emotional. It only makes sense if the customers actually have needs of which they are rationally aware and if these needs are genuinely satisfied by currently existing product and service offers. Especially the communication efforts **for new products** or the innovative features of products and services that have already been introduced to the market fall into the domain of informative positioning. However, these offers need to address a sufficiently strong need: Moreover, the new and innovative offers should be likely to arouse the buyers' interest.

7.3.2 Affective positioning

If the information available on an offer is rather trivial or if the buyers are thought to be indifferent to this information, marketers are well advised to bypass the information issue by positioning their offer as an experiential pleasure. This is a trend that has established itself under contemporary market conditions. In many markets, products are more or less **mature**, of comparable quality and **interchangeable**. The differences in their functional and design features, too, are negligible. This calls for positioning from an emotional perspective rather than from the angle of factual information.

One should perhaps point out that the conditions which require affective positioning are to be found in capital goods markets. The interest which buyers are expected to show is frequently overestimated even by the producers who supply to these markets.

7.3.3 Combined affective and informative positioning

A combination of affective and informative positioning techniques can be particularly beneficial in producer goods markets as this approach is advantageous in two respects: Firstly, emotional appeals provoke higher levels of attention and, hence, enhance the processing of the messages communicated by the producers of capital goods, secondly, the objective, informative aspects of market communications endow their offers with the aura of reputability which is of extraordinary relevance to the marketing of producer goods. Marketers therefore face the challenge of having to counter a communication situation encumbered by information overload by affective communication measures without losing their credibility.

7.3.4 Competitive positioning

Positioning against competitors

This form of positioning highlights all distinct features that distinguish a product or service from competing offers. It has proved to be a promising strategy above all for market challengers who are trying to improve their own position vis à vis the market leader.

Positioning a market leader

As market leaders cater for the biggest market segment, they may experience difficulty in defining their position as unequivocal. Thus, they need to present themselves as a company "in total command" of the market and in a manner which underlines their superior strengths, market experience and competence. They would be ill advised to try and develop specifically tailored strategies for each of their heterogeneous market segments, as this would make their positioning concept as a whole look undifferentiated.

Positioning a niche supplier

Niche suppliers require a highly precise positioning concept which is able to focus on requirements of their small market to a "t". This is one of the advantages they enjoy vis à vis the market leaders. They will always be in a position to adjust their communications effort more exactly to their market segment than those companies that have to serve the entire market or large market segments.

Positioning a market follower

According to received marketing wisdom, attempts to succeed in a market by emulating the strategies of the market leader are highly likely to be doomed (cf. *Ries & Trout,* 1986: 79 pp.). If market challengers imitate market leaders, prospective buyers will probably prefer the experienced, well-versed number one. Challengers need arguments that distinguish them from the leaders and should present a convincing alternative. That is to say they are in need of a better product and better communication messages for their offer. Whereas market leaders may be able to use similar arguments as market nichers, challengers have no alternative but to emphasize their distinguishing features.

7.4 The copy strategy

Since the 90's, the number of **communication tools applied in marketing** has been continuously on the increase. This has led to the fact that, in classical advertising areas, a higher numbers of advertisements cannot automatically produce stronger impacts any more. Although the advertising sector would hotly reject this allegation, one cannot deny that with the rise of private TV, for instance, the same advertising measure has doubled in price. Whereas, in the years before, companies were able to reach all TV viewers in Germany by buying air time on the first and second German channels, nowadays they have to book time with a much larger number of broadcasters. The cost of TV time, however, has not been reduced to speak of. Consequently, we have seen that in all countries that have known a growing proliferation of media variety, advertising budgets have had to be increased for advertising effects that have been slower and slower in producing themselves.

Other cost factors are public relations work, some types of sales promotion and personal selling techniques, which are – like advertising – classic expedients of the advertising business. The **weakening impact of classical advertising** that has been accompanied by a growing number of new design opportunities in the media has given rise to "neo-classical" forms of market communications. These include sponsorship, event marketing, product placement and the multiple expressions of "personalised" mass communication which have become possible as a result of the purchase data now available. The latter pretend to be tailored to the individual buyer but, in real life, "personalisation" follows a strictly standardised and anonymous format.

This current versatility of the communication tools can be seen as a logical response to the dwindling efficiency of advertising, which, nonetheless, has to rise to the challenge of growing information overload. If budget rises in marketing remain at negligible levels, the funds available might simply be spread out over a greater number of communication tools, thereby causing the impact of each individual tool to wane. However, if all tools are appropriately co-ordinated, it might definitely be possible to boost the advertising impact by benefiting from the **synergy effects** that have thus been created. Managing this successfully is the task of a **normative and superordinate communications strategy**, i. e. the copy strategy.

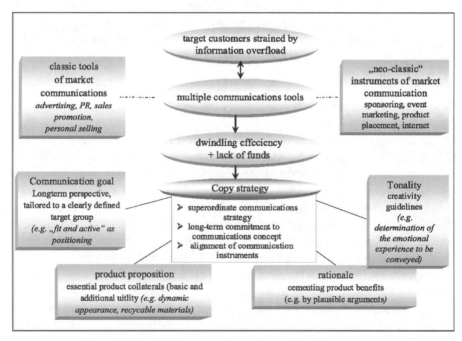

Fig. 7.3. Environment and dimensions of the copy strategy

A company's advertising copy strategy is the foundation for all its internal and external communications from your web site to your product collaterals.

A focused model communications strategy ought to develop a long-term perspective and to embrace the entire communications mix. Communications research (especially that dealing with cognitive response) has shown that long-term communication concepts evoke more favourable attitudes and result in positive learning effects. However, one ought to bear in mind that any communication measure that is implemented over a long period of time and fails to vary its design features will eventually provoke feelings of redundancy and lose some of the favourable impact it previously created. What we are looking for is, therefore, a **communications concept that remains valid over time** but which offers, within its conceptual framework, enough leeway for variations. The **copy strategy** will assist corporations in implementing such a concept.

The copy strategy (which was first published as outlined below by *Unger & Fuchs*, 2005:143–146) consists of four elements:

- **Communication goal:** contains a precise as well as concise formulation of the company's communication goal that is implemented over time and directed at one well-defined target group.
- **Product proposition:** highlights the essential benefit of a product without exposing the specific advertising message which will be issued at a later stage. It is important that this product "promise" is a genuine reflection of at least one utility demand by the target group.
- **Rationale:** justifies the product promise which, if not backed up, boils down to a simple statement. At least during the penetration phase, the customer needs to be given sound reasons for selecting the product in preference to the competition. The proposition needs to sound plausible.
- **Tonality:** refers to the form of creativity desired, the atmosphere and the style of the market communications to be implemented.

How these individual measures are designed in detail is **not** determined by the copy strategy itself. However, if the copy strategy is put into practice in a focused and coherent manner, this will likewise affect its design and, thereby, lead to a recall of the marketing messages and synergy effects. The copy strategy offers the design framework.

Let us now take a closer look at these four elements:

The formulation of the **communications goals** marks the starting point of communications planning. It requires focus and clarity. This is of paramount importance as all parties concerned need to understand the set goals in precisely the same manner and to agree with them. The following persons are involved in the planning and implementation process: persons responsible for the marketing project (e. g. production manager), marketing and possibly sales executives, market research team, advertising agency with budgetary discretion, customer contact managers, creative groups, and at a later stage photographers and radio or TV producers.

The **product proposition** states the essential product collaterals vis à vis the purchasers and ensure consistent messaging across all the media. In saturated markets in which products are technologically comparable and mostly exchangeable, the decisive product attribute can be a very subtle, affective suggestion of credibility, dependability, reputability etc which is communicated as part of the product profile but a lot of other emotional values can be conveyed, such as strength, natural or erotic looks, a dynamic appearance or a sense of security.

Product policy makes a distinction between **basic utility** and additional utility. The former corresponds with the original purpose of the product (e. g. a living room cupboard serves to store objects). In many markets, this utility is provided by virtually all suppliers. This is not the case regarding the **additional utility** of a sales item, however, where comfort, prestige, environmental friendliness etc. may decide on the purchase. In combination with other pieces of furniture, a lounge cupboard reflects a certain lifestyle.

The distinction between basic and additional utilities is, above all, of relevance for consumer goods but will gain impetus for capital goods. Thus, the capability to be easily integrated into an existing production process, to protect the environment or to be recycled can be transmitted as additional collaterals for technological products, as can the longer maintenance warranties. In the last few years, value adding by back-up services or maintenance support has become quite common with technical products, especially with industrial plants and fixed installations.

Successful market communications presents **product utility** as a **unique entity** that differentiates itself from competing products by at least one aspect in the eyes of the buyers. In the **consumer goods sectors**, the differentiation benefits tend to be affective product collaterals. Market communications is to ensure that customers fully realize the uniqueness of the product and – if necessary – to emphasize its additional informative or affective qualities.

The **rationale** is designed to cement the differential product advantages. Its phrasing/wording depends on the degree of interest shown for this product by the target customers. There are high-interest und low-interest products or rather high-involvement and low-involvement sales items as outlined in Section 2.1. Low-involvement items can be justified by statements that appeal to simple feelings. The rationale can always be limited to pictorial messages that are apparent at first sight. High-involvement buyers to whom the purchased product is of significant importance may require rational statements on the product collaterals. Nevertheless it should be stated that the willingness to absorb rational and objective arguments is soften overestimated by marketing executives.

The hope for high involvement may mislead some of the marketing executives in charge of designing the communications measures to believe that there is a general willingness to process advertising information. But even if the level of involvement is clearly very high, there is often little readiness/willingness to absorb the more complex arguments communicated by the media. In such a case, the copy strategy needs to focus on the decisive positioning arguments and to restrict communication to a few succinct, focal statements. It can also try to create a need for information by questioning common assumptions or by stressing the significance of obtaining additional information.

Example:

An actor in a TV commercial asks a young woman: "Do you take vitamin C?"
Young woman: "Yes, of course."
Actor: "Did you know that you body cannot store vitamin C very long?"
Surprise and irritation on the part of the young woman... .

Tonality includes the entire creative make-up of communication measures. It provides guidelines, for instance, for the tone, the moods, the atmosphere and the emotional appeal to be conveyed by marketing communications. This is vital for the collaboration between a company's marketing team and the agency executives which requires a mutual understanding of what the creative realisation of the planned communications measure actually requires. Many problems between advertising agents who are "creative spirits" (aka "creatives") and the commissioning companies they work with actually arise from their diverging views on creativity. As affective design is steadily gaining momentum, the issue of tonality, too, will become more important in future.

The copy strategy is not an uncontroversial subject amongst marketing practitioners. Testing the advertising impact, for instance, or subjecting communication goals to the commercial principles of strategic controlling may be perceived by the creative staff of advertising agencies as an imposition that constrains their imagination. However, the role played by imagination and creativity in professional marketing communications also involves meeting economically measurable marketing objectives and the execution of the communication targets that can be derived from them. The restrictions imposed on creativity by the **copy strategy boosts the efficiency of the** execution of the **communication means**.

The copy strategy requires creative, imaginative and pragmatic capabilities. It aligns all contents, aims and objectives of market communications with advertising and the entire communications mix and details the tasks to be carried out by advertising agencies and by the institutions contributing to the design work.

7.5 Integrated communications

Optimising the individual components of the communications mix is in itself no adequate outcome. The factor that contributes essentially to the success of market communications is the harmonious alignment of all these components over a longer period of time. This is understood by **integrated communications**.

This concept of integrated communications, which is essentially founded on the works of *Bruhn* (2003 b) develops and exceeds the concept of a **normative communication strategy**. It is more comprehensive than the former while relying on the same **fundamental ideas**.

It would be difficult to overrate the information overload that media users are subject to in developed countries. This is why is has become necessary to generate **synergy effects** between as many communication tools as possible. As media diversity and the opportunities to apply new forms of market communication are on the rise, **communication concepts** risk **disintegrating** into an ever increasing number of components on which individual communication measures have little or inadequate impact. As electronic communication is progressively gaining momentum, this process will continue to be of topical significance for some time to come.

"Integrated communications" is a structured planning and organisation process that aims at creating a coherent corporate image from the different sources of the internal and external communications and to disseminate this image to all the company's target groups. (cf. *Bruhn*, 2003 b: 17).

Integrated market communications refers to the same process with regard to a company's external communication (cf. *Bruhn*, 1993 b: 40–47) across all customer contact areas.

The following requirements result from the above definition and the currently existing communication situation in general (increasing information diversity and quantity). They necessitate a certain integrated market communications approach whose goals are listed below:

• consistently messaged corporate image across all the measures taken;

- stimulating an increase in customer interest;
- using synergy effects on applying the communication tools;
- the subsequent boosting of communication efficiency;
- and implementation of cost reduction potentials.

The coordination of the different communication activities that result from the communication tools selected by an organisation can be implemented from a **content, design or time-related perspective** (cf. *Bruhn*, 2003 b: 17 p.):

Content-related integration coordinates all statements issued in the course of the communication process and involves the alignment of all slogans, key messages, key arguments and key images. It is closely related to the copy strategy and to **corporate communication** as a whole. There is not always a clear boundary between content-related and formal design aspects as pictures and graphic designs communicate meanings too.

Design-related integration coordinates the formal design principles which are to warrant the conformity of the corporate appearance. These uniform design criteria (e. g. typeface, size and colour of the scripts as well as the usage of corporate symbols and brands signs) need to be applied across all communication tools.

This is to achieve brand recognition and identification as well as a higher level of penetration in a diffuse and unstructured communications environment and in view of the information overload impacting on the target groups. Unfortunately the significance of a consistent exterior appearance, which is closely related to **corporate design,** still tends to be underrated in marketing practice.

Time-related integration schedules the communication activities and coordinates the timing of all communication means during the various planning stages. It ensures that long-term communication strategies are fully implemented and that the requirements of the cognitive response approach, which will be dealt with at a later stage, are met in the process.

Figure 7.4 below shows the perspectives of integrated market communications and charts the integration process.

Organisational reality offers ample proof of the fact that a considerable number of communications concepts lack even the smallest degree of integration, and some practitioners even speak of the **failure of integrated communications** while quipping that "organisational theory has once again fallen short of business practice". These sceptics ought to hold up a mirror to their own marketing approach. (Up to now), the concept outlined above has proved to be appropriate and suitable and has made a valuable contribution to corporate reality. The fact that it may have failed was probably not due to the (alleged) gap between theory and practice but to inadequate **organisational**

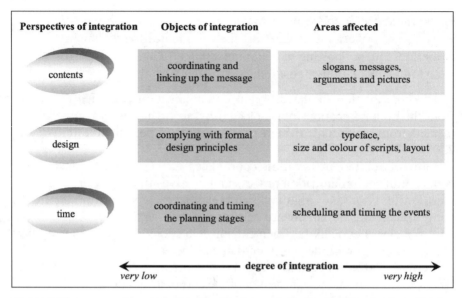

Perspectives of integration	Objects of integration	Areas affected
contents	coordinating and linking up the message	slogans, messages, arguments and pictures
design	complying with formal design principles	typeface, size and colour of scripts, layout
time	coordinating and timing the planning stages	scheduling and timing the events

◄———— degree of integration ————►
very low   very high

Fig. 7.4. The perspectives and objects of integrated market communications (*Bruhn*, 2003 b: 69)

structures in the marketing departments, to a lack of expertise in communications, and maybe to a lack of commitment on the part of the corporations involved. It is apparent that some communication tools still emit contradictory messages or that **advertising campaigns are altered** too frequently. This results mainly from a missing communications strategy in advertising as well as from the high degree of independence enjoyed by the departments that are in charge of communications in business organisations. Advertising, sales promotions and public relations often fail to align their activities.

As companies are undeniably confronted with the growing weight of information input, an expanding diversity of communication tools and increasing competition in the area of communications, we can assume that those corporations which have achieved a high degree of integration between their communication measures and tools will also obtain a bigger market share. By systematically exploiting all possible synergy effects, they will be able to build up and defend sustainable competitive advantages over a longer period of time.

7.6 Multiple choice questions

Question 7/1: Which fundamental communication positions can be adopted by a company?

(a)	Enhancing current position.
(b)	Updating current position.
(c)	Abandoning current position.
(d)	New positioning of current product.

Question 7/2: List some dimensions of the copy strategy.

(a)	Long-term compliance with the communication goals.
(b)	Financial planning of the organisation.
(c)	Product proposition.
(d)	Competitive analysis.

Question 7/3: What are the aims of integrated market communication?

(a)	Uniform product design.
(b)	Standardised personal selling routines.
(c)	Consistent corporate image created by communications.
(d)	Implementing cost reduction potentials.

Question 7/4: Name at least one dimension of content-based integration.

(a)	Statements transmitted.
(b)	Uniform appearance.
(c)	Using communication tools across several planning stages.
(d)	Employing communication means in diferent geographical regions.

Question 7/5: List ways in which a business organisation can position itself by means of communication?

(a)	Informative positioning.
(b)	Irrational positioning.
(c)	Affective positioning.
(d)	Affective and informative positioning.

7.7 Case study

In the last few decades, *Cosmetic PLC* has positioned itself as producer of a broad range of high value hair care and hair cosmetics. Not unlike other markets, the hair cosmetics market has had to confront a solid level of saturation and aggressive competitive activity. Owing to your communications expertise you have been asked to assist this company in developing a communications strategy.

This also implies that you should answer the following question: "Which dimensions of the communications strategy can be distinguished and which are relevant for *Cosmetic PLC*?

Solution

1. Communication strategies represent comprehensive medium or long-term **behaviour guides** which outline how a prescribed set of communication tools and communication vehicles can enable a company to meet

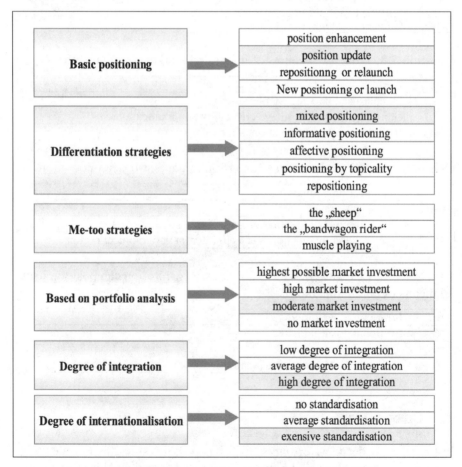

Fig. 7.5. The communications profile of *Cosmetics PLC*

its communication goals. The **advertising goals** can be split up into cognitive objectives (e. g. achieving a 70% level of awareness for their brand *Cosmet* in their targeted group of 35 to 45 year old women), affective aims (e. g. building up a positive image) and conative aims (e. g. generating the wish to purchase this product).

2. The communication strategies of *Cosmetics PLC* can be visualised by means of a strategic profile (as shown in Fig. 7.3).

3. Strategically speaking, *Cosmetics PLC* has decided to update its existing product profile by launching a new hair care product on the basis of the company's current positioning approach (which conveys the idea of "exquisite" hair care). This revised offer will be instrumental in updating their current market position.

4. By strategically opting for a **combination of affective and informative positioning components** *Cosmetics PLC* intends to differentiate its message from those of its competitors. The combination of affective and informative appeals permits the corporation to fulfil a twofold purpose: on the one hand, emotional message components boost attention levels and thereby improve information processing, whereas the information provided by means of communication emphasizes the company's reputation as a trustworthy cosmetics supplier. This strategy will enable *Cosmetics PLC* to counter a corporate environment severely hampered by information overload. Affective communication measures will assist the company in achieving just that without losing its respectability in the eyes of its consumers. **Me-too strategies** would be completely unsuitable for *Cosmetics PLC*.

5. The results of the portfolio analysis suggest that the company should choose the strategic option of **moderate market investment**.

6. According to *Cosmetics PLC,* the information overload imposed on contemporary media users requires the generation of synergy effects between as many communication tools as possible. For this reason, the company requires a **high degree of integration** with regard to the contents, the formal design and the timing of these instruments.

7. In view of the international focus of its communication policies which will require the building up of an internationally consistent corporate image and/or international brands, *Cosmetics PLC* will need to adopt a high level of standardisation for its product range.

8 Media planning in marketing communications

8.1 Learning outcomes

This chapter will explain to what extent media planning is concerned with the various instruments of marketing communications. This will be followed up by a discussion of the most common budgeting procedures. Further focal issues of this chapter will be the design and the evaluation of media plans and media schedules.

In this context, the afore-mentioned competitive positioning strategies will play a major part as will the copy strategy that constitutes a normative communications strategy. The chapter will be concluded by discussing the role of integrated communications in media planning.

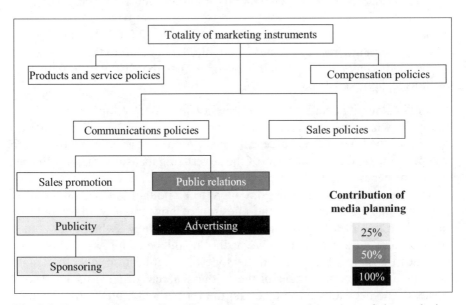

Fig. 8.1. Communication policy: The communications mix as part of the marketing mix (*Unger, Durante* et al. 2006: 1)

On completing this chapter,

1. you will have learned that media planning is not responsible for the totality of marketing communications;
2. you will have encountered the most important budgeting methods;
3. you will know the different stages of drawing up a media plan;
4. you will be in a position to evaluate a media plan.

8.2 The object of media planning

Media planning is significant for the different tools of marketing communications in various ways.

Media planning is not essential for marketing communications as a whole but focuses instead on classic advertising, certain areas of public relations and some forms of sponsorship (e. g. the sponsorship of programmes) and of publicity.

Media planning always becomes relevant

- if air time and media space need to be booked and bought by media planners to be designed and used under the commissioning company's own direction;
- or if the transmission of the messages is performed for financial compensation, with the message design being more or less left to the discretion of the media independents (as this is sometimes the case with public relations and publicity assignments).

Media planning decides on the following question: "Which media will be bought at what time, in which way and how often." This usually depends on the size of the financial resources allocated. A rational approach would be to calculate the budget on the basis of the advertising measures that are considered to be necessary.

The question as to which media ought to be bought touches on the classic issue of media selection, the question of how often media should be booked on that of the media impact. The term "format" which was coined by US marketers refers to how media should be employed. This issue includes the shape, the size and the style of a publication, e. g. the length of radio and TV commercials or the colour schemes of advertisements and posters. The decisions to be taken on the format add a qualitative element to media planning.

8.3 Budgeting

There are a number of budgeting procedures (*Unger & Durante*, 2000: 78 pp.) some of which will be dealt with in the following section. They are:

- the percentage of sales method,
- the affordable method which is also known as "all you can afford" method,
- the competitive parity method, and
- the share of the market method.

All these methods have considerable deficiencies or are insufficient if they are applied on their own.

The latter two approaches are based on the assumption that a company's market share reflects to a considerable extent its advertising share in a market.

8.3.1 Comparing the media impact

It is common practice in advertising to compare a company's weighted media ratings to that of its competitors. There are three different approaches to obtain such an assessment:

- **Share of Advertising (SOA):** this concept indicates the share of a company's own advertising volume in a competitor's total advertising budget. SOA emphasises the fact that a company's own advertising expenditure and that of its competitors both impact on the media impact it desires to reach. However, in order to obtain a genuine evaluation of its position in comparison to the other suppliers in the same market, a company will have to set its SOA rate in proportion to that of its major competitor.
- **Share of Voice (SOV):** this concept explains how "loud" a company's communications are compared with those of its competitors. SOV complements the SOA approach in a significant way since the media expenditure on its own is not a sufficient success indicator with regard to media planning. The gross media reach in one target group is seen as a further indicator of the media effects achieved. In order to monitor the return on a company's advertising investment, the exact percentage of the actual contact opportunities (OTCs, cf. section 6.7: "Formulating media objectives") in a company's own target group is compared with its competitors' rate. A high gross reach can be obtained in two ways: a) it can be the strong impact exerted on a small target group by intensive advertising, or b) the relatively weak media impact per member of a large target group that was exposed to the same amount of media input. The following indicator is intended to take this situation into account:

- **Share of Mind (SOM):** integrates criteria such as reach, frequency and the distribution of contacts. It has already been pointed out that even a comparatively high SOV (vis à vis the competitors) may still mean that the advertising effects achieved have been less intensive than competing media impacts. This figure is determined by multiplying the (high) target group reach by the (relatively low) OTC. The OTC determines which persons can be contacted by communication measures and at what rate of frequency. By contrast, media strategies which are based on smaller reach but higher OTCs, i. e. less media weight, can be successful. Moreover, the total media weight achieved in one's target group is not necessarily a conclusive indication of how the media weight is distributed amongst the individual members. This is considered by the "share of mind" concept which permits the calculation of one's OTC by comparing it with competitive figures. This calculation is generally based on rates that have been achieved with one's own target group as the various competitors may have defined their target groups in other ways. When media planning is carried out it is not possible to arrive at an exact comparative determination of the advertising impact by comparing it with competitive figures. All one can do at this stage is rely on the figures applicable in the past or on hypothetical anticipation of current competitive behaviour. This is why it is advisable to continually monitor competitive advertising activity.

8.3.2 Objective- and task-budgeting

For rationally acting managers there is no alternative but to devise their budgets from a completely goal-oriented perspective. Figure 8.2 overleaf illustrates that marketing objectives represent the starting point of each advertising budget.

Marketing objectives can be quite easily quantified in terms of market share targets from which the sales targets (anticipating the sales volume) are derived. By estimating the consumption intensity mean per user one arrives at the percentage of the users to be won over by advertising. As soon as the target group has been defined, the percentage of potential users within the defined target groups is deducted by integrating the market share data. Systematic market research then uses this data to formulate the required **reach**. The percentage of members in a target group to be reached always needs to be greater than that of the intended potential users. Market research should provide the data which permit an estimation of how big this difference ought to be. All this contributes to the determination of the reach, which is one of the most important media objectives.

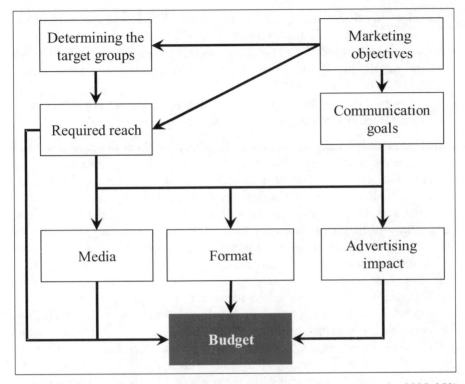

Fig. 8.2. Modelling the process of object and task budgeting (*Unger & Fuchs*, 2005: 350)

The definition of the target groups combined with the determined reach are indicative of what media should be bought. It is undeniable that communication goals, which are instrumental in the inter-media decision, the advertising format and the desired advertising impact on the target audience, should be founded on the marketing objectives. The advertising budget required is set on the basis of the media plan especially provided for this purpose as soon as the company has determined which persons (i. e. which reach in the target group) should be contacted in which media on the basis of what predetermined format and at what rate of frequency (media impact). The crucial decision to be taken in this context is the determination of the necessary advertising impact, which, above all, depends on the following:

- **Intended user behaviour:** The greater the intended change in user behaviour, the stronger is the advertising impact required. If existing behaviour needs to be merely sustained, relatively little advertising impact is necessary.
- **Contents to be communicated:** The advertising impact required increases in proportion with the complexity of the contents to be conveyed.

- **Level of involvement in the target group:** The lower the level of involvement, the more impact is needed.
- **Selected media class:** The less attention a target group is prepared to give to the media during the presentation of commercials, the more media weight is necessary.
- The stronger the **media impact of a company's direct competitors** in its own target group, the more media weight is required.

It is manifestly evident that all the above statements either represent estimates or anticipate trends. But if, in the course of the planning process, agreement can be reached on their contents and consequences, they may altogether add up to a useful and viable recommendation for the media budget to be earmarked. This is an advantage with regard to some of the well-known (idealistic) **optimisation models** which allegedly produce a precise **media** plan, but which presuppose an information level that would be completely unrealistic in everyday business practice.

It should be pointed out to readers who are interested in economic theory that one of the misconceived ideas abroad in Business Studies and Economics is **to overrate how much information is actually available**. All optimisation models presuppose that there is a perfect information input. However, in business reality, virtually all decisions are taken on the basis of uncertain, incomplete and probably often even inaccurate information. This is an undeniable feature that qualifies all routines performed by human beings. Heuristic decision models give due consideration to this fact.

8.4 Drawing up a media plan

A media plan is designed – after the marketing objectives and communication goals have been formulated – to logically pursue the following stages:

- definition of target group.
- selection of the type of media vehicles to be used.
- determination of the advertising platform, i. e. the specific issues and selling points that advertisers intend to include in their advertising campaign, according to the company's design guide. During this stage, media planning and advertising design can be performed simultaneously. On the one hand, the design of advertising measures depends on media planning, on the other hand the design determines the advertising platform.

- formulation of the media impact and the required media reach which are both laid down in terms of OTC rates or figures. The media weight, too, can best be determined by taking the media design and platform into account.
- a case in point is the decision by a company (known to one of the authors) to turn their corporate symbol, and nothing but this symbol, into a quarter-page print advert. This symbol was already making a constant appearance in sales promotions, on packages and in TV commercials but it was felt that customer awareness could be enhanced by extending it to the print media as well.
- the design of media plans assisted by media-dialogue programmes (including media rankings).
  The media plan comprises:
  - a list of the advertising vehicles (e. g. titles of weeklies; names of TV channels),
  - the advertising format,
  - the air times and media space to be bought,
  - cost of space and airtime buying and the budget that derives from this.

Please note: We assume that the budget is not imposed as a definite figure fixed in advance but that it is calculated on the basis of the measures that are considered to be necessary. This approach may not gain the planners "a majority" vote but it seems to be the only one that is appropriate. At this stage, and not before, it a check should be made as to whether the budget is realistic. If not, those in charge should seek to establish whether the amount budgeted is obtainable, otherwise the aims and objectives ought to be revised. On the other hand, if the budget is definitely fixed, planners should find out whether and how it can be aligned with the aims to be met.

- evaluation data: costs and media performance ratings, costs per thousand (CPTs), opportunity-to-contact figures (OTCs), reach and gross rating points.
- other data which cannot be discussed here (cf. *Unger, Durante et al.*, 2006).

The approach outlined above is depicted in Fig. 8.3. overleaf.

Before a detailed media plan is drawn up, the media vehicles considered to be suitable are broken down according to their ranking order. They are then evaluated in terms of costs and ratings in order to narrow down the options for their selection. This is followed up by a finalized media plan which also includes alternative plans.

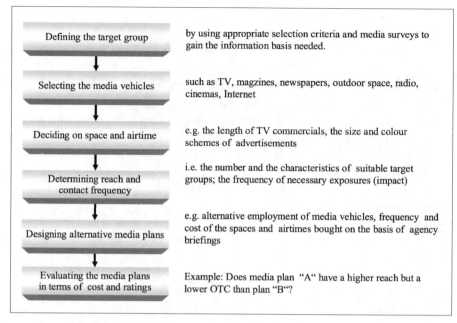

Fig. 8.3. Charting the process of media planning and evaluation

8.5 Evaluating the media plan

As a rule, media plans are evaluated in terms of cost and efficiency.

Please note that media efficiency is not identical with media effectiveness, which seeks to establish how well an advertising message is carried in the media.

Ratings

Gross Rating Points (GRPs) represent the overall reach effected by a media plan. They equal net reach (i. e. the total reach less allowance for duplication) x OTC mean per actually reached target group member. In Fig. 8.4 plan 2 is the best performer having achieved a result of 37.8 (i. e. 5.9 x 6.4). The difficulty here lies in the fact that GRPs can be calculated by multiplying a high reach by a low OTC mean but also by multiplying a high OTC mean by a low reach. This indicates that the significance and usefulness of GRPs tend to be overestimated in practice.

It is much more important to decide which effective reach is considered to be necessary to meet the marketing objectives and at what minimum, ideal or maximum frequency rate the members of the target group should be contacted. Media plans count as successful if a reach seen as necessary

Target groups			
age	20 to 49		
net income per household	2.500 €		
size of target group	9.3 millions		
	Plan I	Plan II	Plan III
Budget in euros	**1.330.800**	**1.336.000**	**1.304.500**
Vehicle 1/1 4c			
magazine A	**9**	**6**	**9**
magazine B	7	6	3
magazine C	8	6	6
magazine D	8	6	6
magazine E	3	0	0
magazine F	5	3	0
magazine G	9	9	9
magazine H	3	6	0
magazine I	3	0	3
magazine K	0	3	6
magazine L	0	6	0
Net reach (in %)	**56,1**	**63,7**	**61,2**
Net reach per person (in millions)	**5,4**	**5,9**	**5,7**
OTS rate	**6,7**	6,4	**6,3**
GRP figure	**34.8**	37.8	**35.7**
Cost per 1.000 readers (in euros)	255,92	**226,27**	229,96
Cost per 1.000 contacts (in euros)	**38,30**	35,35	**36,50**

Fig. 8.4. Presenting alternative media plans (simplified version)

has been effected and if most of the targeted persons have been contacted at the ideal rate of frequency. This is expressed by the concept of "contact classes".

Such contact classes could be mandatory guidelines and they might look like the example given below. This is assuming that **a minimum amount of five contacts** is necessary in order to reach the target group in an effective way.

Less than effective reach (5 contacts or fewer)	0,6 million persons
6 to 7 contacts	1,2 million persons
8 to 9 contacts (seen as ideal rate)	3,0 million persons
10 to 11 contacts	0,8 million persons
12 or more contacts (input seen as too high)	0,3 million persons
Total	5,9 million persons

In the case shown here, a total of 5,9 million people have been reached in the target group. However, for 0,6. million of them this contact was not an effective one. 3,0 million persons were contacted at the planned efficiency level and a further 2,0 million with an acceptable rate of efficiency. For 0,3 million people the contact rate was too frequent which may mean, on the one hand, that financial resources have been wasted or that for the latter group the saturation threshold has been exceeded so that the effect achieved has been lessened or is negative. Judged from the "efficiency" angle, a media plan is ideal if it reaches as many persons as possible at the ideal rate of frequency and if its OTC hardly deviates from the rate of frequency.

Costs

In order to be able to compare the different media on an equitable basis, marketers look at how much it would cost to reach 1.000 members of one specified target group. The "cost-per-thousand" concept is fundamental to media buying. This term can be abbreviated as CPT or CPM (the M representing the Roman numeral for thousand). It divides the cost of advertising (or any other item of marketing communications) by the number of the members of the target audience reached.

Media cost over **media reach** is calculated as follows:

$$\frac{\textbf{cost of budget} \textbf{ x } \textbf{1,000}}{\textbf{(absolute) reach}}$$

$$\frac{1.336.000 \text{ x } 1.000}{5.900.000} = \textbf{226,27}$$

In our case, plan 2 is the most cost-efficient because the cost per user (i. e. reader) amounts to € 226,27.

A second question marketers ask is how much it would cost to achieve 1.000 contacts within the same specified target group.

The calculation of **media cost** over **media contacts** is equally straight-forward:

$$\frac{\text{budget} \times 1{,}000}{\text{(absolute) reach} \times \text{OTS rate}}$$

$$\frac{1.336.000 \times 1.000}{5{,}900{,}000 \times 6.4} = \mathbf{35{,}35}$$

With the cost per 1,000 contacts totalling only € 35.35, plan 2 is again the most cost-efficient.

Let us now return to the calculation of the GRP as this will show us that the denominator in the afore-mentioned equation equals the GRP value and can therefore simply be inserted instead of *reach* multiplied by *OTS*. This facilitates our calculation.

$$\frac{\text{budget} \times 1.000}{\text{GRP}}$$

$$\frac{1{,}336{,}000 \times 1{,}000}{37{,}850{,}000} = 35.35$$

Last but not least, one can take into account that the cost per 1,000 audience members is known as the OTS rate. For this reason, the cost per 1,000 users can simply be divided by the latter.

$$\frac{\text{CPT users}}{\text{OTS}}$$

$$\frac{226.27}{6.4} = 35.35$$

Which plan is best?

In view of both ratings, plan 3 is in a disadvantageous position compared to plan 2. Moreover, the advertising cost would be slightly higher. Plan 3 should therefore be dismissed as an alternative. Plan 2 has a better reach compared to plan 1 but has a slight disadvantage where its OTS is concerned. The decisive figure is the GRP which definitely tips the balance in favour of plan 2. Additionally, it is advisable to consult some breakdowns of contact classes.

8.6 Multiple choice questions

Question 8/1: Which marketing tools are involved in media planning?

(a)	Public relations.
(b)	Advertising.
(c)	Product policy.
(d)	Sponsorship.

Question 8/2: What tasks and areas are affected by media planning?

(a)	Media selection.
(b)	Messages.
(c)	Format.
(d)	Frequency.

Question 8/3: What budgeting approaches are applied in media planning?

(a)	The percentage of profits method.
(b)	The affordable method.
(c)	The competitive parity method.
(d)	The market share method.

Question 8/4: Which of the following answers are correct?

(a)	Share of Advertising (SOA) refers to the share of a company's own advertising volume in the total budget spent by its competitors in the same market.
(b)	Share of Voice (SOV) signifies "gross advertising expenditure".
(c)	The OTC or "opportunity to contact" rate determines which persons are to be reached at what rate of frequency.
(d)	Share of Mind (SOM) offers information on the distribution of the advertising weight across the individual members of a target group.

Question 8/5: What can be measured by CPT?

(a)	The cost efficiency of media plans.
(b)	The cost effectiveness of media plans.
(c)	The effect of any item of marketing communication on the target group.

8.7 Case study

Cosmetics PLC advertises its products intensively in order to defend its position in a very tight market. Its annual advertising expenditure has so far accounted for 5 per cent of the revenues achieved in the previous year.

	Women's Realm	Lifestyle	Fashion Today
Cost per advertisement (€)	5	5.5	???
Number of readers	300	370	280

Fig. 8.5. The media data of *Cosmetics PLC*

You have been provided with the following data:

1. Use the data to assess *Cosmetics PLC's* approach in allocating its advertising budget.
2. Your recommendation is definitely to allocate future financial resources for advertising in line with the advertising aims and objectives formulated by the company and to choose the advertising measures accordingly. Please justify your decision.
3. You are suggesting that advertisements should be placed in the following three magazines: *Women's Realm, Lifestyle* and *Fashion Today.* You would like to evaluate your magazine options on the basis of cost of the contacts they effect per 1,000 readers. You are currently negotiating the cost per advertisement with the magazine *Fashion Today.* How much would you be prepared to pay to this magazine?

Solution

The volume of the advertising budget would ideally be calculated on the basis of the cost incurred by implementing the advertising measures derived from *Cosmetics PLC's* advertising aims and objectives. These costs include, in particular, the expenditure on the advertisement design, space and airtime costs, the consultation fee paid to the advertising agency and the share of the expenditure incurred by the company's advertising department.

1. The **share of the market approach** employed by *Cosmetics PLC* is the most pragmatic heuristic method to decide on the total spend on advertising. The essential advantage of this procedure lies in the fact that it is easy to apply, its biggest disadvantage being its lack of an apparent **causal relation** between the volume of the **advertising budget** (i. e. the cause) and the **actual turnover achieved** (i. e. the effect). Moreover, if the receipts from sales decreases the advertising budget might be reduced as a result, and this could, for its part, accelerate the existing downtrend thereby creating a vicious circle.
2. Alternatively, *Cosmetics PLC* could determine its total advertising spend on the basis of the projected sales volume or of the financial resources

available. It could employ the market share method, the competitive parity method or cost its advertising measures in accordance with the advertising objectives it has set. All these approaches require little market information and can be used independently. According to *Bruhn* (2003 a: 231 pp.) these **heuristics** are founded on simplified budget standards and on the principle of "satisficing". In other words, they opt for "satisfying" solutions rather than for the one that is considered to be "optimal".

3. Furthermore, *Cosmetics PLC* could resort to **optimising approaches** which rely on certain response functions in advertising and allow a company to determine optimal outcomes by means of marginal analysis.

4. If media budgeting is executed in accordance with the **"measures meet objectives"** (or "objective and task") approach, the advertising goals of *Cosmetics PLC* will form the starting point of all costing calculations. This will be followed up by a breakdown of the measures required to meet these goals. The essential advantage of this method lies in the fact that the cause-effect relations are immediately apparent. However, there is a disadvantage, too, namely that it necessitates **sufficient information about the advertising impact** of all individual media tools. In order to bypass this hurdle, companies tend to resort to their previous experience in this area.

5. *Cosmetics PLC* would like to decide in favour of *Fashion Today* but this would require that they should renegotiate a new "cost per thousand" total. The new figure needs to be lower than that of *Lifestyle* magazine, i. e. less than € 140.

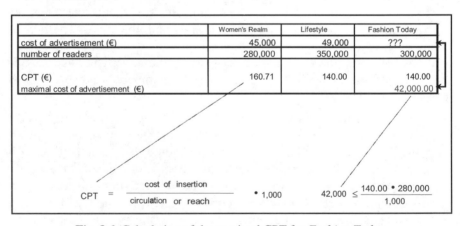

Fig. 8.6. Calculation of the maximal CPT for *Fashion Today*.

9 Designing market communications

9.1 Learning outcomes

This chapter will focus on the fundamental principles of communication design which form the basis of the tools that companies employ to master their communication tasks. These tools will also be discussed.

On completing this chapter,

1. you will have encountered the manifold types of advertisements that are placed in magazines;
2. you will have learned which aspects are decisive for the design and the layout of TV commercials;
3. you will know which are the most common types of radio commercials;
4. you will be aware of the design guidelines that are to be complied with in poster advertising;
5. you will have learned who a company's public relations work is directed at;
6. you will be in a position to assess which tools are appropriately used in direct marketing;
7. you will know what the term "publicity" refers to; and
8. you will what the term "event marketing" stands for.

9.2 The communications mix

The communications mix represents a concrete set of instruments which companies employ to master their **communication tasks**. This tool set is a comprehensive and complex one. The dynamic developments experienced by the conventional media (e. g. new types of advertising on TV) as well as the new media (e. g. Internet communication) have opened up new avenues which companies are able to explore when communicating with their target customers. Moreover, new forms of advertising, such as event marketing, are constantly being designed in order to meet the changing requirements of target groups that are becoming more and more differentiated.

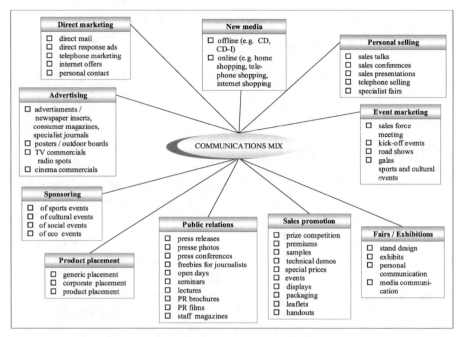

Fig. 9.1. The elements of the communications mix

Selecting the most efficient and effective combination of communication instruments from this pooled source and gauging their most appropriate usage in compliance with the specific corporate communication aims represents the biggest challenge that a communications manager now faces. The **complexity of this challenge** not only springs from the high number of tools currently available (e. g. advertisements, sales promotion, public relations, product placement, sponsorship, trade fairs and exhibitions) but also from the fact that each tool can be applied in a large variety of ways (see Fig. 9.1). In addition, there are the cumulative interrelations between the tools arising from the combined usage of communication tools that need to be taken into account (see section 6.5. Integrated market communications).

9.3 The fundamental principles of communications design

As far as the design of advertising measures is concerned it is difficult to overrate the genuine lack of interest on the part of the target audiences. This is why designs benefiting from **affective expedients and pictures** are of the highest significance. Activating elements are particularly indispensable in order to achieve the desired effects. Music, humour, lively illustrations, unusual or erotic images are popular design elements. Advertising has developed into "a world of beautiful pictures". Moreover, there are attempts at emphasising the persuasive power of commercials by integrating plays on words. This has been successful to a point where certain advertising slogans have become "cult". As a considerable degree of saturation has been reached in advertising, different communication tools have gained in importance. However, this has often entailed a severe loss of clarity in individual marketing concepts. The large variety of media and of communication tools has led to an increasing number of long-range communication strategies which combine all available communication measures.

Mass communication requires an **experiential, picture-enhanced** type of communication which does not be mean that companies should abandon verbal messages altogether. The latter should simply be used sparingly in mass communication via the media. The emphasis on pictures in marketing communications also applies to the design of corporate brands (cf. 6.4.1 Defining corporate identity.).

The statements made above are not only of significance to the marketing of consumer goods but also to that of capital goods. Many marketing practitioners assume that business customers take a more genuine interest in the capital goods they acquire and that advertising should therefore offer more factual information. However, this assumption has been empirically proved to be incorrect. *Jeck-Schlottmann* (1988: 33 pp.) was able to show that even customers who are genuinely interested in the products they buy, only glance briefly at adverts. They, too, prefer affective pictures to copy, which they perceive only fleetingly, and affective images to factual photos or diagrams. The importance of affective, picture-supported advertising in the business-to-business market has also been confirmed by the recent research of *Lassoga* (1999).

This provides us with conclusive arguments about the design of market communications and of advertisements. The most important contents ought to be transmitted as **affective picture messages which are clearly structured** and easy on the eye. Due to the afore-mentioned low level of interest in advertising messages, marketers are obliged to design the message in a way which is capable of arousing attention and of fuelling the **"activation"** process. This can be achieved by means of affective pictorial components, colour schemes and creative techniques and images. If the pictures are unique, lively and appealingly presented, they offer considerably more advantages to market communications than the copy of the advertisement. They arouse attention, are easier to memorise than verbal information and can be more quickly processed even if the interest threshold is relatively low. It is more difficult to escape from an intensive combination of pictures than from a text. In practice, the members of a target group may be a lot **less willing to absorb information** than managers are prepared to believe. This is why quite a few communication designs are encumbered by too many pieces of information, and this frequently results in the fact that a great number of essential messages are ignored. We can further assume that the effects resulting from pictures are generally capable of lowering the resistance threshold they are facing and that affective picture elements will emotionally enhance even the most **objective product assessments.** This presupposes, however, that the pictures selected have strong links with the product they promote. As a rule, it is important that the entire creative effort which is meant to inspire attention and to appeal to the respondents should to be closely related to the product they represent and to the actual advertising message. An error frequently committed in market communications is that the actual message is partially superimposed with creative designs. What is remembered in such a case is the excellence of the advertisement at the expense of the sender of the message.

If emotional and creative picture-based communication and corporate strategic communication aims are successfully integrated, this can in-fluence product preferences and product positioning in a given market. Market surveys have shown that – especially under low interest condi-tions – illustrations and pictures produce better memorisation results than words and phrases. This applies in particular to the perception of advertising messages.

However, picture-based designs on their own cannot suffice in bringing about the desired advertising effects. **Clear images** need to be created for the target audience: "The halting success of adventure-oriented marketing measures can be directly attributed to the lack of internal brand images and corporate images." (*Kroeber-Riel*, 1986: 92).

Successful picture-driven communication is inspired by liveliness, richness, independence, a clear structure, novel or strange elements and graphically portrayed configurations, the latter referring to the multiple **interaction of the various picture elements** with each other. The essential issue is the integration of all elements into one contextual framework. The stranger this context appears to be, the better are the learning outcomes which can be expected. Many people would probably find it difficult to memorize a list of animals in a set order. But most readers of this chapter are likely to recall the four animals in the fairytale of brothers Grimm '"The travelling musicians of Bremen". The clearer, more agreeable and familiar the visual images are, the more one can count on their success as a market communications tool. Market communications therefore face the task of having to conjure up positive images that can be internalised and memorized. If the images projected about products and corporations are incoherent or diffuse, all ideas connected to the advertised product become exchangeable and cannot be

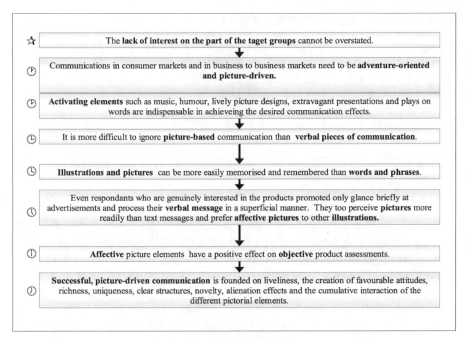

Fig. 9.2. Summing up the essentials findings on communications design

unequivocally associated with one specific offer. This is counterproductive with regard to the unambiguous product profile that a company needs to maintain in a competitive market environment.

The **composition of the pictorial portions** – which should preferably be unusual too – is of specific significance to advertising. Let us look at the following individual items, for instance, namely a monkey, a cigar, a hat, a football, a bike, a pair of sun glasses, a pair of boxer shorts and an umbrella, which hardly any viewer would perceive as a holistic entity. However, we would easily be able to imagine and to remember the picture of a cigar-smoking monkey wearing a funny hat, dark sunglasses and boxer shorts while riding a bike (with a football strapped on its back) and waving an umbrella in his hand.

Image you are drawing a creative flower pot. What thoughts would cross our readers' minds. They would perhaps conjure up the most beautiful flower pots with exotic and picturesque flowers. Compare this to the illustration below which also represents a flower pot – only one seen from underneath. Which picture would longer in your mind?

The extraordinary importance of picture-prompted communication does not signify that marketers should completely refrain from using textual components in market communications. This approach has occasionally –

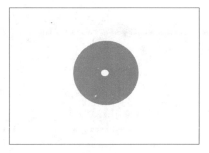

Fig. 9.3. A flowerpot seen from underneath: an example of an ideosyncratic illustration.

and unsuccessfully – been tested in the consumer sector. It is of crucial importance that pictorial and textual elements should be combined in a manner which produces synergy and cumulative effects. Picture and text-based information processing should therefore be aligned with each other. A focused processing of all the pieces of market communication is only possible if the messages are supported by textual as well as pictorial portions.

In a nutshell: The following factors are decisive for the success of market communications in the **business-to-business sector**: Picture-driven messages, uniqueness and creativity as well as the integration of creative features and message contents. It seems crucial to confront the consequences of information overload which apply to all sectors of communications and, hence, to practice what the consumer sector has been preaching all along; on the other hand, the marketing of capital goods needs to address its target groups in the serious and trust-inspiring manner that its customers have come to expect. Marketing industrial goods on the basis of affective messaging that relies exclusively on moods would be completely inadequate. Informative messages need to be designed in a way which is attractive enough for them to be perceived and learned in spite of the information overload that is currently superimposing itself.

9.4 Printed advertisements

Before the ascent of private TV channels, consumer magazines were considered to be the most important media vehicle and they still play a considerable part in communications. Most of them offer ample opportunity for a large number of advertisements, inserts and other supplements; some can only accept printed advertisements owing to their lack of technological sophistication.

Magazine advertisements conventionally use one to four colours to create a **large variety of shades**, themost simple distinction being that between black and white and multi-coloured advertisements. Black and white prints enhanced by one additional colour are popular, too. The space charge for black and white ads may be lower but so are usually the advertising effects obtained. Coloured ads are assumedly memorised with greater ease and speed but the black and white portions may stand out more in a multi-coloured environment.

The various **sizes of advertisements,** some of which are presented in Fig. 9.4, represent another multi-facetted design opportunity. There is virtually no limit to the options available. Most advertisements use range A as a standard. They may be full page (A0), half page (A1) or quarter page (A2) or may match any appropriate proportion of a full page, usually starting from an A5 size which represents 1/32 of a page. They may also be double page spreads (DPS) or even span several pages across a magazine.

The **number of colours** which an advertisement deploys as well as its **size** are usually assumed to reflect positively on its **effects.** However, this type of rough and ready judgement can be problematic as it focuses nearly exclusively on size as an assessment criterion. Other options, for instance **advertisements** that are placed in **solus positions** or are, in other words, completely surrounded by editorial or margin (cf. Fig. 9.5), have apparently been able to attract a high level of attention, too.

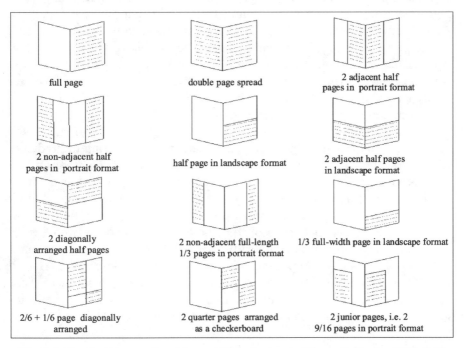

Fig. 9.4. Varying sizes and positions of advertisements (*Unger & Fuchs*, 2005: 186)

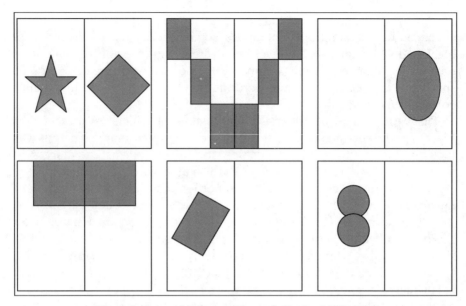

Fig. 9.5. Unusual formats (*Unger & Fuchs*, 2005: 187)

Advertisements that enjoy an interesting **format** (e. g. landscape format, checkerboard patterns or diagonal arrangements) can strongly appeal to potential customers as can the innovative "junior pages" (see Fig. 9.4). Advertisements presented in portrait format are equally likely to attract considerable attention. More care needs to be exercised when it comes to very small advertisements (covering 1/3 of a page or less) as their advertising impact will probably quickly vanish. Advertising agencies have recently tended to use even more extraordinary formats in order to boost the level of attention they intend to attain. (see Fig. 9.5).

Otherwise identical advertisements can adopt different formats in the same magazine. Such a sequence can induce the respondents to gradually take notice of a significant detail. To this purpose, we should perhaps imagine that diagram 9.6 (1) contains a machine shown from a distance whose details are not discernible but which has been photographed in an exciting way that catches and holds the observers' attention. Diagram 9.6 (2) subsequently offers a clearer outline of the whole machine and diagram 9.6 (3) finally exposes a blown-up technically sophisticated machine component.

Figure 9.7 displays some examples of **gatefolds**. These are oversized pages that can unfold to their left or to their right. If more than two of these pages are connected, the advertisement can cover a space of six pages altogether and would therefore be extremely difficult to overlook.

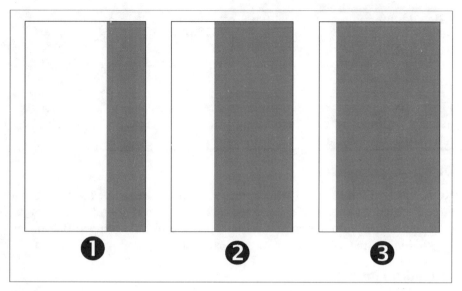

Fig. 9.6. A sequence of advertisements using different full-length portrait formats in the same edition of a specialist journal (*Unger & Fuchs*, 2005: 188)

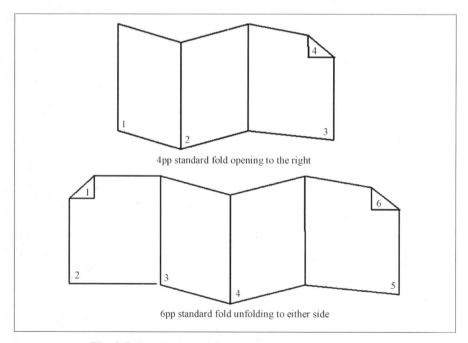

Fig. 9.7. Standard gatefolds (*Unger & Fuchs*, 2005: 189)

In addition to the traditional types of advertisements shown in the exhibits above, there are a number specific variations that will be dealt with in the following:

Ad(d) a card

Figure 9.8 represents an advertisement that contains a clear "call-to-action", namely a reply card to be returned to the advertiser. This approach is referred to as "Ad(d) a card".

Direct-response items

Reply cards are not the only direct response item that can be attached to an advertisement. Other such items may be coupons, address stickers or stamped addressed envelopes (SAEs). They are usually "tipped on" insets or otherwise attached to the major advertisement.

Tipped-on items

These are small items, such as postcards or merchandise samples that are "tipped on" to the larger-sized main advertisement by a gluer or are otherwise attached. They can easily be peeled off or detached thus facilitating the response desired, i. e. their immediate return to the advertiser.

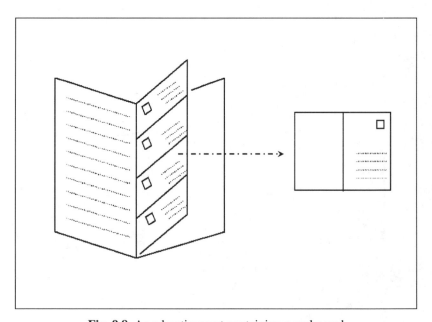

Fig. 9.8. An advertisement containing a reply card

Inserts

These are usually finished leaflets or prospectuses which are supplied to the publisher and placed loose in the non-classified, run-of-paper section of a newspaper or magazine.

Extra colours

If companies are prepared to bear the cost, there is always a possibility to supplement the four conventional colours of a print advert by one or several special pigments, such as fluorescent or metallic colours, the latter being especially suited to emphasise the relationship between the advertisement and the product in the capital goods sector. Some shades, such as bright oranges, cannot be managed without difficulty in a four-colour print and are therefore added as a special colour feature if they happen to be important for the brand.

Advertorials

Some print advertisements are designed to look like press editorials. However, if they are published they are subject to a legal code of practice which requires that they are identified as advertising features. It is an illusion to believe that this type of advert conveys the credibility of third-party endorsement more than others. Most readers spot the heading of "advertisement" which adorns such advertorials immediately. If press advertisements are intended to appear in magazines, they should preferably be presented as genuine newspaper articles.

Free merchandise samples

Samples constitute yet another supplement to regular advertisements. There are quite a few product samples which can easily be "tipped-on" to the pages of especially consumer magazines. Offering industrial goods as samples would be much more difficult to imagine. However, merchandise samples would seem to be at least a theoretical option in commodity markets where raw materials, operational resources and auxiliary supplies are traded.

Perforations and punch-outs

A certain part of the advertisement can be punched out, for instance, in the shape of the promoted product. The cut-out part could be folded out to create a three-dimensional pop-up advert. Moreover, a sequence of perforations could allow the readers a glimpse at the contents of subsequent pages.

The most important elements of print advertising are:

1. the artwork,
2. the headline or sub-headline,
3. the body copy,
4. the logo.

It has been pointed out before that images are always the first communication items to be perceived and processed. They are closely followed by the headings or, alternatively, the sub-headlines. The body copy is taken in last. This is why the pictures, headlines or sub-headlines need to be capable of communicating the essential message of an advertisement on their own.

However, *Bernhard*'s research (1978) indicates that it is advisable to place "headlines" below the pictures or to their right as they are absorbed more often in these positions. The brand mark, the corporate signature or an additional slogan are often inserted in the bottom right corner as advertising

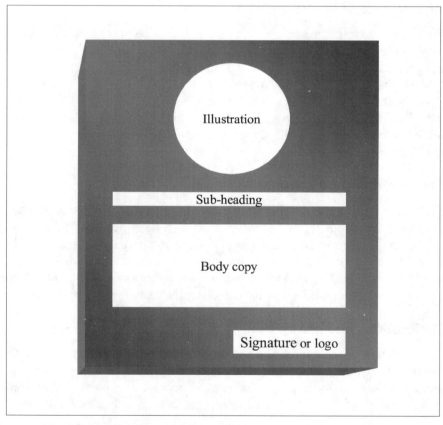

Fig. 9.9. The classic advertising structure (*Unger & Fuchs*, 2005: 191)

specialists believe that readers throw a last glance at this part of an advertisement before they turn the page and that this "last impression" sticks.

The eyes of the readers therefore tend to follow this "natural" order of preference:

1. picture,
2. headline or sub-headline,
3. body copy,
4. signature or brand name.

This leads to the classic structure of vertically designed advertisements. The copy, i. e. the verbal portion of an advertisement, should be short and easy to follow. The logo, i. e. the signature of the commissioning company, concludes the advertisement. Research into the effects of advertising has shown that the human eye first stops at the pictures and then moves mostly downwards towards the name of the advertising organisation. As pictures are perceived first and the eye movements, in accordance with the reading routines in western cultures, follow a top-down route, pictures ought to be enhanced by a sub-headline rather than a headline. Otherwise headings might simply go unnoticed. The copy or copy line should be placed under the artwork; the brand names or corporate logos should occupy the bottom right corner.

Specific advertising features in newspapers

To some extent, newspaper advertising is dissimilar to that of magazines as the environment provided by the target audiences is completely different. Newspaper readers expect more information and coloured advertisements seem to have less impact on them than on the readers of consumer magazines. However, these statements cannot be generalised. They are probably only justifiable where the daily and weekly papers are essentially comparable to their contemporary German counterparts. They do not apply to North American newspapers such as *USA TODAY*.

Newspapers offer some additional options to insert advertisements which can be distinguished according to their format or position. These are, *inter alia*:

- full position advertisements: usually appear in the run-of-paper section of a newspaper where they occupy a special position, e. g. the top middle part of a page or another marginal space, so they are surrounded by editorial on three sides.
- full-length advertisements in portrait format, i. e. advertisements that occupy one or several full-length columns of a newspaper; they border on the adjacent editorial on either their left or right hand side.

- full-width advertisements in landscape format, i.e. advertisements which are mostly spread across the bottom part (occasionally also the top part) of a newspaper page; they border on the adjacent editorial in the top (or bottom) part of the page.
- special position advertisements, i.e. advertisements that are placed; for instance, in one of the four corners of a newspaper, next to a specific feature, the front or the back page.
- double page spreads that span two pages across an open newspaper.

Because of their good quality, "high fidelity" and "insetter" adverts should be mentioned, although these printing methods are now the exception rather than the rule in newspaper off-set printing. Insetters are separately pre-printed illustrations which are integrated into the high speed printing process. Insetters are electronically controlled thereby ensuring a perfect fit with the type area and making full use of the type area and the chosen newspaper format. They have evolved from high fidelity techniques. The latter are also based on intaglio printing. The prints are produced on a separate paper roll which is then used in the main printing process. Contrary to insetter adverts, high fidelity ads cannot be gauged to fit the type area perfectly, they therefore need to be smaller than the area to which they are transferred.

9.5 TV advertising

The concept and the design and of TV commercials are guided by two aspects in particular. Firstly, they need to be aimed at overcoming the **lack of interest on the part of the viewers** who might be generally uninterested in advertising and be busy with other matters when the commercials are on, and secondly, TV advertising **requires its own particular approaches**. Most TV commercials run between 7 and 60 seconds (most of them last 30 seconds) and therefore require a more precise scheduling than short movies. For this reason, TV commercials are usually not planned in time units but according to the number of pictures broadcast per scene (e. g. 25 pictures per second). TV advertising enables advertisers to make minor or apparently unimportant details the focus of attention. A strand of "brittle" hair can create an effect that is more dramatic than an unfavourable hairstyle. Thus, enhancing small details and turning minor figures into TV heroes contributes to the outstanding opportunities offered by independent TV advertising.

A **catchy idea tailored to the specific features of TV**, the advertising vehicle, forms the foundation of each and every skilful TV commercial. (*Fechler*, 1984: 1328–1330). Not only the design of the commercial and the pictorial and tonal sequences have to be right but the message itself needs to be adapted to this medium. If possible, each commercial should concentrate on one idea only as quite a few commercials are hampered by **idea overkill,** whereas those that are short of ideas and devoid of action are the exception rather than the rule. One central focus is a lot more effective than too many and tailoring the advertisement to the specific requirements of TV is a lot more important than broadcasting a string of verbal messages.

These are examples of successfully adapted ideas:

The factual message …	**tailored to TV**
• Whiskas is an excellent cat food.	• Cats know the difference!
• Kit Kat chocolate bars boost your energy.	• Have a break, have a Kit Kat.
• Toyota cars are (more) reliable.	• The car in front is a Toyota.
• Duracell are long-life batteries.	• No battery is stronger longer.
• Radio Times is reliable and up to date.	• If it's on, it's in.
• O2 offers a perfect mobile phone service.	• O2 can do.

Inspired TV slogans can develop into proverbial sayings (provided they are supported by an adequate budget):

- Let your fingers do the walking. (*Yellow Pages*).
- Consider it done. (*UPS*).
- Nothing runs like a Deere. (*John Deere tractors*).
- Getting There Is Half The Fun. (*Cunard Line*).
- All the news that's fit to print. (*The New York Times*).
- Where do you want to go today? (*Microsoft*).
- It's good to talk. (*British Telecom*).

Other famous examples of priceless TV stars were the "Dulux Dog", the "PG Tips Chimps" (tea) as well as the animated "Michelin Man", the brand symbol of the tyre producer. Inspired verbal adaptations are "whiskers", which left a lasting impression as "Whiskas", "kitten and cat" which re-emerged as "Kitekat" and "Sunkist", the juice pressed from oranges "kissed by the sun".

By contrast, some images flop for cultural, operational or other reasons. The purple "Milka Cow" did not grab the attention of British TV viewers and the much ridiculed *British Rail* slogan "We're getting there" made a rather dubious contribution to an already controversial public service.

Original ideas make advertisements genuinely independent so that, in the long run, there is less ad-wearout and a higher degree of acceptance. If this is the case, these adverts are capable of providing the continuity that is required in market communications (this issue has already been dealt with) and of **generating favourable product attitudes** on a large scale. TV commercials can be highly **entertaining** and interesting, and these are assets that advertisers will need to nurture even more in future. Otherwise viewers will "zap" to the increasing number of alternatives that present themselves on TV.

This is the reason why TV commercials absolutely need to propagate **one single central idea** that has been tailored to their specific environment and advertisers might be well-advised to invest more time and creativity into this task than in devising picture and sound sequences. Like the cinema, TV is one of the most versatile media. Moving images, spoken or sung words provide the fundament of advertising. But good TV advertising can aim more highly as it is also capable of acoustically transmitting the desired positive product attitudes and atmosphere. Health, happiness, relaxation, social recognition, worries, speed, freshness and virtually all emotions can be converted into **acoustic signals**. The sound of TV commercials, above all, should receive due consideration (*Fechler*, 1983: 1330). Acoustic signals might catch the viewers' ears and, subsequently, their eye(s) and thus induce them to "look up from the crossword they are doing". "Only acoustically prompted activations offer the chance of arousing interest in potential viewers that happen to be in the vicinity of the TV" (*von Keitz*, 1983 a: 344). TV commercials are often listened to rather than watched, and more than one "household name" owes its breakthrough to TV acoustics. One case in point is the TV (and radio) spot for *Heinz* beans, which claims that:

"A million housewives every day pick up a can of beanz and say:
'Beanz means *Heinz*',"

This jingle remained popular even years after the company had stopped broadcasting it and is still remembered today.

It goes without saying that this kind of commercial is also most suitable for radio broadcasts.

From a dramaturgical perspective, the **initial and the final seconds** of the commercial are of the greatest significance. During the initial stage, advertisers need to stimulate the viewers' interest in a way that makes (potential) viewers feel personally involved. Ideally, the latter should be under the impression that they will miss out on something if they switch off.

The final stage ought to provide the viewers with a lasting impression that can be recalled. The interest engendered at the beginning has to be maintained throughout the commercial. Attention can be rekindled by occasionally focusing on different emotions.

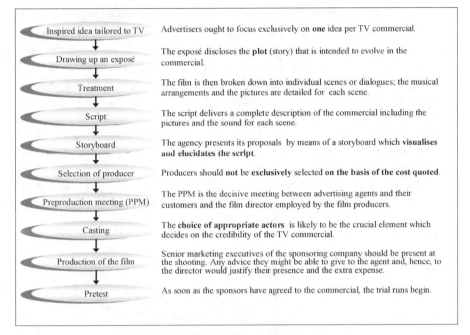

Inspired idea tailored to TV	Advertisers ought to focus exclusively on **one** idea per TV commercial.
Drawing up an exposé	The exposé discloses the **plot** (story) that is intended to evolve in the commercial.
Treatment	The film is then broken down into individual scenes or dialogues; the musical arrangements and the pictures are detailed for each scene.
Script	The script delivers a complete description of the commercial including the pictures and the sound for each scene.
Storyboard	The agency presents its proposals by means of a storyboard which **visualises and elucidates the script.**
Selection of producer	Producers should **not** be **exclusively** selected **on the basis of the cost quoted.**
Preproduction meeting (PPM)	The PPM is the decisive meeting between advertising agents and their customers and the film director employed by the film producers.
Casting	The **choice of appropriate actors** is likely to be the crucial element which decides on the credibility of the TV commercial.
Production of the film	Senior marketing executives of the sponsoring company should be present at the shooting. Any advice they might be able to give to the agent and, hence, to the director would justify their presence and the extra expense.
Pretest	As soon as the sponsors have agreed to the commercial, the trial runs begin.

Fig. 9.10. The genesis of TV commercials

The following expedients are suitable to this purpose:

- surprising and unusual presentation,
- sequential changes of scenes (also in short intervals),
- acoustic signals,
- humour,
- eroticism,
- children,
- animals (cf. *von Keitz*, 1983 b: 29).

Caution needs to be exerted to prevent the constant change of scenes which is intended to attract the viewers' attention from becoming an end in itself which swamps or marginalises the actual message of the commercial. This message needs to be given special care and attention so that it becomes the focal attraction of the commercial.

Von Keitz (1983 b) who has conducted extensive research in the above area stipulates the following design principles: The more certain elements of a TV commercial stimulate the activation process, i.e. attracting a person's attention, the easier they are memorised and remembered. It has been pointed out before that it is these **intensively experienced** and **affectively appealing** moments that strongly accelerate the activation process. A commercial, and hence the messages it seeks to transmit, is remembered longer if it starts by sending out an extraordinary stimulus Empirical research has confirmed that the integration of activating elements has a positive impact on learning efforts in general. The better these activating elements are integrated in the message to be acquired, the more successful is the learning effort. Another aspect that ought to be borne in mind is that TV viewers cannot rewind the film they are watching. An incomprehensible statement cannot be replayed, a superficially pursued scene is irretrievably lost – at least till the next commercial break.

The ascent of private TV companies will increase the diversity of TV advertising as it offers more opportunities to tailor TV spots to specific programmes and to include them in currently running programmes. Companies will also be able to sponsor entire programmes.

9.6 Radio advertising

The most common type of radio advertising is the single "radio spot" whose airtime normally takes up **20 to 30 seconds**. Similar to the commercial breaks on TV, radio commercials are allocated airtime slots. Apart from these classic spots, special types of radio commercials are available, some of which are listed below:

In addition to the commercial breaks, some German channels – state-owned and private – offer complete advertising programmes by means of entertainment shows which also integrate radio spots. These are slightly longer **programme spots that** contain a pre-produced spot which the speaker introduces and refers – in one way or another – to his or her currently running programme.

Two components of the same radio commercial can also be inserted as **tandem spots** into the above programmes. They can be placed before and after a musical number, for instance, which interrupts them for 2 to 3 minutes. The second tandem components is developed on the basis of the first one; it does not make sense to simply play the same spot twice.

This procedure is also suitable for **teaser spots** that are followed by central or **main spots**. The teasers may be the shorter components their major function being to incite the viewers curiosity for the ensuing centrepiece which carries the advertising message. Conversely, the main part of the central spot can go on air first and be followed-up by a **"reminder"**.

The **double spot**, another popular type, consists of two identical parts that are played at different times in the commercial section. The term can also signify that the same spot is broadcast twice, e. g. after two or three different spots, in the same block, a procedure that also makes sense. Compared to commercial slots, marketers expect a considerably higher level of acceptance for programmes that integrate advertisements into entertainment broadcasts. Double spots are therefore intended to increase the degree of awareness in commercial slots.

By way of conclusion, the following specific options should be mentioned whose major function is to deviate from standardized radio commercials and to attract additional attention: There are, for instance, the conventional **live spots** (aka live readers) that are delivered – seemingly "off the cuff" – by the speakers at the radio stations, the **sales promotion** activities specially **designed for airtime** and finally the **infomercials** that contain more information and may merge the spots of several advertisers or for various products into one programme. Moreover, there are the live announcements made in many shopping centres which point out special marketing activities (e. g. attractive offers) or the occasional contests and sweepstakes and celebrity presentation. This type of advertising requires local control and might be of increasing importance owing to the proliferation of private radio stations.

Designers of radio commercials need to bear in mind that this type of advertising is restricted, to a large extent, to **audio messages and acoustic**

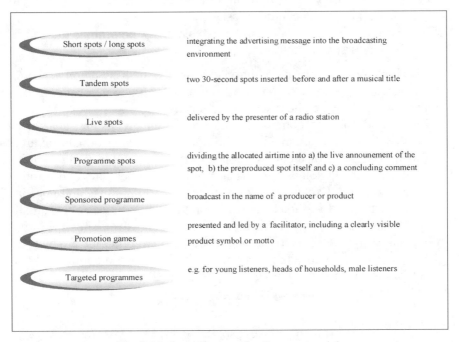

Short spots / long spots	integrating the advertising message into the broadcasting environment
Tandem spots	two 30-second spots inserted before and after a musical title
Live spots	delivered by the presenter of a radio station
Programme spots	dividing the allocated airtime into a) the live announcement of the spot, b) the preproduced spot itself and c) a concluding comment
Sponsored programme	broadcast in the name of a producer or product
Promotion games	presented and led by a facilitator, including a clearly visible product symbol or motto
Targeted programmes	e.g. for young listeners, heads of households, male listeners

Fig. 9.11. Special types of radio commercials

presentation. Owing to the transient nature of the message and the fleeting exposure of the target audience to it, there has to be a focus on **highly intensive sound signals** which should always be given prominence. Too much information can "muddy" the central statements of commercials. Designers therefore need to exercise more restraint than usual when dealing with the audio media. Apart from the accuracy of the details to be conveyed, the quality of the musical appeal that sustains this transmission is of paramount importance. Sounds are the decisive success factor in advertising. Moreover, the fact that the listeners' attention is easily distracted requires **frequent replays**. listeners need to be given **repeated and intensive indications** in order to be able to identify audio messages. These can be theme music, popular advertising jingles, the slogans of well-known brands and similar assets that are apt to increase the level of awareness on the part of the listeners.

As for the dramaturgical structure of the spots, there are two classic approaches:

1. Firstly, strong indicative incentives are offered at the beginning of each spot which are designed to immediately capture the listeners' attention and sustain it throughout the spot. However, listeners always may miss or misunderstand the initial stages of audio commercials. This can be compensated for by frequent replays of the entire spot or by repeating its essential contents and central messages.
2. Secondly, radio spots can **build up tension** by presenting the central message by way of conclusion.

Tension boosters can be additionally applied such as emotive words, catch phrases, speech and sound pauses, tonal variations, changing beat and volumes, semantic alienation and sound effects.

The essential design components of radio commercials are, apart from the voice, all possible sound effects and of course all types of musical tunes and melodies. Some of them are subject to the contemporary trends in advertising. A capella songs, for instance, are sometimes "in" and at other times less popular. Excellent advertising adopts a long-range and goes beyond such fads and fashions. Extravagant sound effects can substantially facilitate the listeners' identification with certain advertising measures. A popular design element to be mentioned here are brand or product **jingles,** one of the famous examples being the *Heinz* tune mentioned above. An other case in point is the *Haribo* jingle which using the same tune in most European countries claims:

"Kids and grown-ups love it so, the happy world of Haribo."

Such theme jingles are of tremendous (financial) value to companies once they have established themselves in the listeners' minds.

Alternatively, instrumental music can be used by advertisers to create individual tunes or to emulate popular entertainment music. It is important to ensure that the melody chosen matches the product. If a product really becomes associated with a well-known tune, this represents a considerable advantage for the overall effect of the advertisement.

Kaloff (1982) points out an essential issue with regard to the design and the development of radio spots. The appeal created by the sounds of a radio commercial cannot be transferred to its written draft. This might mean that the essence of the design may be lost on its way through the decisional hierarchies of the sponsors where decisions may be take without by consulting the creative experts. The optimal design is often not accomplished before it reaches the agents' studio. However, it is less crucial for the effects achieved by radio spots that their messages should be **objectively accurate** than that their presentation should be **credible**. The sound appeal of a radio spot cannot be assessed by comparing it to the factual contents of the copy strategy (which stipulate, for instance, how often a brand name should be mentioned). Such an assessment should be rather be based on the question whether the verbal and acoustic signals represent a persuasive match in terms of the atmosphere created in the advertisement. This can only be tested in a studio but obviously needs to be line with the strategic communication goals.

9.7 Posters and outdoor boards

Posters and outdoor boards share some of their features, such as the way in which they are produced and the fact that they are presented by an agency, with advertisements in the print media but as far as their design is concerned, different rules apply, at least in part. Contrary to press adverts, one cannot assume that if the need for information intensifies more complex pieces of information can be conveyed. In any case, the contact established between the viewer and the advertisement is extremely short-lived and **superficial**. This means that the following design principles should be observed:

- The message should be extremely concise and compact; it should be whittled down to/reduced to a few essential statements.
- Pictures take absolute priority as the driving elements of communication.
- Headlines need to be short and clearly understood; they ought to appear in the upper part of the poster as this area is looked at and registered

more often. If the poster forms part of a series, the name of the expedient could constitute a permanent feature, perhaps in combination with a consistent sub-heading. It can be placed in the lower regions. If the design of serial posters is salient enough to warrant recognition, it is sufficient for the permanent elements to be occasionally perceived by the respondents.

- The copy is of minor importance.
- The piecing together of several smaller pieces to compose the poster results from the technical limitations of poster production and represents a poster-specific problem. The individual pieces sometimes overlap when the posters are billed. Specifically important components of the picture such as human eyes and mouths or corporate logos should therefore not be placed at the points of overlap.
- Poster advertising, too, thrives on the combined blessings of consistency and variations within the given strategic framework of market communications, a framework which helps to avoid redundancies. However, in cases where a topical issue needs to be transmitted, individual posters can be designed and used over a limited period of time. The posters may extend an invitation to important events or represent a piece of communication in reaction to a public relations problem that has suddenly occurred. They may also form part of a political campaigns.

9.8 Public relations

Public relations comprises all communication efforts of an organisation with its public. They include the representation of the organisation as a whole, the formulation of its own interests and building up the organisation's image over time. As far as these goals are concerned there is no difference between consumer and business to business marketing.

Watzlawick once maintained in his now famous statement that "it was not possible not to communicate". Likewise it is impossible not to have public relations, the essential question being whether these relations are result-focused and favour a systematic approach. Each (business) organisation forms part of its public environment and each of its statements which is perceived by its publics influences the way in which the entire organisation is perceived from outside. Public relations seek to establish goodwill and mutual understanding between the organisation and its publics. Although the PR efforts are also directed at the sales market, like all instruments of marketing communications, they include all the other markets with which the organisation exchanges people, goods and services, such as the employment market, the supply market, the financial market as well as the political and the entire **social environment**. In addition, public relations

formally represent an organisation's long-term interests, a task which includes, for instance, influencing media reports about unexpected negative developments in terms of the organisation's own policies. This necessitates a sound and active relationship with the media on a permanent basis and a great deal of sensitivity when dealing with their representatives. Building up relationships of this nature is, in a nutshell, the essential quality of PR work which disposes of multiple and versatile tools:

- advertisements in the print media,
- press releases,
- photographic services,
- open days,
- press conferences,
- public interviews or statements of senior executives,
- annual statements of account,
- corporate magazines or newsletters,
- building up contacts with personalities and organisations that are relevant to one's own.

The messages may also be directed at a **company's own staff**. This is referred to as "internal PR" or as "internal marketing". In these cases, PR is converted into an instrument of corporate identity.

9.9 Publicity

In the consumer sector, "publicity" signifies placing pre-edited articles, which are presented as news stories, about an **organisation** or its **products** (i. e. product publicity), or both, with mass media vehicles. Publicity, which is free of charge, also has an important part to play in business-to-business markets where specialist journals, which have always concerned themselves with technical reporting represent important instruments of publicity.

In order to get the news to the press, companies either invite editors to their premises and arrange for product demonstrations, thereby inspiring the latter to write press articles, or they provide the journalists with the relevant pieces of communication and photographic materials. Press articles enjoy a high degree of credibility and are read more eagerly than the information contained in conventional ads which are hampered by the fact that they are labelled as such. The more the text and the illustrations comply with the requirements of the corresponding subject editors, the more likely is their prompt publication.

Publicity, in its simplest form, has met with increasing difficulty in recent years, as editors tend to erase all brand names and names of corporations from the articles to be released (cf. *Holscher*, 1993: 699) as a direct mention of these names would be an infringement of current legal practice. It is important in this context to underline the **informative character** of the news story, which may focus on technological innovations and corporate news that are of relevance to the entire sector of industry, and to **conceal** or blur the obvious intention to promote certain names or products. Offering information about novel products, reporting on corporate events or discussing newly developed sophisticated technological features is accepted practice and legally admissible. Furthermore, companies can create such events for the benefit of media reports. This is referred to as "event marketing".

Product publicity should pay attention to the fact that while products need to be **visualised** this ought to be accomplished in a manner that differs from their corresponding advertisements especially if these advertisements are placed in the same publication. If this is not the case, it would fully reveal the advertising intention and would be absolutely detrimental to the credibility of the news stories or produce other negative effects. Ideally, product publicity items and advertisements should not appear in the same medium but product publicity should precede conventional advertising in specialist magazines. The advertisements can then emphasize the central statements made earlier. In this case, the advertisement becomes a concise version of the preceding article. Communication research clearly indicates that repeating non-identical but similar messages which additionally spring from different sources (such as the editor's address under the publicity article and the name of the commissioning company in the advertisement) can considerably increase the cumulative effects of marketing communications. This is due to the fact that articles receive a lot more attention than advertisements. Generally speaking, the level of attention that is given to advertisements of capital goods is often **overestimated** by advertisers. For this reason, focused product publicity can be an ideal means to deliver specialist information to a targeted audience.

The following three factors contribute to the effectiveness of publicity:

- Publicity makes the general public realise to what extent the corporation is imbedded in its economic sector and its social environment, e. g. as an employer and tax payer.
- It gradually builds up a corporation's image profile, market position and establishes its name and reputation.
- It transmits concrete product information which in the medium-term is aimed at boosting the sales volume.

Publicity should be integrated in a holistic public relations concept. It will be met with success, if it is founded on a well-coordinated cooperation with the subject-editors of the relevant publishers. This requires constant face-to-face, written or other forms of contact with the editors in charge as well as the appropriate formulation of the editorial text and the information on the pictures. It might also involve exclusivity agreements concerning the publication of certain pieces of information. as well as the regular supply of information about all developments regarding the organisation, even if the latter are not directly intended for publication.

The number of articles that publishers allow to be printed in their specialist journals may largely depend on the extent to which these publications are booked as media vehicles, although such requests will hardly ever be expressed directly. This has led to the practice of inserting **"alibi ads"** in exchange for the opportunity to include editorial articles. However, it would be illegal to make such an agreement on an official basis.

The **reasons for press activities** are provided by the marketing mix. They may be based on:

- product policies: new designs, novel products or more advanced production processes.
- distribution policies: special exhibitions at international trade fairs, opening up of new distribution channels, the signing of a franchising agreement or comprehensive staff development measures based on corresponding HRM policies.
- communications policies: opening ceremonies for in-company exhibitions, the start of advertising campaigns or the design of a new corporate signature.
- pricing policies: fixing new price terms, general reporting on the developments of the pricing system of a certain sector of industry or in combination with different product policies, implementation of a new pricing strategy in combination with a new product range (e. g. offering semi-professional goods at more favourable prices or prestigious up-market sales items as innovative products).
- market research: Market studies and provides relevant information at regular intervals which is welcome to the print media.

In addition to their regular personal contacts with the media, many companies hold press conferences, in order to pass on research-based information to the print media. These contacts are just as important as press conferences which may simply be pure acts of goodwill designed to improve the basic atmosphere between the representatives of the media and the corporations.

9.10 Direct marketing

Direct marketing refers to all types of communication directed at individual addressees. The *Direct Marketing Association* understands this term as denoting an **interactive system** of marketing, which uses one or several advertising media to achieve a measurable reaction (e. g. the placing of an order) on the part of its targeted customers who can be reached virtually everywhere (*Kotler & Bliemel*, 2001: 1108). Direct marketing makes use of the following instruments: direct mail, direct response press advertising, telephone marketing (which can be legally complicated), telemarketing, direct on and offline marketing (e. g. offers via the Internet or *Compuserve*), door-to-door and personal selling. Direct marketing in consumption markets differs from that in capital goods markets. Firstly, the marketing of consumer goods tailors its designs to their respective consumers, and secondly, it needs to take into account the greater number of its respondents. Direct marketing will increase owing to the new media (Internet), the growing number of possibilities to process customer-specific data and an oversupply of advertising measures.

9.11 Product placement

Product placement is a typical instrument of consumer goods marketing (cf. www.productplacementawards.com). It refers to the process of **effectively placing a company's products or services as requisites** in TV or cinema movies, TV serials, video clips or theatre productions. Most of these products thus placed are branded, i. e. trade marks, but advertisers and their sponsors might also think of introducing non-branded products into a movie in order to raise acceptance for a whole class of products. It should be emphasised that whereas product placement pursues goals that are similar to those of advertising in general such as raising the levels of product awareness and adoption, it is not perceived as an advertising measure by the target audience as it appears as part of a TV plot or a programme that is not immediately associated with advertising. Its intention to influence the audience by communication is thus well concealed.

Product placement has been a common feature of cinematic productions since the beginning of the fifties when Ford pioneered it by providing the film studios with cars (*Auer, Kalweit & Nüßler*, 1991: 49). In recent years it has been rediscovered especially for TV productions but also for entertainment shows, video clips and, above all, movies.

The significance of product placement has grown in recent years as a result of the high level of saturation in advertising. By benefiting from a large range of opportunities to arrange for **branded names** to be seen "coincidentally", advertisers can bypass negative responses such as consumer reactance. Moreover, there might be an additional positive feedback from the TV or show programmes chosen and the image of the stars that feature in them.

There are three types of product placement (*Berndt*, 1993 a: 675):

- Placing generic products: These are unidentifiable products which either belong to a generic product type or to an entire sector of industry. It is in particular the market leaders and the household names (such as "Hoover" which has become a synonym of "vacuum cleaner") that profit from such placements. If the leading actor of a TV series, for instance, repeatedly eats wine gums, this might reflect positively on the general consumption of gummibears in general, and on the Haribo brand in particular. And the fact that Telly Savallas kept eating hard-boiled lollipops in *Kojak* can be considered as a kind of anti-marketing as these sweets are obviously meant to be a substitute for smoking.
- Placing corporations and their services: This type of placement usually restricts itself to briefly flashed-in company names and corporate symbols (*Bente*, 1990: 30). The services supplied by these corporations can be "placed" too, as they are, for instance, in the German TV prime time soap *Traumschiff* (i. e. Dreamboat) in which the luxury liner *MS Astor* promotes the cruises offered by the shipping line *Hapag Lloyd*.
- Product placement in the narrow sense of the term includes only well-known brands which are easily identified and recognised and therefore preferred items for placements by the advertisers. This type of placement, which especially favours branded everyday items as well as automotive products, is popular with movies to which it adds a touch of realism (*Soukop*, 1993: 28). It is equally suited for the introduction of innovative products. A well-documented case in point is the JVC camcorder that was used in the movie *Back to the Future*. This camcorder was the first not to require an extra adapter tape but recorded on full-size video tapes that could be played back and slotted in any video player that used the same format. Thus, this film creatively stimulated attention by presenting an innovative product to the audience which was not available at any point of sale before the movie was launched (*Auer, Kaltweit & Nüßler*, 1991: 83).
- *Pepels* (1994: 346) also adds "placement of innovative products" and of "messages" to the above list.

There are three possibilities to integrate products in the plot of a movie:

- On-set placement refers to products that merely serve as props for the storyline of the film in which they appear (*Bente*, 1990: 32). They are, so to say, replaceable accessories and their placement has no direct relation to the plot.
- Creative placement denotes the more or less artistically intensive integration of products, which play a marginal role, into the storyline of a movie.
- Image placement is another name for a type of product placement, which completely integrates one company's well-known product into the theme and the contents of an entire film. Image placement represents the highest degree of integration. Well-known examples of image placements are the role of the coke bottle in the film *The Gods must be Crazy* and the VW model starring in *Herbie the Beetle*.

By integrating products into adventure-focused stories, the feelings and the atmosphere evoked in the film can be transferred to them so that they become associated with images, experiences and moods. This is known as **added affective utility**. In any case, advertisers justifiably assume that by placing products in an emotionally appealing environment they can exert a positive influence on the product assessment by the consumers. For the same reasons it seems problematic, from a marketer's point of view, to arrange for products to be recognized in movies that contain tragic scenes or critical messages.

Seen from the perspective of motivation theory, products should be placed in a film plot in a manner which allows them to convince the viewers that they are capable of meeting their needs and to benefit from the **normative example** of the actors. At the same time, one should bear in mind that the motivation to buy the placed brands have to be in harmony with the motivational complexity felt and shown by the movie actors (*Soukop*, 1993: 44).

One can further assume that positive product placement engenders **agreeable product associations.** If a product appears often enough in a situation which holds a pleasant experiential appeal, it evokes the same kind of expectations in the viewers. The feelings associated with the product, e. g. success, eroticism, intensive feelings, beauty etc. can be enhanced by adept product placements.

On the other hand, the impact of product placement may be considerably weakened by what is referred to as the **boomerang effect**. If product placement is seen as an illegitimate or inadmissible form of manipulation, this might produce untoward results which were not anticipated by the marketing department. Boomerang effects can be caused by the following **errors** which are **to be avoided in** the area of **product placement** (see Fig. 9.12).

9.12 Sponsorships

Sponsorships (cf. *Fachverband Sponsoring & Sonderwerbeformen*) are contributions in cash or in kind made to people or organisations with the expectation of achieving corporate goals and in return for prominent public recognition of this support. There are several forms of sponsorship which include support for the world of sports, the arts and other relevant areas of society. The recipients of sponsorships and the sponsors enter a contractual business relationship which precisely determines the level of the sponsorship and the expected benefits, e. g. wearing the logos or brand signs of the sponsors on their sports equipment, mentioning the sponsorship activities in their newsletters, brochures and advertisements as well as on the tickets for the sponsored events. The sponsors, for their part, can highlight the support they give in their own advertisements (e. g. sponsorship of the top national football league or a title sponsorship of a cup final). The essential principle of sponsorship is that of **"give and take"** (cf. *Bruhn*, 1998: 240). There is a fundamental distinction between sponsorship and charitable donations which do not carry any expectations of public recognition. Unlike **donations** and philanthropic **patronage**, sponsorships are devised as a tool of the marketing communications mix.

The sponsorship of sports events, which seeks to profit from the positive image of the sponsored event or of the sportsmen to be sponsored, is seen

> ➤ The same brands appears too often in the shot.
>
> ➤ The time during which a product is displayed in sequence seems unnecessarily long, at least from a viewer's point of view.
>
> ➤ The placement of the products in the shot is blatantly obvious.
>
> ➤ The link between the actors and the brand is exaggerated and felt to be engineered.
>
> ➤ The brand is arbitrarily integrated into the plot; it interrupts the course of action and looks unrealistic or unsuitable.
>
> ➤ There is an overkill of product placements in the film.

Fig. 9.12. Errors to be avoided in product placement

as an opportunity of image transfer by means of marketing. The **question as to if and how this positive image can be transferred** from the sports arenas to the sponsoring companies is the decisive criterion in choosing a sponsoring partner. When they support sportsmen, sponsors always risk being affected by sudden popularity swings caused by or related to the recipients of the sponsorship (e. g. footballers, clubs, fashionable sports). In order to protect themselves from the negative marketing and media leverage caused by performance lows of individual athletes or from the affairs of sports idols, some sponsors concentrate their activities on sports events and on the promotion of (hopefully) exemplary teams. Currently they are also focussing on junior teams such as the one established and promoted by General Motors in Germany (i. e. *Opel*). A special risk involved in sports sponsorship derives from its growing attractiveness. This has led to such extensive sponsoring activities in sports that achieve a high media leverage such as alpine skiing and car racing that it has become difficult to identify individual sponsorship measures. The sponsorship of such high profile sports only recommends itself to companies whose products are household names or which are fully committed to these sports.

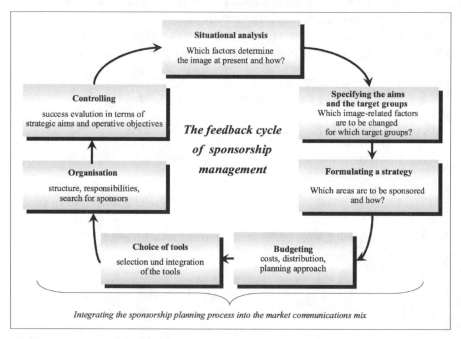

Fig. 9.13. Mapping the sponsorship planning process from a corporate perspective (adapted from Bruhn, 1998: 61)

Cultural sponsorships includes all arts and all forms of cultural expression be they locally important or of international renown. This form of sponsorship, which has recently gained in importance, can be of interest for SMEs in the **business-to-business sectors** if these companies wish to build up a positive image in their **local communities**. They can accomplish this by promoting theatres of some local standing, or culture and arts societies. Museums that include substantial technological exhibits or technological museums also constitute interesting locations for producers of capital goods.

Environmental sponsorships is designed to highlight a corporation's stakeholder orientation which is beginning to play a more important part in view of the growing sensitivity that communities are developing for ecological issues. The related **social sponsorships** allows companies to demonstrate their interest in societal problems and their willingness to contribute to their mitigation or solution. By these means, sponsorship becomes an **instrument of community orientation** in marketing. The advantages of social or environmental sponsoring lie mainly in the fact that companies do not depend so much on certain events or persons but are able to commit themselves to solving social problems that are considered to be important for their communities at large.

Marketing needs to clarify to what extent the solution of ecological and social problems can be aligned with the corporate philosophy. Social and ecological commitment can be integrated successfully in corporate strategies if the sponsors are in some way linked with the area they are sponsoring. Local and regional involvement can derive from the company's major field of activity. The wood processing industry, for instance, might like to sponsor projects for the protection of the forests; manufacturers of solar equipment might launch an environmentally-oriented competition on energy-saving. Moreover, such relationships can be built up with targeted customers, especially between companies that supply consumer goods. They might, for instance, define young people as target groups and offer support for their training and further education programmes. Producers of industrial goods might sponsor projects for their target customers in the processing industries, suppliers of plastic articles might support joint recycling programmes with their communities.

The sponsorship of social, cultural and sports events can be viewed **critically** if the members of a community suspect that the sponsors intend to exert their influence in these areas. This risk obviously exists and, in sponsorship practice, there are numerous examples that sustain such claims. If companies consider their sponsorship activities to form part of their community image building strategy, they can easily defuse such arguments by choosing therecipients of their sponsorship accordingly. If sponsorship is intended to create a community-friendly corporate image it should always seek to be highly credible and sufficiently independent of short-term economic aspects.

A relatively novel field which has been largely overlooked until now is the sponsorship of the scientific projects which offers interesting perspectives to SMEs as well as major corporations operating in capital markets. **Scientific sponsorship** can assist universities in raising funds, a prospect which will be of increasing importance in view of the budget shortages in the sector of higher education. Companies may benefit from this form of sponsorship by supporting research projects that will give them the competitive edge over their competitors. *Hermanns & Suckrow* maintain in their study on this issue (1995: 126 pp.) that companies that sponsor institutions of higher education are facing objections which primarily concern the independence of scientific research and academic teaching. Universities, on the one hand, need to overcome their reservations about unjustifiable interference by the sponsoring corporations, companies, on the other hand, need to reconsider their view of universities as a drag on industry's resources and see them as research partners, who are able to transfer considerable knowledge to businesses in practice.

Sponsoring addresses a fairly broad **target group** and is, therefore, unsuitable for business-to-business enterprises that serve a small and limited market segment. However, it may be worth the consideration of the major players in the industrial sector, such as the truck producers *Iveco Magirus* and the producers of construction materials *Raab Karcher* which have repeatedly provided sponsorship for sports. This form of sponsoring is certainly also advisable for companies which wish to reach a large number of medium-sized producers or service providers on a nationwide basis.

As sponsorships aims to achieve long-term image effects, it seems extremely difficult to monitor and **evaluate its success**. Evaluation requires a systematic planning process which is founded on an **image-related situational analysis**. The planners would have to specify exactly which factors determine the image and to what extent they should be changed and by when. The overall **sponsorship aims** would be derived from this analysis. It is not possible to meet economically quantifiable and measurable short-term objectives such as increase in the sales volume, the market share or a company's competitive position by offering sponsorships. Sponsorships will only be able to make a contribution to these objectives over time and in combination with all the other communications and marketing tools. The definition of the target group, too, is a significant aspect in defining the sponsorship aims. The target customers should be defined just as precisely as is the case with advertising and marketing as a whole. On the basis of these aims and in relation to the specified target group, a **sponsorship**

strategy is formulated. It contains the central issues of the company's commitment which regards in particular the area to be sponsored (e. g. arts, sports, social or ecological environment, the media). The necessary **sponsorship budget** is then allocated in line with the formulated strategy and the **sponsoring measures** to be taken are determined accordingly. Subsequently, contacts are established with the prospective recipients of the sponsorship and a sponsorship agreement is drawn up.

Seen from the perspective of integrated communications, **intermeshing** a company's sponsorship activities with its other communication instruments is of specific significance. The diversity of communication measures in general and the variety of sponsorship opportunities in particular require this interlinking in order to ensure the synergetic enhancement of the overall impact of marketing communications. Sponsorship planning as detailed above is charted in Fig. 9.13.

In a nutshell: Sponsorships concentrate on the areas of sports and arts, on the social and ecological environment and the media. They are directed at individuals, groups, organisations and events. This is graphically represented as the **sponsorship mix** in Fig. 9.14 which has a horizontal and a vertical dimension.

In terms of sponsorship efficiency, companies need to focus on those sponsorship areas and activities which correspond best with the goals

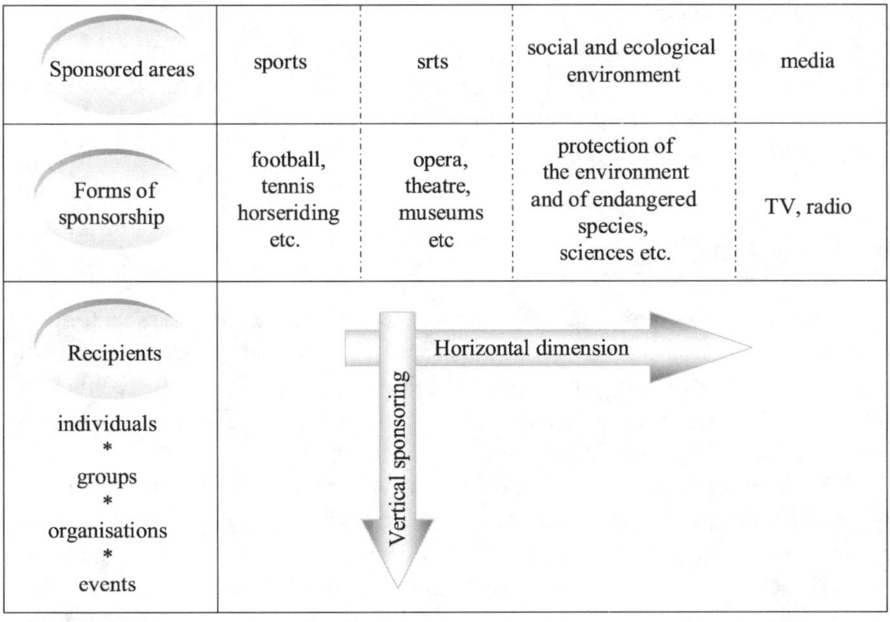

Sponsored areas	sports	srts	social and ecological environment	media
Forms of sponsorship	football, tennis horseriding etc.	opera, theatre, museums etc	protection of the environment and of endangered species, sciences etc.	TV, radio
Recipients individuals * groups * organisations * events				

Horizontal dimension

Vertical sponsoring

Fig. 9.14. Structure and dimensions of the sponsorship mix. (*Bruhn*, 1998: 460)

formulated with regard to their image and which involve their target groups as much as possible. The options concerning the recipients of the sponsorships depend, firstly, on the sponsorship budget available and, secondly, on the opportunity to reach the desired target groups.

9.13 Event marketing

Event marketing signifies planning and staging events which make a company their centre of attention. Event marketing emanates from the experiential orientation of marketing. The targeted persons are transformed from passive onlookers to active participants who experience the world of corporations, their products and brands. The event thus becomes the medium as well as the message.

Zanger & Sistenich (1996: 235) list the following criteria to define and differentiate the term "event marketing":

- Events are initiated by companies on a no-sales basis.
- Events differ from the everyday experience of the participating target group.
- Events which stage the world of brands, convert advertising messages into experiential appeals and interactive encounters.
- Events are tailored to the target groups with whom they seek to establish intensive contacts.
- Events are interactive and invite active customer participation.
- Events are components of the overall concept of integrated corporate communications (which determines their contents while allowing for an independent organisation).

9.14 New media

Although the new media have not yet outgrown their early years as tools of market communications they have ushered in new and sometimes alternative communication opportunities and have opened up new avenues of interchange with targeted individuals and groups. Their considerable bandwidth includes two main groups (cf. Fig. 9.16).

Offline media use data platforms from which stored information can be retrieved on request and which do not interact with other systems. They include ordinary **floppy discs** (generally available but with little storage capacity), **CD ROMs** that have a much higher capacity and are suitable for multimedia applications, **CD-Is** (interactive CDs, high capacity, require a CD-I

Type of event / Target group	sales force meeting	kick-off event	presen-tation	road-show	gala	con-gress	work-shop	sports event
owner			●		●			●
staff	●	●	●		●		●	●
suppliers		●	●		●			●
dealers		●	●	●	●		●	●
journalists		●	●	●	●	●		●
customers		●	●	●	●	●		●
public		●		●				●

Fig. 9.15. Matrix relating target groups to event types (*Unger & Fuchs*, 2005: 311).

player connected to a TV screen) and **hard discs** (high capacity and mobility if combined with a laptop). Companies use laptops to support communications with their **sales force** and to provide them with electronic sales folders. This permits customised product presentations and sales negotiations. **PC-supported** or **CD-I-based** point-of-sales (POS) systems can even be used in busy locations (such as airports and trade fairs) and on a company's premises (e. g. in entrance halls). **CD ROMs** are increasingly produced as catalogue substitutes and can store and reproduce advertising games.

Online systems, by contrast, provide a connection with other systems that can be accessed and used for communication. TV-based online systems rely on digitalised TV equipment and allow the viewers to compose their own programmes at any time. Online media offer companies an ideal platform to publish their self-image and to present themselves and their products to the public. There are no constraints concerning the space for these presentations. The Internet is an excellent instrument of international public relations. It offers marketing information to a company's international customers. Online websites are linked to all areas of marketing. By offering special services and simple ordering routines companies raise the attractiveness of their online offers. Moreover, direct contacts and the evaluation of online-interviews give companies access to market data. **Interactive TV** facilities, such as on-demand services (i. e. the individual combination of programmes) or home shopping channels are ushering in a new era which holds future opportunities that are difficult to appreciate at present.

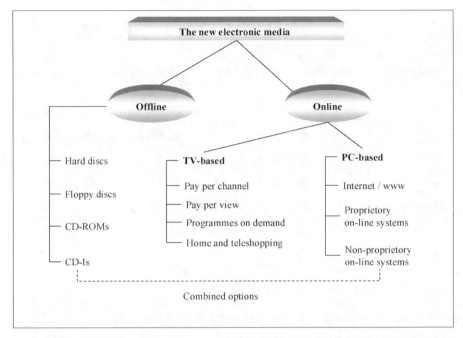

Fig. 9.16. The new media: on overview (*Unger & Fuchs*, 2005: 315)

The new media enjoy the following advantages. They are:

- multi-functional as they permit the simultaneous usage of different communication activities, e. g. individual or multi-user chats, internet conferencing, emails, news groups, intermercials;
- interactive facilities which enable users to send and receive information;
- digitalised as they rely on standardised transmission techniques and allow further electronic processing of the information received;
- multi-medial by integrating different media, e. g. texts and data into video and audio sequences;
- topical due to the fact that they constantly update their information base;
- individualised by barring or restricting access to certain pieces of information;
- internationalised due to the global existence of online services.

The new media excel by their high degree of **innovation** and the **fascination** that emanates from this. Companies use them to **build up a more favourable image** knowing that this fascination will eventually wane and the new media will lose their momentum as image boosters. Nonetheless, the new media have enabled companies to customise their offers to meet the requirements of **targeted user groups** or even of individual users.

There is no time limit (such as shop opening hours) which imposes itself on electronic business activities. The information offers can be permanently updated; it transcends national borders and thereby considerably encourages the internationalisation of business organisations.

In spite of these advantages there are snags involved in the usage of the new media which demand that companies develop a new understanding of their market communications. This means that users have come to expect **constant information updates** and **prompt replies** to their requests and will not be impressed if companies fail to deliver. Moreover, they may be overwhelmed by the **huge amount of information** in the Internet.

9.15 Combining the media

Let us start by looking at the classic combinations of the media mix which result from the relationship between the different media vehicles and the design of the advertisements. This relationship is particularly close between **poster advertisements**, which can usually be reissued in the print media, and **press advertisements**. By contrast – as we have already pointed out – in order to reproduce newspaper adverts as posters the advertised message needs to be more concise. Outside shopping centres, for instance, it would be a good idea to position enlarged versions of advertisements as posters.

Print advertisements and TV commercials also enjoy good relations. Commercials conjure up "inner images" in consumers (*Kroeber-Riel* & *Weinberg*, 2003: 242 and 350 pp.), which can resurface as adverts in consumer magazines and on posters. These images rely on prominent personalities or well-coined phrases; alternatively they can be taken from the key scenes of the respective commercials. Good commercials thrive, in any case, on such scenes which are deeply etched into the viewers' memory and which can be reproduced on posters outside major points of sale. The efficiency of the combination of TV and magazine advertising, which is quite popular at present, depends to a large extent on the distinctiveness of the images they project.

Last but not least, there is the **combination of radio and TV commercials** whose common features are the sounds, the spoken words, the jingles and the tunes. TV commercials supplement each other in as far as the TV version is a more intensive experience and the frequent replays of the same spot in the radio counter their speedy demise. All the options mentioned above need to be specially devised and – as has been pointed out before – occasionally varied to make the best use of their specific advantages and to achieve the most effective results.

9.16 Multiple choice questions

Question 9/1: Which of these statements on communications are correct?

(a)	The significance of a picture-supported affective design of advertisements is often overestimated.
(b)	Mass communication requires picture-supported approaches that make an experiential appeal to the respondents.
(c)	Business-to-business marketing needs to include more information than consumer marketing.
(d)	The readiness of the target audiences to receive information is often overrated.

Question 9/2: Which is the "natural" route that viewers follow?

(a)	Artwork.
(b)	Headline.
(c)	Copy.
(d)	Logo.

Question 9/3: Which of these statements on TV commercials are correct?

(a)	TV audiences are highly interested in the commercials.
(b)	Quite a few TV commercials suffer from idea overkill.
(c)	From a dramaturgical perspective, the initial and the final seconds of a commercial are of specific importance.
(d)	Statements that have been misunderstood cannot be repeated.

Question 9/4: Which of these statements on product placement are appropriate?

(a)	Generic placement signifies placing well-known brands.
(b)	Corporate placement restricts itself to briefly flashed-in names or symbols of companies.
(c)	Image placement means embedding a product creatively in the storyline.
(d)	On-set placement refers to the placement of products as props which support the course of action.

9.17 Case study

Cosmetics PLC has been an established producer of a broad range of high-value hair care products and cosmetics. The product managers for the areas "hair care", "hair colourants" and "hair styling" have been assigned the planning and implementing of their own communications campaigns. In addition to the more conventional forms of advertising, *Cosmetics PLC* organises regular events which involve fashion-conscious celebrities and offer information about how to use the company's products.

1. Which forms of communication are we dealing with here and to what purpose have they been chosen by *Cosmetics PLC*?
2. Are there any other communication tools that *Cosmetics PLC* could make use of?

Solution

1. The events which *Cosmetics PLC* organise for their customers on a regular basis fall into the category of "event marketing". They constitute the platform on which *Cosmetics PLC* present their products in an experientially pleasing and interactive way. The communication messages such as "fashionable" and "stylish" show that *Cosmetics PLC* has opted for an affective approach which aims at creating positive product attitudes and experiential appeals that the target groups can associate with.
2. *Cosmetics PLC* could additionally envisage setting up stands at **trade shows** and **exhibitions** in order to present their product range and their state-of-the art application techniques. Although **sponsorship** is a comparatively new marketing approach, it should be considered too, as it promises to consolidate product awareness and offers an opportunity to intensify contacts with customers and other addressees. Moreover, it could improve staff motivation and the level of corporate identity at *Cosmetics PLC* **Multimedia communication** should be looked into as well, especially the production of CD-ROMs for the provision of product and user information. This medium represents a mobile communication facility that is independent of the print media and enjoys a high storage capacity. It is therefore ideally suited for semi-profes-sional customers whose selective need for information it can satisfy by providing a customised interactive platform. This CD-ROM would be in line with the following communication aims agreed on by *Cosmetics PLC:*
   - affective aims: i. e. exerting a positive influence on the customers and by making an experiential appeal to them (e. g. by showing them a video clip which highlights beautifully groomed hair in various styles and situations),
   - cognitive aims: arousing the customers' attention and interest in new hair care products and instructing them about the application of hair colourants,
   - conative aims: changing customer behaviour by making the information on your company's products and their applications permanently available. This might lead to more purchase intentions.

10 Collaborating with agencies

10.1 Learning outcomes

This chapter will first describe the generic tasks of communication agencies and then move on to the criteria that are decisive in choosing such an agency. The different forms of cooperation that exist between the sponsors of advertising measures and communication agencies will conclude the chapter.

On completing this chapter,

1. you will be aware of the fact that business organisations and communication agencies pursue both common as well as independent goals;
2. you will be able to judge what kind of expertise and experience communication agencies provide for their customers;
3. you will be able to distinguish the principal forms of collaboration with communication agencies;
4. you will be familiar with the individual component of "agency briefing";
5. you will know what kind of services communication agencies are able to offer;
6. you will have learnt how these services are evaluated and how much is paid for them;
7. you will be familiar with the guidelines that apply to the collaboration with such agencies;
8. and you will know that constructive criticism is crucial to the cooperation with agencies.

10.2 Advertising agencies versus communication agencies

The collaboration between the advertisers and the communication agencies is a business partnership with both parties pursuing mutual goals in addition to their own aims and objectives (which are mostly profit-targets). However it is impossible for each party to meet their independent objectives if the common goal of successful communication is not achieved.

Communications agencies have developed in recent years from the former advertising agencies whose major task used to be (in the fifties) to carry out the media bookings for the advertiser. By way of compensation, they received a commission from the publishers or broadcasters which usually amounted to 15% of the booking price. Later on, these agencies started designing the advertising measures themselves. Nowadays, these service providers operate as intermediaries and consultants in all areas of marketing communications. Apart from booking the advertising means with publishers and broadcasters, they submit design proposals to the management and coordinate the production of the different pieces of communication, a process for which they sometimes also take responsibility. The broad range of services they offer exceeds marketing communications to include, for instance, the implementation of product design measures, devising packaging or branding techniques or motivational measures for the sales force (e. g. provision of sales literature or the organisation of sales force meetings). This is why the term communication agencies is more appropriate and now also more common.

10.3 Arguments in favour of collaborating with agencies

Each communication activity, such as advertising, sales promotion, packaging and the supply of sales literature, with a company's partners in the marketplace seeks to provide information and, thereby, to exert influence. If this attempt is to be successful, it requires a fair amount of **expertise**. Communication agencies, which are used to tackling the complex issues involved in communications, have acquired a considerable amount of experience. Agencies benefit from the fact that they need to solve communication problems in completely different fields. They can **transfer the knowledge** they have gained to currently existing problems and thus make a creative contribution to their solution. The production of communication means, too, demands special knowledge and capabilities such as the conversion of drafts into prints, the production of illustrations, photos or films. For this reason, make or buy decisions in communications should not only be based on **cost considerations** but should also take **quality** and **effectiveness** of communication measures into account. However, owing to their activities in a large number of economic sectors, agencies hardly ever have the necessary detailed expertise required by each specific sector of trade and industry. This will have to be provided by the marketing management of the advertising organisation.

There are two possibilities to work with communication agents. If the design work to be carried out is of an occasional nature, advertisers will place

project-by-project orders. However, it is always sensible to cooperate with one agency on a **retainer** basis, especially if projects have been successfully conducted in the past. The more projects they have completed for one client, the easier is it for the agents to understand the new task and the more efficient future cooperation will be. Past experience also has a harmonising influence on the style of the different assignments which increases their overall efficiency. Moreover, long-term cooperation with communication agencies is usually supportive of a long-term communications strategy. If there is a higher number of assignments to be carried out, a long-term regular cooperation on a contractual basis should be considered.

10.4 Criteria for agency selection

If substantial communications budgets are at play, companies send out an **issue brief** to the selected agencies and invite them to a competitive **pitch** in the course of which the agencies present their campaign proposals. In France and Germany, agencies receive an agreed contribution towards the pitch which is frequently entirely at the expense of the advertiser.

In the UK clients and agencies fundamentally disagree about this issue, with the clients usually refusing to pay. In any case, the pitch is cost-intensive, even if the presentations are short and even if only a small number of agencies take part. And there is the unresolved question as to whether one pitch presentation can be a conclusive and reliable indication of a harmonious future cooperation. Major corporations which are experienced in working with agencies therefore maintain business relations with a pool of agencies whom they invite to pre-pitch meetings about their planned projects. The eligible agencies are then short-listed and invited to a briefing meeting.

The **brief** contains the following elements:

- a thorough situational market analysis,
- a competitive analysis which may include wholesalers, retailers and end consumers,
- a precise definition of the target audiences,
- the marketing communications objectives based on the target markets,
- a detailed product description,
- the budget available,
- the timing and the schedule of the project, and
- its most important item, the desired advertising design.

In order to achieve optimal results, communications agents also need information about previously conducted advertising measures and those that are planned to run simultaneously. The more detailed the information given to the agents, the better results can be anticipated. Marketing management itself needs to be fully aware of what can be expected of the planned communication measures. This is an absolute prerequisite it the agencies are to achieve optimal design results.

Furthermore, agencies ought to be in a position to query the brief in order to eliminate possible misunderstandings. Independent of the permanent or occasional nature of the cooperation, the following credentials play an essential role in the selection of agencies:

a) Competencies and services offered

An agency's service offer includes the following:

- Consultation on all matters related to communications and, if need be, also on questions of marketing. The main task of the agency is the design, the layout and the realisation of advertisements, public relations, sales promotion, sponsorships, event marketing and packaging.
- Media planning. This includes proposals as to what media vehicles should be booked, the performance appraisal of these media vehicles, the booking of the advertising measures with them and the subsequent liquidation and invoicing.
- Market and advertising research. Agencies can make a contribution to the aforementioned research areas; they can also offer advice on trade fairs and trade shows, product development and the design of the product range.
- The size of the agency ought to be in proportion with the volume of the order to be placed. Otherwise minor customers may not be given enough attention by major agencies, or small agencies (four to six staff or fewer) may not have the experience required for big orders. Highly specialised agencies may be not be advisable either as their perspective of the order might be too narrow. On the other hand, it might be sensible to commission specialists for the organisation of sponsorship, event marketing and product placement. In any case, collaboration with more than one agency at a time requires a high level of coordination which might be at the expense of the integration of all communication measures.

b) Quality of staff

Agency staff must be qualified to perform consultation work and should, above all, have sufficient experience in their field. Clients should make sure that there is enough contact with the most competent and senior staff.

Collaboration with an agency, which mainly consists of customer consultation and the provision of creative services, requires a high level of personal trust.

c) International networks

Many agents have signed cooperation agreements and undertaken world-wide joint business ventures and it is exports and imports that can benefit from this most. The employment of globally operating agents makes sense if the advertising budget amounts to several million euros per year. If this is not the case, SMEs in particular should rather opt for medium-sized agencies which form part of an **international cooperation network**.

d) Location

The opinions on this issue are divided. On the one hand, consultancy may definitely be more difficult to perform remotely than locally, especially as certain questions may require immediate attention. On the other hand, distance is no real issue in view of the opportunities offered by telecommunications.

As soon as the selection process has been completed, the cooperation – be it on a jobbing basis or a long-term arrangement – is usually continued on the basis of a contractual agreement.

10.5 Remuneration

The contract stipulates the exact nature of the assignment and remuneration. Agents traditionally received a commission of 15 per cent from media owners on each booking they made for their clients. Alternatively agencies contract-out work (e. g. print or video production) to third party suppliers and mark up the purchase cost by 15 per cent for their supervisory and brokering tasks. However, owing to the fact that the commission method has encouraged expensive out-contracting with third parties and that many agencies now are full-service or through-the-line providers that operate in all areas of communications, this remuneration method is now being replaced by fixed time charges or fixed fees plus performance-related pay.

If fixed fees are negotiated, the 15 per cent commission is fully passed on to the client. Given due consideration to the expenses incurred by the agents which depend on the volume of the budget, some clients will allow them to add a mark-up of 5 per cent to the retainer they have agreed on. Fixed fees seem to be more appropriate for creative work, such as the artwork of an

> ➤ Range of services availbale
> ➤ Creative potential
> ➤ Awards received and prizes awarded by the advertising sector
> ➤ Advertising and product experience
> ➤ Size
> ➤ Location
> ➤ Competencies in the service required
> ➤ International network and experience
> ➤ Existing customer base
> ➤ References
> ➤ Duration of collaboration agreements
> ➤ Market achievements of the customers
> ➤ Reliability
> ➤ Meeting the deadlines
> ➤ Personal relations
> ➤ Versatility
> ➤ Qualifications of staff
> ➤ Staff turnover in the past
> ➤ Cost consciousness
> ➤ Compliance with the brief
> ➤ Usage of information provided
> ➤ Work approaches

Fig. 10.1. Selection credentials for agencies (*Unger & Fuchs*, 2005: 448p.)

advertisement, as the price of the design of an advertisement should not depend on the number of its insertions.

Fixed fee arrangements force the agencies to reveal the complete cost incurred for each assignment to their clients. This and the usual time charges for an agency's primary activities is a fairly reliable basis for the costing of agency services. However clients ought to bear in mind that creative tasks **cannot** always be calculated to the exact hour. In the long run, agencies will provide satisfactory services if the fee they receive is felt to be an adequate reward. It therefore seems advisable to collaborate with them on a trial or jobbing basis before a long-term contract is signed.

10.6 Project-by-project contracts

It there is only one specific job to be carried out, advertisers should specify, even before the task is awarded, exactly how much the contracted-out portion will **cost** and which **type and quality of service** will be expected for the agreed fee. "Package design" is too vague a task description. Instead they should determine:

- the manner in which the proposals are to be presented, e. g. as sketched drawings or as a master layout which resembles the final version or has the quality of the completed print out;
- the number of alternative proposals that are to be presented to the client;
- the number of new proposals to be submitted after changes demanded by the customer have been made. It may not be enough to present several alternatives on only one occasion, as new questions may arise from this one presentation for the customer which might affect the original task description. An additional fee might have to be negotiated for this eventuality;
- the time in which the new proposals are to be made and the deadline for the final approval and production of the communication tools;
- the expected cost of work contracted-out to suppliers (production of prints, photos, illustrations and videos) and of the agency's coordination work including those of the third-party suppliers. The agency can be requested to submit a complete quotation before it is awarded the contract. If illustrations are required, draft copies can be demanded beforehand. These are indicative of the style of the final version and thus save cost and time.

10.7 Ground rules of collaboration

10.7.1 Presenting, evaluating and selecting agency proposals

As a rule, a proposal made by an agency is only as good as the information the latter has received. For this reason, a precise and comprehensive **brief** lays the foundation for the agency's work. This is why, in practice, it seems reasonable to demand that the agency should be involved in the drawing up of the brief.

The first step towards the final selection of alternative communication measures is the **pitch** meeting at which the agencies present and expand on their proposals. All senior executives involved in this selection process ought to be present at this meeting so that they can voice there objections directly. As most proposals are subsequently revamped and resubmitted, they should be thoroughly discussed during the first presentation.

Evaluating creative achievement in advance is difficult and this applies even more to the projected impact of communication measures in marketing. To reduce the risk of failure and to eliminate errors beforehand, agencies therefore often provide scamps for pre-vetting purposes. Other research procedures applied to assess the advertising reach will be explained in detail in the module on **Market Research**.

Agencies can be consulted on the methods conducive to pre-vetting. In any case, they should be fully informed about the results. This seems the only way in which marketing managers and communications agents can jointly benefit from the results for further reference. As **advertising research** can be very cost-intensive, checklists such as the one suggested in Fig. 10.2 tend to be used to assess the plausibility of minor communication ventures.

The final decision on the proposed measures needs to involve the agency. If the agency is seen as a competent and expert partner there is no reason why it should not be included in the decision making process. Product and sales managers certainly are well versed in the question what kind of information the buyers ought to be given, but the agency may know more about how this informed should be conveyed and companies should benefit from the agency's communications experience. A team decision seems to be most appropriate.

> Customer needs represent focal area

> Clearly expressed product utility

> Independence of design

> Ability to arouse interest

> Picture-enhanced

> Copy and illustrations supplementing each other

> Readability of all elements of the copy

> Compliance with long term strategy

Fig. 10.2. Checklist to evaluate advertisements

10.7.2 Producing the communication means

The production of the communication means should likewise involve consultations with the agency. Agencies who are permanently requested by a large number of sponsors to produce communication means enjoy a high level of expertise. Company departments or executives will not often be able to provide the same subject knowledge and should not be called upon to do so as this would create an unnecessary rivalry with the agency. Executives sometimes attempt to compete with agencies, for instance, by buying printing material at more favourable prices. This can be to the detriment of quality and hence of the communication effects. For this reason, the agency should be consulted as an **external advisor** even in such seemingly trivial matters. Those in charge of the design should be involved in its technical implementation. The agency can best contribute its expertise as an independent adviser if it is not involved in the production of the communication means.

Scheduling must allocate enough time and leeway for the creative and productive work. The ad hocery which sometimes hampers the production of the communication means also springs from inadequate planning and the lack of discretional discipline. Even if the job is completed in the very nick of time, time pressure is always at the expense of quality.

10.7.3 Continuity of collaboration

It is manifestly obvious that the most successful consumer brands have evolved and benefited from **long-term relations with individual agencies**. Communication works and needs to be developed over time, its continuity being the prerequisite for its success.

Changes in management that often entail changes in the communications style of the company and hence in its agencies, tend to be mixed blessings. Long-term communication goals, corporate, product and brand images as well as corporate identity may be severely affected. The allegation that an agency's creativity could dry up, which is sometimes put forth to justify a change in agencies, is somewhat dubious. In practice, agencies employ many creatives on a freelance basis for their own work as well as for out-contracting. Customer consultants are responsible for the design tasks, whereas the creative groups can be swapped around to various tasks. This is less detrimental to the continuity of communication.

Rather than indulging in **frequent agency changes**, the existing cooperation should be analysed on a regular basis and continually improved by a mutually developed routine which ought to become part and parcel of a process which would allow all parties concerned to tackle and resolve problems objectively and efficiently. The following questions, for instance, could be routinely discussed:

- Which are the strengths the agency has shown in handling the tasks which it is currently performing?
- Which weaknesses have been identified in handling the same tasks?
- Is the agency professionally run?
- Has it been sufficiently informed?
- Is it making good use of the information provided?
- Are the regular meetings efficient from either partner's point of view?
- Is the company benefiting enough from the specific expertise of the agency?

However, if the collaboration remains unsatisfactory in spite of these routine checks and if an extension of the cooperation seems unlikely, changing agencies should obviously be considered.

10.7.4 Handling criticism

Agencies ought to be entitled – and perhaps encouraged – to comment critically on a company's marketing and communications approach; other-wise they cannot fulfil their function as independent consultants.

However, constructive criticism only thrives in a climate of mutual trust. If this can be created, the collaboration with agencies can become a future-oriented venture, provided the agency's staff have the necessary expertise. Medium-sized companies, in particular, can benefit from the pooled expertise of agencies – not many of them do so at present. The economic dependency of the agencies, which makes them susceptible to threats to terminate the relationship, is not a sound basis for constructive criticism.

In human resources management, participative leadership is now seen as superior to power-coercive styles (even if this may not always reflect HRM practice) and this seems to be the right avenue to take in marketing, too, if companies wish to cooperate efficiently with agencies and build up successful long-term marketing communications.

10.8 Multiple choice questions

Question 10/1: What are the arguments in favour of collaborating with communication agencies?

(a)	Subject knowledge and expertise.
(b)	Transfer of experience from different areas.
(c)	Continuity of the communication strategy.
(d)	Organisational aspects.

Question 10/2: What are the criteria for selecting communications agencies?

(a)	The range of services they are able to offer.
(b)	Their staff.
(c)	International network(s).
(d)	Relationship with local stakeholders.

Question 10/3: Which statements on the remuneration methods for agencies are correct?

(a)	The commission method inspires agencies to commission cheaper productions.
(b)	An increasing number of companies pay agencies a fixed fee or retainer.
(c)	Remuneration should depend on how often the advertisement is broadcast, printed or billed.
(d)	The negotiation of the fee requires that the agency should present a breakdown of the cost incurred for the assignments specified by the sponsor. .

Question 10/4: What are the ground rules to be considered when co-operating with communication agencies?

(a)	Agencies should not be involved in the drawing up of the brief.
(b)	Companies should attempt to create rivalry between the collaborating agencies and their own advertising departments.
(c)	The most successful brands in the consumer sector have evolved from long-term relationships with agencies.
(d)	Agencies should be entitled to comment critically on the marketing and communications approach of the collaborating company.

10.9 Case study

For decades, *Cosmetics PLC* has been well established as a producer of a broad range of a high quality hair cosmetics. You are in charge of the company's communications and you have read in the trade journals that "most briefs are inadequate and that the agencies have to try and acquire the information they need for their design proposals themselves." You suggest that your company should reduce such communication problems by professionalizing its briefs.

Please outline the structure of a written brief.

Solution

The brief contains the tasks assigned to the agency by the company. It may be communicated in writing or result from a work session with the agency. In both cases it is necessary that it should be as comprehensive as possible in order to warrant the quality of its creative realization. *Cosmetics PLC* achieves this aim on the basis of the following checklist (*Unger & Fuchs*, 2005: 451):

Situational analysis

- Market development and forecasts (total market, segments)
- Turnover achieved (total market, sales areas, sales volume and sales receipts)
- Development of market share (by distribution channels)
- Development of distribution (in figures, weighted by sales areas and distribution channels)
- competitor analysis (brands, producers, market share, marketing mix)
- Own expenditure on advertising in the past (including communication strategies and their implementation)
- Final comparison (SWOT analysis)

Marketing aims and objectives

- Previous sales targets (stating the difference between actual sales and targeted sales)
- Projected market objectives (turnover, distribution, market share)
- Communication aims (regarding buyers, line traders, market segments)
- Product positioning (product benefits, assumed and desired user evaluation compared to that of major competitor, packaging text and own product design comparared to that of competitors)

3. **Requested creative realisation**
   (assignments for the agency)

- Communication strategy (e.g. copy strategy)
- Media strategy
- Media design, line trade, key accounts, consumers; details on individual advertising means (posters, ads, radio spots, TV commercials)

- Sales promotion: sales literature for the dealers, product cataloguess for the sales force
- Public relations, including product publicity to be designed by the agents or a third party
- Other media
- Information on creative realisations that were totally rejected by the customer

4. **Target groups**

- Socio-demographic features
- Psychographic features: attitudes, motives, purchase or usage obstacles, values
- Consumer behaviour: complete customer data obtained from panel research

5. **Budget**

- Total budget
- Allocation to the elements of the communications mix and the mediy types relevant for advertising
- Scheduling the budget allocations

6. **Schedule**

- Scheduling the first pitch
- Further presentations after customer approval of the changes to be made
- Decision taking on the part of the customer
- Scheduling the production of advertising means (photos, final drafts, test prints, radio and video recordings, customer approval, scheduling the correction period, booking the media
- Scheduling the employment of the communication tools

Fig. 10.3. The structure of the brief

11 Specific issues in international marketing communications

11.1 Learning outcomes

This chapter will demonstrate the complexity of international communications management and will then outline the trends which underpin the widely discussed issue of globalisation as well as the ground strategies of international market communications. Moreover, it will deal with the factors that mostly determine the level of standardisation of the internationally applicable communication tools.

On completing this chapter,

1. you will know which factors add to the complexity of communications management in an international context;
2. you will be able to appreciate which environmental developments can result in the internationalisation of market communications;
3. you will be in a position to assess the impact of an international management focus on market communications;
4. you will be aware of the difference between a standardized and a differential international communications strategy;
5. you will have learned what the transferability of communication concepts depends on;
6. you will be able to gain an idea of what arguments are usually propounded in favour of or against standardized cross-cultural communication;
7. you will be familiar with those communication tools which are suspected of being unduly national or too parochial.

11.2 Managing international market communication

Many people are involved in the planning, the implementing and the control of international market communications. This and the huge amount of data and facts relevant for the different national markets account for the high degree of complexity that the management of international market communications are facing.

The manner in which enterprises tackle this challenge depends first and foremost on their global strategy and organisation. In other words, their corresponding communications strategy, be it standardized or differentiated, often depends on whether it is based on centralised or decentralised structures which, for their part, are indicative of the overall internationalisation strategies of these enterprises.

In this context, it is the relationship between the communication departments of the parent companies and the subsidiaries which is of paramount importance. Is there a controlling system which has empowered the central communications department with responsibilities and discretional power or have these been more or less delegated to the subsidiaries which take the important decisions? And what is the strategy regarding the collaboration with external agencies?

There are several options concerning the selection of agencies: they may be centrally controlled internationally operating agencies or national agencies embedded in a network based on partnerships all over the world. On the other hand, they may be nationally based agencies that are employed by the communications departments on the spot. The type of cooperation adopted also depends on the degree of standardisation or adaptation of the communication strategy in which it is embedded (see also *Mooij*, 1991: 335pp.). This also applies to advertising and, at least indirectly, to the question as to who is responsible for booking the media and where they should be booked.

The decisions about centralised or decentralised discretional powers within the organisation and the kind of cooperation envisaged with external communications agents are essential parameters for the process of planning, execution and control of international market communications, that is to say for the fundamental management tasks in this area. This process is outlined in Fig.11.1.

The above process starts with the international marketing aims and objectives, which are founded on the overall corporate goals and structures, and an analysis of the organisation's existing communications approach. The situational analysis of communications includes the most important variables that impact on a communication policies. These are, *inter alia*:

- the management focus (international, multinational, global),
- the level of standardisation or adaptation of the brandnames in question and of brand positioning,
- the structure of the markets served (geographical and cultural boundaries, size, potential, market share, consumer behaviour, distribution system etc.),

- competitive analysis (strengths, weaknesses, positioning, conformity of public appearance compared to the company's own image and degree of popularity,
- national and cross-border media systems.

This analysis should be backed by a comprehensive number of relevant and up-to-date pieces of information about global developments. However, it is not always easy to obtain this data, as international market research is not without its deficiencies when it comes to data alignment and the harmonisation of the research tools. The analysis is intended to provide relevant information concerning international corporations and their environment.

On the basis of the aims and objectives formulated by the international marketers and the cross-border situational analysis, companies can decide on their international communication goals and their customers to be targeted. Whether these goals can be messaged uniformly throughout the company's markets depends on the specific situation in each country (e. g. the degree of maturity a product has reached in its life cycle in different European countries). Building up an image as an environmentally friendly company throughout Europe would be such a consistent goal.

Situational analysis

- Market development and forecasts (total market, segments)
- Turnover achieved (total market, sales areas, sales volume and sales receipts)
- Development of market share (by distribution channels)
- Development of distribution (in figures, weighted by sales areas and distribution channels)
- competitor analysis (brands, producers, market share, marketing mix)
- Own expenditure on advertising in the past (including communication strategies and their implementation)
- Final comparison (SWOT analysis)

Marketing aims and objectives

- Previous sales targets (stating the difference between actual sales and targeted sales)
- Projected market objectives (turnover, distribution, market share)
- Communication aims (regarding buyers, line traders, market segments)
- Product positioning (product benefits, assumed and desired user evaluation compared to that of major competitor, packaging text and own product design comparared to that of competitors)

3. **Requested creative realisation**
   (assignments for the agency)

- Communication strategy (e.g. copy strategy)
- Media strategy
- Media design, line trade, key accounts, consumers; details on individual advertising means (posters, ads, radio spots, TV commercials)

- Sales promotion: sales literature for the dealers, product cataloguess for the sales force
- Public relations, including product publicity to be designed by the agents or a third party
- Other media
- Information on creative realisations that were totally rejected by the customer

4. **Target groups**

- Socio-demographic features
- Psychographic features: attitudes, motives, purchase or usage obstacles, values
- Consumer behaviour: complete customer data obtained from panel research

5. **Budget**

- Total budget
- Allocation to the elements of the communications mix and the mediy types relevant for advertising
- Scheduling the budget allocations

6. **Schedule**

- Scheduling the first pitch
- Further presentations after customer approval of the changes to be made
- Decision taking on the part of the customer
- Scheduling the production of advertising means (photos, final drafts, test prints, radio and video recordings, customer approval, scheduling the correction period, booking the media
- Scheduling the employment of the communication tools

Fig. 11.1. Planning international market communications (*Unger & Fuchs*, 2005: 641)

On determining the target groups, marketers need to answer the question whether there are **supranational market segments** which are sizeable and homogeneous enough – that is to say whose media usage and consumer behaviour patterns are identical – to be targeted in a similar way. If such supranational target groups are non-existent, country-specific target consumers need to be identified. This is also important if the ensuing **communication of positioning strategies** is to be harmonized. One of the most essential strategic decision an international marketer has to make is whether to standardise the communication mix, to wholly or partially adapt to the local markets or to opt for a hybrid form.

The choice of **communication tools and methods** to be used in international campaigns is even more difficult than that employed in national campaigns. Each instrument and each method has advantages as well as disadvantages. Before decisions are taken they ought to be assessed against the set communication goals. What tool or method mix is selected depends, *inter alia,* on the corresponding product-market constellation, the push or pull strategy applied, the life-cycle phase of the product, the level of involvement on the part of the targeted audiences and the decision taking process of the consumers (*Mooij*, 1991: 381). These criteria can differ from one national market to the other. Depending on whether these markets re similar or different, marketers will then realise identical, similar or different communication programmes in their respective markets.

Based on these programmes, a task-centred and result-focused budget will then be determined and evaluated which, for its part, will evidently constitute the foundation for the **communications budget** and the allocations made to each country market. In practice, however, task-orientation is not always the overriding concern; and the following approaches may be used:

- The budget represents a percentage of the sales.
- It is based on competitive parity, i. e. it equals the competitors' expenditure or represents an approximation thereof.
- An apparently affordable budget is allocated.

If budgets are determined according to any of these methods, marketers will need to examine whether the amount allocated will cover all the measures necessary to meet the communication goals. If this is not the case, a realignment of the goals with the budget is advisable.

The allocation of the total budget to each country is usually made in an equally pragmatic way which includes

- sharing the budget out equally between all countries,
- calculating it as an appropriate proportion of the sales,
- competitive parity budgeting (see also *Berndt*, 1993b: 787).

The decisions that have been taken on the above concepts form the basis for the **realisation of the communications design** not only with regard to the contents (e. g. an identical product presentation or positioning world-wide while developing country-specific features) but also to the collaboration with agencies (e. g. enlisting the services of one global player, of a lead agency).

An effective and successful implementation of international communications, be it founded on standardised strategies or not, always requires a sound **organisation** and close cooperation between the central and the peripheral, i. e. local, functions of the communications agencies involved. According to *Mooij* (1991: 385) clear directives and close contacts between all parties concerned are apt means to improve such cooperation.

The last stage concerns the question of **how communication effectiveness** can be evaluated. Unfortunately there are no uniform evaluation methods used on the international stage. The two most popular approaches are **sales and recall surveys** whose results can be relied on when communication strategies are revamped and subsequently adjusted. However, transnational comparisons to assess the advertising reach of international campaigns are impossible without prior harmonising of the different research approaches.

The basic structure of the planning process that underlies international marketing communications is not fundamentally different from that of national marketing communications but includes further variables which add to the complexity of such a process.

11.3 Analysing the starting position

As early as the eighties, the large number of new developments (see Fig.11.2) provoked a heated debate on the internationalisation of marketing strategies and activities which has continued to this day. This includes a highly intensive discussion of the **internationalisation of market communications** in general and of advertising in particular.

The more essential communications are for a company and for a national economy as a whole, the more the issue of cross-border market communications will become relevant and need to be given prominence.

Worldwide advertising campaigns are not exactly a novel concept. Some companies, namely *Coca Cola* or *Marlboro,* started communicating their products and services by launching global actions decades ago. *International Marketing* was added to the curricula of US universities as early as the 1950's when North American companies began their rapid international expansion. This discipline of Marketing concerns itself with the

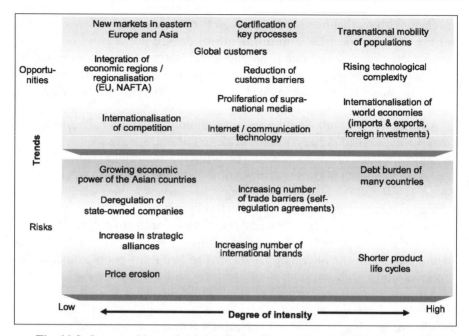

Fig. 11.2. Opportunities and risks analysis of internationalisation (an example)

question when international marketing concepts and methods are transferable to foreign markets and when they need to be adjusted. Its fundamental issue therefore was the search for the parameters of individual country markets and of the relevant supranational determinants of world economy. This approach implies that owing to the multiple socio-cultural and socio-economic structures and processes that make international operators more dependent on their international context and business environment, the nature of **international marketing** is highly complex.

Figure 11.3 visualises the fact that international companies may wish to "diagnose" the globalisation potential of their industries in order to obtain information about the **equilibrium between overglobalisation and underglobalisation**. An ideal strategy would anticipate a perfect balance between the a company's degree of globalisation and the globalisation potential of its industry. In the above example, corporations A and C have succeeded in placing themselves in such a situation. Corporation A shows a small degree of globalisation which mirrors that of its industry (e. g. frozen food) whereas corporation C (e. g. a software provider) is globalised enough to benefit from the strategic advantages offered by its highly globalised sector. Corporation B is strategically impeded in its **international efforts** because its level of globalisation is too low for it to take advantage

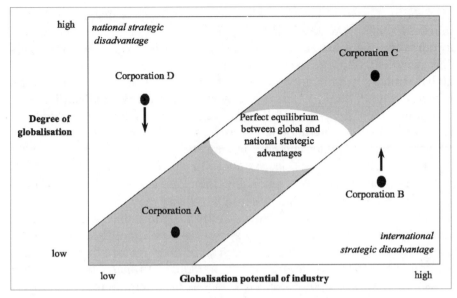

Fig. 11.3. Challenges to international enterprises (*Yip*, 1995: 40)

of the standardisation potential of the industry it belongs to. Corporation D, by contrast, is over-globalised compared to its economic sector, in other words, it has not adjusted its marketing strategy to the country specifics as much as would have been necessary. Corporation D is therefore hampered by **national** disadvantages (*Yip*, 1995: 41).

11.4 The international management focus

11.4.1 Fundamental principles

International Marketing is situated between the extreme positions of domestic, which directs its activities exclusively at the home market, and global marketing (see Fig. 11.4) which assists a company in using its assets and expertise to formulate global strategies. We would like to point out that multinational and global are not synonymous: "The multinational corporation operates in a number of countries, and adjusts its products and practices in each – at high relative costs. The global corporation operates with resolute constancy – at low relative cost – as if the entire world (or major regions of it) were a single entity; it sells the same things in the same way everywhere. Which strategy is better is not a matter of opinion but of necessity" (*Levitt*, 1995: 11). Global marketing does not signify that all the markets in the world have to be catered for, serving **a great number of markets** is enough (*Weinhold-Stünzi*, 1996). Moreover, it is the **strategic importance of a market** which is the decisive factor (*Yip*, 1995: 34): "This may mean entering a market that is unattractive in its own right, but has a global strategic significance, such as the market of a global competitor." *Hünerberg* (1994: 31) assesses the degree of **internationalisation of a company** according to the results of its entrepreneurial operations and to its key targets such as international turnover, relative market share in foreign countries, degree of international sourcing etc.

The majority of corporations are not so much confronted by the question as to **whether** they ought to globalize their operations – and hence their market communications – but rather **in what way** they will be able to manage their worldwide activities successfully and **how** they will meet their aims. Figure 11.4 visualises the **stages of internationalisation** which a company can go through. These stages can be characterised by corresponding **management orientations** which in addition to managerial expertise reflect a further corporate success factor of international enterprises, namely "the commitment of the latter to regarding international operations as an explicit element of corporate strategy." (*Dichtl & Müller*, 1992: 442).

Internationalisation processes are in need of being "triggered off" (*Douglas & Craig*, 1995: 29) or of "change agents" (*Czinkota & Ronkainen*, 1993: 254): "For change to take place, someone or something ... must initiate it

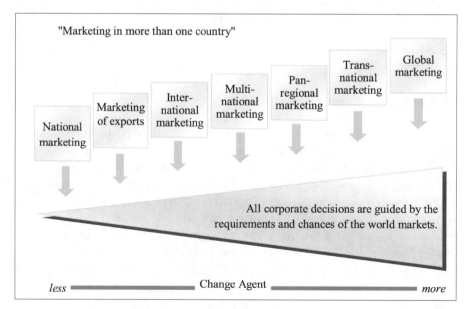

Fig. 11.4. International management orientations

and shepherd it through to implementation. This intervening individual or variable is here called a **change agent**." There are **internal forces** driving the change process which may be, for instance, international market opportunities which a chief executive was able to identify in the course of a business trip abroad, the recruitment of new staff who are experienced in working abroad, the saturation of the company's domestic markets, customers going international, risk diversion, the arrival of a new market entrant in the domestic market or export incentives offered by the government. **External forces** may be the following developments (*Yip*, 1992; *Yip*, 1995: 41): converging standards of living and lifestyles (e. g. *McDonald's* in Paris and *Perrier* in the US), acquiring global customers by increasing the number of trips abroad, international distribution channels, increasing production cost accompanied by a decreasing life cycle, the creation of trade barriers, new market entrants, technological progress (e. g. new means of communication). **The intensity of the driving forces/change drivers depends on the level of internationalisation a company is going through** (*Douglas & Craig*, 1995: 33).

11.4.2 Ethnocentric enterprises

Ethnocentric enterprises are inclined towards pursuing international strategies which are characterised by their rather strong focus on the parent company's business activities and in which the selling to the domestic market takes priority over catering for foreign markets. This is also referred to as "domestic market extension". Accordingly, there are only **minor efforts** made to align the marketing mix (e. g. the individual communication elements) to the foreign markets. Affiliated foreign companies are restricted to their function of "simple sources of quick profits" (see Fig. 11.5). Their pieces of communication mostly represent directives which flow – not unlike one-way traffic – from the corporate headquarters to the affiliations and the business routines and systems predominant at the parent company are adopted unchanged. This know-how transfer is supported by senior executives appointed by the parent company as these are considered to be the most capable persons to ensure the pursuit of the goals and directives issued by the headquarters.

11.4.3 Polycentric enterprises

Polycentric companies which are also referred to as "multi-domestic", "multi-national" or "multi-local" have realized that the **particular feature of each host country** should be given due consideration. Setting up foreign

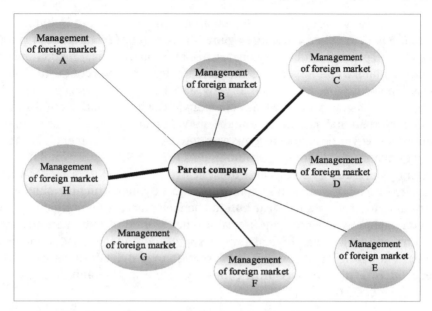

Fig. 11.5. An ethnocentric enterprise

affiliations or subsidiaries aims at building up a national image "on the spot" in order to be met with the same acceptance as local business organisations. These subsidiaries are given considerable discretional leeway and act as autonomous national businesses. *Yip* (1992: 10) comments on their competitive behaviour as follows: "…a multilocal strategy treats competition in each country or region on a stand-alone basis, while a global strategy takes an integrated approach across countries and regions". This is achieved by appointing local managers for the subsidiary who are widely experienced in serving the national markets or in dealing with the local legislation and human resources. The function of the headquarters is, by contrast, to optimise each national strategy and to merge it into a **multinational strategy**.

11.4.4 Geocentric enterprises

Geocentric enterprises seek to achieve global efficiency for the totality of their operations in the world market (*Cateora & Graham*, 1999: 22): "With this orientation a company attempts to standardize as much of the company effort as is practical on a worldwide basis. Some decisions are viewed as applicable world-wide, while others require consideration of local influences. The world as a whole is viewed as the market and the firm develops a global marketing strategy. Firms with this orientation would be classified as regiocentric or geocentric." Corporations that fall into this category are *Levi Strauss, Revlon, Toyota, Ford, McDonald's* and *Coca Cola* as they have been selling their **relatively standardized products** all over the world: "The ideal is a standardized core product that requires minimal local adaptation. In practice, some multinationals have pursued product standardization to a greater or lesser extent" (*Yip*, 1995: 34). Globalisation strategies aim at integrating all corporate activities into one consistent and holistic system thereby seeking to improve the organisation's international competitiveness. As a matter of principle, market share targets are therefore formulated on the basis of a uniform strategy that is geared towards the world market and refrains from taking specific national needs into account. Companies that are intent on implementing an optimal global strategy are therefore willing to accept suboptimal national business activities. The competitive advantages they anticipate are founded on the following three key factors (*Hill*, 1994: 136; *Czinkota, Ronkainen, Moffett & Moynihan*, 1995: 120):

* eonomies of scale, i.e. global cost leadership by benefiting from large-scale operations or specialisation advantages (e.g. *Benetton*, *Philips*);
* economies of scope, i.e. raising the innovation potential by learning or by pooling resources and know-how to realize differentiation benefits (e.g. worldwide quality leadership as intended by *IBM* or *Kodak*);
* structural hedging, i.e. handling risks by transferring the production facilities to the markets and currency zones where they are distributed (e.g. *Honda* in the US).

The "global mania" of the 1980's, when many companies uncritically adopted global marketing concepts in response to the saturation of their existing markets and an increasingly fierce competition, showed that this approach was unsuitable for the large number of companies that were not ready to fully exploit the international potential on offer. There were in particular two problems that made themselves felt (*Morrison, Ricks & Roth*, 1998: 275), a) buyer behaviour is genuinely divers in many foreign markets, and b) managing and co-ordinating or integrating global enterprises remains difficult.

The theoretical fundament of the globalisation hypothesis is *Levitt's* convergence theory. This approach is founded on the assumption that **potential target groups in highly developed markets increasingly resemble each other**. This applies in particular to the highly important markets of the US, Europe and Japan where the demographic characteristics of the consumers groups (stagnating population growth, near-identical standard of living and level of education) are increasingly convergent. Moreover, uniform lifestyles are encouraged, especially of the younger generation, by the ascent of sophisticated communication systems (e.g. satellite TV).

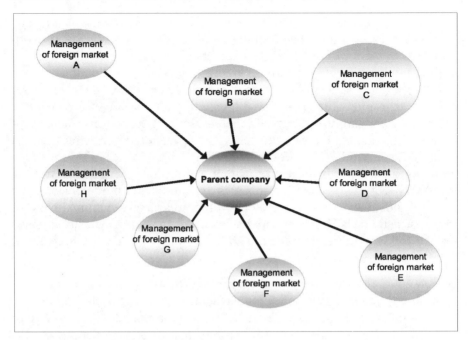

Fig. 11.6. A polycentric enterprise

These developments will result in increasingly convergent consumer behaviour. This also applies to the business-to-business markets where the requirements of internationally operating investment organisations, for instance, are being aligned and where technological standards are being harmonized.

A critique of this hypothesis is that it represents a **gross simplification**. It is debatable whether there is any foreign market in which all relevant consumer characteristics occur simultaneously or are even remotely similar. This also applies to capital goods if one takes into account the different structures of the DMUs involved in the purchase decision and the individual attitudes of the key persons in the purchasing process. A further reservation concerning this hypothesis is that many markets show an increasing fragmentation and regionalisation of the demand pattern rather than homogenisation.

Meffert & Wagner (1986) arrive at the conclusion that there are market segments, whose need and demand patterns are similar and that targeting these cross-cultural groups in the same way would therefore make sense. On the other hand, their objections are that the convergence theory has been formulated in too sweeping a way and that it is questionable whether it is applicable to many economic sectors.

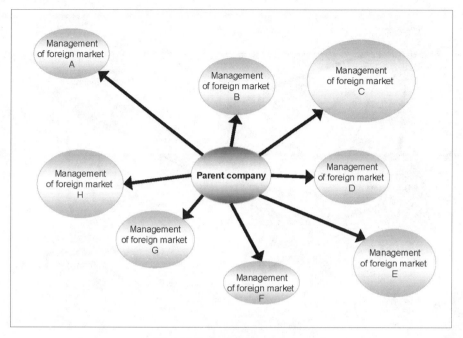

Fig. 11.7. A global enterprise

11.4.5 Transnational organisations

Transnational organisations transcend global perspectives. This concept – which is becoming more and more important as a result of the undifferentiated globalisation pursued by many companies – recognises the significance of a company's proximity to its local markets. "If one interprets the development trends in the world markets correctly, management is currently facing the specific challenge of having to bridge the gap or establish an equilibrium between the conflicting interests of those who want to realise global cost advantages and those who favour national or regional adaptation and, thereby, worldwide learning.

In practice, this signifies that in **areas of contention where global competition and local needs collide** – in other words, at times when hybrid strategies are required – companies need to look for "fit-all" solutions: One such widely traded formula is "Think global, act local", a phrase that was coined by the Japanese internet pioneer *Izumi Aizu* in 1985 in Tokyo (according to business folklore while he was opposing the destruction of his local forest). Such solutions demand that global perspectives should be adopted and that the new product and service opportunities should be systematically identified and exploited all over the world.

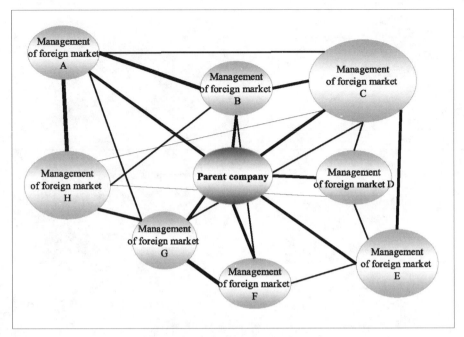

Fig. 11.8. A transnational enterprise

Last but not least, they require that **national or regional concepts should be fitted into global strategic framework**: "Our definition of 'transnational' is that it is a company organized to secure all three benefits. Namely that it has multinational flexibility, global efficiency and innovation transfer back and forth, not only from the headquarters to the national units, but also as soon as something is learnt from one unit, it is transferred throughout the corporation globally" (*Kotler*, 1997: 85).

11.5 International communication strategy

Owing to the wide acceptance of *T. Levitt's* convergence theory, the concept of global marketing was also transferred to the area of communications where it has been propagated/heralded in particular by the advertising agencies. *Saatchi & Saatchi*, for instance, placed an advertisement in *The New York Times* and *The Times* as early as 1984 under the headline "The Opportunity for World Brands" whose purpose it was to present themselves as the first ever global advertising agency. This was evidently intended to be an argument for selling their agency services in more than one country or even worldwide.

11.5.1 Fundamental strategies

Two fundamental strategies of international marketing, and, hence, of communications, can be roughly delineated, namely those of standardisation and of adaptation.

Standardised, global communications strategies distinguish themselves by resolutely applying the same communications policy worldwide. In other words, the same advertising mix is employed even in the most divers regional or country markets on the basis of one single communications concept. A TV commercial, for instance, would be broadcast simultaneously in all targeted markets and an advertising campaign would be launched all over Europe without having been tailored to specific markets. Such a standardised strategy can be executed successfully provided that either the object in question, its perceived utilities and its target groups are identical. or that its targeted consumers can be reached by the same communication means, i. e. the same media, or that their behavioural make-up is similar. Caution needs to be exerted when emotional expressions are to be conveyed, for instance, as they can differ from culture to culture (*Fuchs*, 1995).

Adaptation strategies develop country-specific concepts and implement individual communications policies in each country.

These two international communications policies occupy the opposite ends of a scale which also includes a great number of "glocalisation" strategies. One of them would involve the **standardisation of only a few communication instruments** (see Fig. 11.9), which occurs when global advertising strategies are supplemented by locally adapted sales promotions, another one would be to opt for hybrid solutions when choosing the individual communication instruments.

Tostmann (1985) identifies three concrete types of advertising executed internationally:

- advertising without prior adaptation to specific countries, e. g. a TV commercial which is broadcast via satellite to several countries or an advertisement that is placed in a medium accessible to an international audience;
- linguistically adapted advertising, i. e. the contents and visual portions of an advertisement remain unchanged whereas its linguistic aspects are adapted. Appropriate translations are of paramount importance for this type and must be cross-checked on the spot.
- situationally and/or culturally adapted advertising which retains its basic design but adjusts its verbal and visual messages to country specific conditions.

In addition, there are quite a few **hybrid forms** in use such as the *Citroën* TV commercials that are uniformly broadcast in all their target

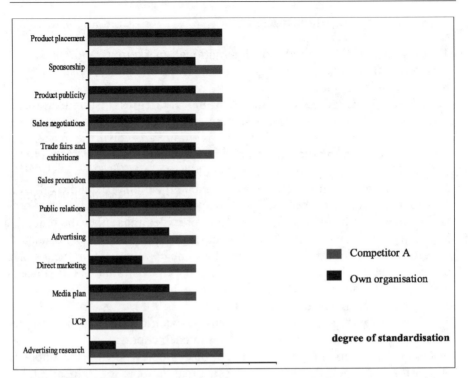

Fig. 11.9. Standardisation problems in the area of communications (an example)

markets, whereas their advertisements and posters are integrated into tailored national campaigns.

A study conducted by *Hite & Fraser* (1988) in multi-national US corporations suggests that marketing practice is definitely moving away from the largely standardised forms of international advertising towards a **combination of standardised and adapted features.** A German survey of 125 internationally operating producers of capital goods (*Langner*, 1996) has arrived at similar conclusions: only about 20 per cent of companies pursue a standardisation strategy.

11.5.2 Transferability of communication strategies

According to *Althans* (1982) the following criteria determine whether communications concepts are internationally applicable: the specific features of the object of a company's communication policy, the nature of the supplying company itself and of its environment as well as that of the consumers (see Fig. 11.10).

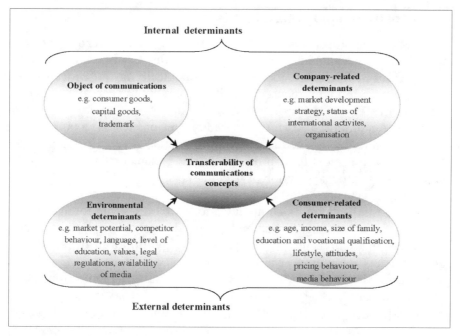

Fig. 11.10. Factors that impact on the transferability of communications concepts (adapted from *Althans,* 1982)

a) Product-related determinants

The determinants related to the product, i. e. the object of communication, depend mostly on whether these objects are consumer goods, capital goods, brand marks etc. (see Fig. 11.11) which may all require different communication activities. If an image is to be communicated, long-term measures need to be put into place and short-lived consumer goods can be supported by means of sales promotion. In the capital goods sector, personal selling may be the method of choice.

Transferability is only warranted if identical or similar **product attributes** and **utilities** can be communicated in the different foreign markets. In some countries, bicycles may be associated with leisure time activity and sports, in others they constitute the primary means of transport. **Lifecycle stages,** too, need to be taken into consideration. If a product has just entered the initial phase of its lifecycle in one country but has reached a stage of growth or maturity in another, the tasks faced by communications differ substantially and, as a result, foil all attempts at standardisation.

b) Company-related determinants

A company's approach to cross-border business is one **internal determinant**. This includes its international marketing function and how it is conducted. Does the company, for instance, strategically favour **concentrated market expansion** (i. e. focused activity in only a few markets) or does it follow a **strategy of diversification** (i. e. extensive expansion to a lot of markets)? According to *Althaus,* focused expansions lead to a higher level of adaptation to the targeted local markets whereas diversified approaches tend to require standardised procedures to a greater extent owing to the rapid and sequential acquisition of new markets.

The extent and the significance of a company's international business activity also impacts on its communications strategy. If its foreign activities are of little standing, for example, it would probably opt for standardised marketing approaches. A company's **designation and organisation**, too, can affect its international communication activities. The framework provided for the design and the development of all communication activities depends on whether the decisions with regard to its communications are taken by a company's central or local functions and on this company's cross-border approach (e. g. ethnocentric, polycentric or geocentric). These

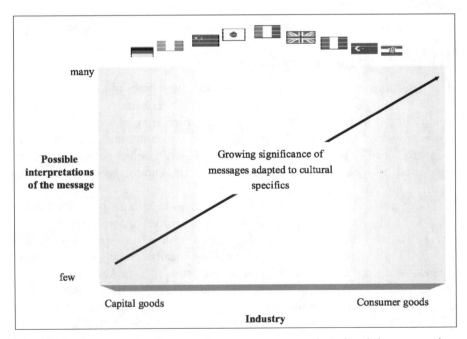

Fig. 11.11. The connection between the message communicated and the communication object (*Hoecklin*, 1998: 97)

complex decisions also include the question as to how the company intends to collaborate with its advertising agencies.

c) Environmental determinants

In addition to a company's individual national markets, which constitute an important environmental force, there is the international market environment with its variables which describe the multi-facetted relationships between countries in political, economic and cultural terms and which *Althans* (1982: 22) categorises as follows:

- socio-economic variables,
- socio-cultural variables,
- natural and technical variables,
- political and legislative variables.

The socio-economic determinants include the existing economic framework such as the domestic market potential and the variables that define it, competitive behaviour, especially in the area of communications, the salience and the "noise" level required to make one's message stick out and be heard, the media system and the advertising infrastructure. Especially the media system, which can be described in terms of cost, and the availability of services and media vehicles are of importance as the transfer of campaigns requires that the media systems should be comparable.

Socio-cultural determinants are *inter alia* language, level of education, nonverbal communication, religion, values and attitudes.

The **natural and technical** determinants comprise variables such as geographical proximity of the business location, a region's climate (and its possible impact on media usage), its topographical aspects and the degree of technological development. The latter aspect affects, in particular, the type and the quality of the communication channels and communication means available.

Environmental determinants include a country's **political situation and its legislative regulations**. There is, for instance, the political risks analysis, which, however, is of less interest in this context than the crucially important legal regulations which restrict the manoeuvring space of the advertisers. In addition, there are the questions concerning media accessibility and the legislation which regulates or excludes the advertising of certain products and regulates the design of the media means (e. g. by outlawing comparative advertisements).

d) Consumer-related determinants

Consumer-focused criteria address the question as to whether and to what extent the target audiences in the individual countries can be described by similar criteria and which communication reach in the groups thus described can be expected. The determinants relevant here are: demographic, socioeconomic, psychographic and behavioural patterns.

There are two methodological approaches to define and characterise these target groups.

- The two-stage segmentation uses cluster analyses to identify groups of similar countries (segmentation of the world markets). This is followed up by a cluster analysis of consumers in each country cluster or each individual country.
- The one-stage integral segmentation describes consumers or members of intended target groups worldwide according to the criteria mentioned above.

In Europe, there is the consumer screening method used by the French *Research Institute on Social Change* (RISC) which interviews 30,000 persons annually and which has typified three main consumer groups (*Tietz*, 1990).

- The traditionalists account for about 30 per cent of Europeans; they are often citizens of senior age with a simple educational background who look to traditional values and behaviours for guidance and are content to conform with social conventions. They are averse to risk-taking and show little willingness to encourage change.
- About 40 per cent are **transformationalists** who seek to move beyond the polarities of traditionalism and globalism. This steadily increasing group of Europeans accepts the complexity of change, maintaining that new power configurations and the multidimensional interpenetration of economic systems will engender more interdependent and integrated cosmopolitan communities.
- The globalists make up about 30 per cent of Europeans. Their level of education tends to be above average and they occupy the upper income brackets. They are change drivers who welcome plurality of expression, technological sophistication and cosmopolitan lifestyles.

In addition, there is the value-oriented typology of *Euro-styles®* that was jointly provided by the *Centre de Communication Avancée (CCA)*, located in Paris, and *EuroPanel™*, established in the 1960's as a merger of 15 European research institutes and now covering 26 European countries.

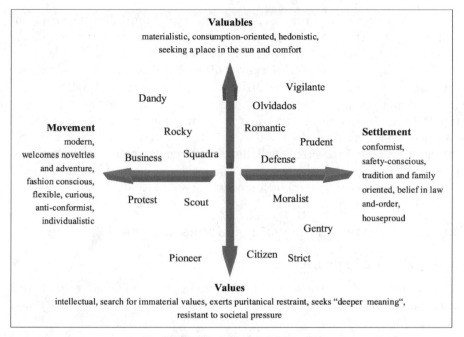

Fig. 11.12. The map of Euro-styles

The socio-style method was first used in France in 1972 and since 1989 in other European countries. It divides the **pan-European**, national and regional populations into six socio-cultural **mentalities** and 16 **lifestyles** which occur in all European countries with diverging national distributions (see Fig. 11.12).

The *GfK Group's* lifestyle research was updated in 1995 and its label was changed to ***Euro-socio-styles***®. This revised typology is based on 24,000 interviews conducted in 15 European countries which contained questions on the respondents' consumption, purchasing and media behaviour, their standard of living as well as their attitudes to market communication activities. It captured 1.5 million items of data on attitudes, behaviour and motives regarding various fields of everyday life which were converted into a three-dimensional map that offers strategic and operative guidance to marketers.

This map indicates the position of each socio-style in the pan-European psychographic landscape. Its axes represent independent fundamental human orientations. The horizontal axis indicates the opposite positions of **movement** and **settlement**, the vertical one the force field of **values** vs. **valuables**.

This map can be superimposed by an imagined third dimension which symbolises the discrepancy between emotional or spontaneous behaviour and rational deliberation (*Müller & Kornmeier*, 1996b: 20).

The fact that such **identical cross-cultural target** groups exist or are developing is essential for the efficient implementation of standardised transnational communication campaigns. *Levitt* (1983) describes the creative task of advertising as "recognising and targeting the basic preferences and needs that are shared by all human beings in spite of their existing differences. This is the great challenge faced by advertising in our day and time"; a thesis which often has been critizised and seems to be refuted by the reality of evident cultural differences.

11.5.3 The pros and cons of standardised communications

a) Arguments in favour

The supporters of the standardisation strategy in communications put forward the following arguments:

a1) Homogenisation of markets and needs

When looked at closely, the convergence theory outlined above (which is supportive of standardisations) is not based on the premise of a worldwide market unification but on **worldwide market segmentation**. Its acolytes argue that in spite of their cultural particularities, there are consumers whose attitudes to certain products show a significant resemblance across all countries so that national target group patterns are superimposed. These **cross-cultural target groups** are likely to respond positively to a standardised communications mix so that different national communication concepts do not need to be devised.

a2) The need for cross-border communications

The necessity to develop cross-border communications is a further substantial argument in favour of standardisation. This development is seen as vital in response to the widely covered issues of the information highways, the multimedia and digital TV; moreover it is intended to counter the cross-border **media overspill** which has been accompanied by the ascent of cable TV and the subsequent increase in the number of foreign broadcasts.

a3) Conformity of external appearance and design

Cross-border communications encourage the intercultural exchange of information. This also offers the opportunity for consumers to encounter different advertising concepts which have been developed autonomously. Consumers of a branded product in country A, for example, can come face to face with an advertisement from country B whose message may to a greater or lesser extent deviate from what they are used to. This can result in **misunderstandings, irritations** and **uncertainty** in these consumers. Internationally standardised adverts, on the other hand, offer a uniform appearance and thereby facilitate the building up of a consistent international corporate image or trademarks.

a4) Cost reduction

As early as the 1980's when *Althans* (1982: 161) conducted his survey, low cost was one of the major arguments in support of standardisation, and cost factors have since then gained in significance. Cost advantages can be realised when advertisements are designed, produced and placed in the media.

Cost can be saved during the **design** stage as standardisation allows only one agency to be entrusted with the design of an advertising campaign instead of employing local agencies in each country. **Production** cost can be reduced by the multiple usage of advertising means. Instead of producing several different national commercials, for instance, companies can simply produce one which is repeatedly released internationally.

Cost advantages in **media buying** may result from the growing internationalisation of the media providers. Many publishers, for example, seek to market their national successes internationally (e. g. *Cosmopolitan*) and sometimes offer favourable terms to those customers that also place adverts in the international editions. *Theis* (1994), too, points out, that the mergers of major national newspapers into European advertising pools will boost the international market offers in future.

a5) Reducing the risk by rerunning successful campaigns

The argument that re-using successful campaigns reduces the risk of failure is based on the assumption that "the selling concept that propels in its first market will be the selling concept that succeeds in every other market at least 60 percent of the time" (*Wells, Burnett & Moriarty*, 1992: 679).

The campaigns of *IBM, Ford, Waterman, Seiko* and many others have used successful national advertisements internationally. This seems to substantiate the claim that the repeated running of a campaign allows its international success to be predicted with a certain degree of accuracy.

Pros	Cons
▪ **Homogenisation of markets** e.g. the existence of identical cross-cultural target groups	▪ **Questionable validity of the convergence theory** e.g. in view of the cultural differences apparent between countries
▪ **Cross-border communications** e.g. "media overspill" by satellite TV or tourism	▪ **Media aspects** e.g. divergent national medis systems and usage patterns
▪ **Uniform design** e.g. to avoid misunderstandings and irritations on the part of the consumers	▪ **Legal framework** e.g. regulations regarding the accessibility of media and the advertisments for specific products
▪ **Cost reduction** e.g. by repeatedly using the advertising means or when buying advertising space and airtime	▪ **Product-related aspects** e.g. culture-free products or culture-bound products
▪ **Rerunning successful campaigns,** e.g. to ensure their future success	▪ **Company-related aspects** e.g. the level of awareness for the company's name and association with its image
▪ **Streamlining organisational tasks,** e.g. by universal guidelines and harmonised quality standards	▪ **Competitive aspects** e.g. the number and profile of local competitors

Fig. 11.13. Pros and cons of standardised international market communications

a6) Streamlining organisational procedures

Last but not least, it can be argued that the standardisation of communications allows the streamlining of planning, coordination and monitoring processes and, hence, a simplification of internal procedures. This is encouraged by universal guidelines and harmonised quality standards (*Mooij*, 1991: 143). On analysing 38 US and European multinationals, *Harris* (1996: 554) found that "the research results indicated in several instances that standardization is employed as a part of a general organizational drive to achieve greater co-ordination, rather than specifically to improve advertising efficiency and brand performance".

b) Counter arguments

The arguments against standardisation focus on the following:

b1) The questionable validity of the convergence theory

A fair number of critics doubt that there are identical cross-cultural target groups marketers can communicate with by emphasizing the complexity of cultural aspects and differences (see Fig. 11.14).

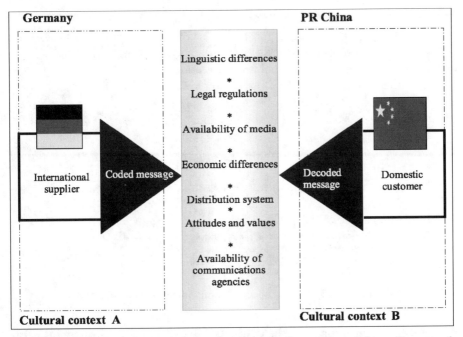

Fig. 11.14. Impediments to international communications (adapted from *Terpstra & Sarathy*, 1997: 609)

If one is to provide "evidence" for the convergences in different markets, it is certainly not enough to rely simply on socio-demographic data; further cultural and market-related data should be collected (*Zandpour*, 1994). *Argyle* (1982) has pointed out the essential cultural differences which generally impede intercultural communication and activity. They also apply to market communications.

First and foremost, it is the **language** which represents the most obvious barrier between cultures (see Fig. 11.15). Language is not only difficult to **translate,** it also causes **interpretation problems**. Danes, for instance, will understand terms such as "work" or "luxury" differently from Mexicans. Using English as a *lingua franca,* which some marketers hoped would overcome these difficulties, has severe limitations, too, as there are multi-facetted comprehension problems. In future, however, English might be useful in standardised communications, in particular to target younger audiences.

Argyle (1982) also underlines the fact that **behavioural rules**, such as eating and drinking habits, the scheduling of appointments and the choice of gifts, can prove to be stumbling blocks in cross-cultural communication as divergent habits between cultures often lead to difficulties and misunderstandings.

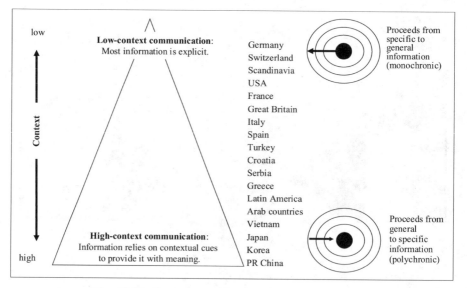

Fig. 11.15. Country specific communication behaviour

A further aspect concerns the distinctly divergent patterns of **social relationships** formed at work, with the family, with friends and acquaintances or in hierarchical societal structures. Communication messages, which make use of these patterns can be well-received in one culture but provoke objections in another.

According to *Argyle* (1982), **ideas and values** which represent broad societal guidelines are another area of cultural contention. A case in point are environmental topics. There is, for instance, a clear divide between France and Germany concerning environmental concerns. Divergences also stretch to the evaluation and acceptance of advertisements: In the UK, for example, advertisements are more welcomingly received than in Sweden or France.

Motivations are the fifth criterion that distinguish cultures. In some countries, an employee's performance level and its respective material rewards are – on average – rated very highly, whereas in other countries remuneration is connected to the social status of a person's family.

Finally the area of **non-verbal communications** should be mentioned. This aspect is of paramount importance as market communications increasingly rely on visualisation and picture-impact. In addition to the phylogenic patterns, which affect human beings in a homogeneous manner, there are, above all, the cultural specifics to be taken into account when messages are visualised. In central Europe, for instance, **territorial behaviour** makes interlocutors take a **distance** of about one arm's length between themselves, any shorter space would be experienced as "breathing on each other" and therefore disagreeable. This may be different in Arabic countries where the distance is much shorter. This signifies that an Arab and a central European might interpret pictures showing two people in conversation differently. Other image, too, need translation and counter-checking. In Thailand, tigers embody danger and do not signal strength as they are intended to do in the European *Esso* adverts. Thus, the cognitive and affective reaction of the recipients may differ considerably according to their cultural region (see *Dmoch*, 1996).

Many cultures differ enormously in the above areas which are crucial for effective market communications. These differences can result in wrong interpretations and weaker attention levels for international campaigns. Even in relatively similar markets such as the US and the UK distinct cultural divergences manifest themselves. This is expressed by *Caillat & Mueller* (1996: 86): "In two countries where most marketing factors are strikingly similar – physical environment, economic development, industry conditions, marketing institutions, language and legal restrictions – the differences in culture alone are significant enough to warrant a specialized advertising approach". From a cultural angle, *Müller & Kornmeier* (1996a; 1996b) arrive at a similarly sceptical verdict on standardisation strategies. They maintain that problems intensify above all when marketers opt for experience-centred, **affective positioning**, as this type of positioning resorts to culturally conventionalised codes and is thus jeopardized by the differences in meaning. However, these authors take a more positive view on the usefulness of standardisation in informative advertising and updating strategies.

b2) Media-related aspects

Another major argument against standardisation strategies concerns the media and, in particular, the media reach in different societies. It includes four major aspects:

Firstly, there are the **organisational structures** within the individual national **media systems**. Secondly, national **media politics** can shackle communications, e. g. by country-specific regulations that limit the availability of TV airtime. A number of questions need to be addressed in this context: Is there a two-way media system as in Germany or are there more private providers as in the US? Are national politics supportive of the new media and communication networks? Do media politics impact on the opportunities that present themselves to market communications facilitate or prevent standardisation? Thirdly, there are **country-specific differences** in the range of media vehicles available, e. g. the number of cinemas and poster boards (see Fig. 11.16). Finally, there are the considerable differences in the **media usage patterns** in the individual countries. Great Britain is consid-

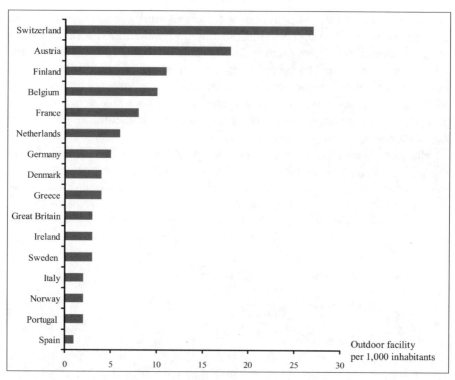

Fig. 11.16. Outdoor advertising facilities available per capita in western Europe 1992 (Berndt, Altobelli & Sander, 1995: 192)

ered to be a classic example of a newspaper-consuming country. Accordingly, one paper is bought per adult, whereas in Spain the ratio is merely 1:9. These diverging user patterns result in huge difficulties when pannational media plans are devised. They also influence the employment of the media types in the country markets.

These problems are intensified by the fact that there are currently no transnational media which would allow a complete coverage of the target audiences. Media structures are, on the whole, country or region specific. However, the new media promise to open up new transnational avenues.

A further deficit is the lacking international **comparability of media data**. Most media-analyses, whose methods vary from case to case, are country-based. In Denmark and the Netherlands, for instance, interviewees are 13 years or older, in Turkey they are included from the age of 19. TV usage data, too, are captured by different tools. They are can be monitored electronically or logged in user diaries Although transnational media analyses of certain regions (e. g. Europe or Southeast Asia) are available,

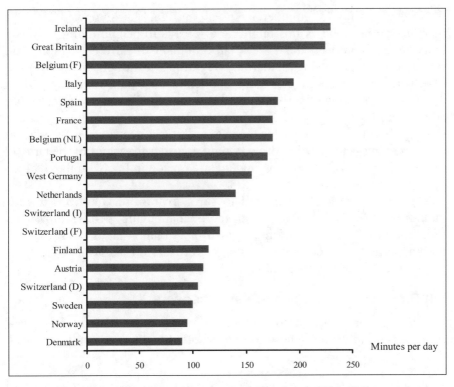

Fig. 11.17. Mean TV usage time (*Hasebrink*, 1995: 199)

they only provide data on a limited number of basic entities rather than on entire populations.

In a nutshell, as national and cultural differences continue to dominate media advertising **a uniform international media market** is as yet a castle in the sky.

b3) Legal framework

Opponents of standardisation also mention the legislation governing market communications in general and advertising, sales promotion, and some PR activities in particular. The different legal procedures to enforce corrective advertising may serve as a case in point here. Even in the economic region of Europe, which is characterised by continuous integration, there is **no uniform advertising legislation**. There are, for instance, at least partial legal divides, concerning the issue of the media classes that can be employed in advertising. Some countries regulate which advertisements can be placed in which media, others how certain products are to be advertised. The following examples may serve to illustrate this:

Norway has no TV commercials at all and Italy has outlawed TV commercials on pet food as this might be offensive to people living at subsistence level. Moreover, there are a large number of different national and international "advertising regulations" regarding the design and the wording of advertising messages. The same applies to misleading and competitive advertising. Although the EU has issued a common directive on misleading advertising, specific legal regulations are determined by national jurisdiction. In Germany, for instance, judges seeking a decision on whether an advertisement is misleading or not would consider the views of the targeted minorities; in France and Italy judgement is made in line with the majority opinion of the end consumers.

The legal situation with regard to **sales promotion activities** in individual countries is similar if not more challenging. *Wells, Burnett & Moriarty* (1992: 685) therefore can justifiably claim that as a result of this unfathomable situation "international advertisers do not fear actual laws; they fear not knowing those laws".

b4) Product and company-related aspects

Finally there are relevant product and company-related arguments against standardisation. Before they are branched out internationally, products

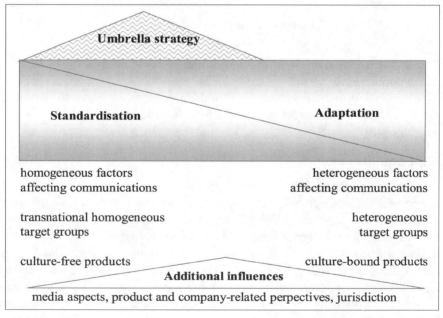

Fig. 11.18. Factors affecting international communications strategies (*Unger & Fuchs*, 2005: 640)

should be divided into **culture free products,** e. g. petrol, which are not bound by cultural specifics, and **culture bound products** such as food.

Communications also depend on the **degree of awareness** a corporate **name, image** and/or **brand** have achieved in individual country markets before communication activities are undertaken there. If there are severe discrepancies these will affect the standardisation option and its communications performance as a whole.

By way of conclusion, it seems doubtful whether standardised cross-cultural campaigns arc sensible in view of the problematic issues discussed above. The question as to which strategy can be implemented depends on a number of variables. Figure 11.18 outlines the essential factors providing the prerequisites for genuine or partial standardisation or adaptation strategies. However, there is no foreseeable tendency towards consumers that can be uniformly targeted across national boundaries. Even if homogeneous cross-culture groups or national subcultures exist they do not represent a genuine perspective to communications at present.

For the time being, internationalisation by adaptation strategies which are embedded in a consistent umbrella structure will therefore be the hallmark of international market communications. Nonetheless marketers should increasingly concentrate on the common assets of internationalisation: "… if you look for differences you will always find them. Equally if you look for similarities you will find them" (*Lannon*, 1991: 161).

11.6 Selected tools of international marketing communications

In the past, the discussion surrounding the internationalisation of communications focused on advertising while allocating a marginal role to other communication tools such as sales promotion, public relations or product placement. However, faced with the growing importance of these tools in current media systems and in increasingly internationalised societies the question whether these tools can be internationalised needs to be addressed. For this reason, those tools that are thought to be deeply engrained in their national or local background will be duly considered. Bearing in mind that business organisations strive to ensure the conformity of the image they communicate to their various publics, these tools ought to be assessed in terms of the internationalisation potential they hold.

11.6.1 Public relations (PR)

"International public relations differs from domestically related activities only in the sense that it seeks to build cultural, geographical and linguistic bridges between stakeholders outside the country of origin" (*Fill*, 2002: 423). It can be defined as the deliberately planned and continuous supply of information that expresses the vested interests of the organisation's stakeholders and aims at creating and consolidating a positive image of a social system (e. g. a corporation). Alternatively it might have to tackle and rectify an existing negative image (*Kunczik*, 1992: 33p.). There is a rough distinction between "corporate public relations" and "marketing public relations" (*Mooij*, 1991: 280pp.), the former always concentrating on the corporate image as a whole, the latter essentially on marketing its products and/or services.

Global corporations understand that their success also depends on how they are viewed externally, i. e. in the markets in which they operate. Their image, be it local or global, is becoming more and more important for them.

Figure 11.19 highlights how going international and undertaking co-operations and acquisitions extends stakeholder demands and expectations. *McFarlin & Sweeney* (1998: 231) maintain that "One aspect of the ´profile of the 21st-century expatriate manager´ is to be able to deal with the various stakeholders of a local market."

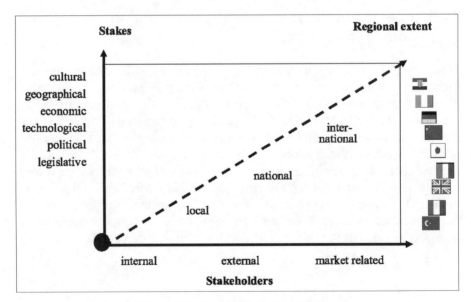

Fig. 11.19. International stakeholders

Companies can opt for one of the following international PR strategies:

- strategies, which are founded on ethno-centric attitudes,
- polycentric strategies, which are adapted to each country's specific features,
- regional strategies, which are tailored to regional markets (e. g. EU, Southeast Asia), and
- global PR strategies which attempt to cover the world markets (*Kunczik*, 1992).

International PR activities need to be adapted to country-specific situations; socio-cultural differences need to be taken into account and most activities need to be tailored to local interests such as those expressed by the media.

The organisation of the PR function in an international business, which like that of advertising can be central or local, depends on the underlying corporate structure.

11.6.2 Sales promotion

The significance of sales promotion has considerably increased in the past decades. It is no longer perceived as an expedient of short-term **tactics** but as a strategic instrument that allows a company to build up sound relations with its sales force, its line traders and customers.

Mooij (1991, S. 260 ff.) defines two main categories of promotional activities for end users: firstly, the impact-driven, short-range classic promotions, and secondly the **value promotions** or **loyalty promotions**, which are image-centred and often combined with other communication instruments such as advertising and public relations. Classic promotions are often regarded as a tool restricted to a regional or local environment. According to *Mooij*, this stronger domestic emphasis is due to the regional needs, the competitive situation and the legal regulations they have to comply with.

By contrast, *Mooij* considers value promotions as suitable for internationalisation. Marketers therefore ought to check whether it is advisable to internationalise this type of promotional activity and to integrate it into a superordinate standardised international campaign.

Differences and similarities in the distribution systems of each country and in the local purchasing behaviour, provide the framework for the development of promotional activities, a framework to which the overall strategy needs to be adapted. Moreover, decisions need to be taken on the nature of the co-operation with the agencies. In this area, too, an increasing number of agency networks has been formed, for instance in order to carry out joint European marketing tasks.

An example of such a thematically integrated campaign is the launch of *Natrel Plus*, a male deodorant produced by *Gillette*, which involved the broadcasting of an identical TV commercial in most European countries. In order to create a consistent image throughout this economic region, all individual national promotion measures took their cue from this campaign, issuing the same message and employing the same positioning methods.

11.6.3 Direct marketing

Direct marketing measures have so far been mostly used in the business-to-business sector, i. e. with specific target groups. They are suitable in markets in which small segments can be distinguished and where appropriate data bases can be built up. They are an excellent means to support exports, especially where national distribution systems have not yet been established.

In international business-to-business markets, by contrast, direct marketing measures are the exception rather than the rule. However, it would be possible to thematically integrate direct marketing measures into a superordinate international advertising campaign and to adapt them to local requirements.

As direct marketing mostly relies on copy writing, due consideration should be given to the correct phrasing and translation of the advertising message. Furthermore, the internationalisation of direct marketing activities should address the following questions:

- Is the hierarchy of decision criteria in the business-to-business sectors different, for example in the buying centres of the individual countries?
- How are direct marketing activities perceived and rated in these countries?
- Are the incentives offered equally rated in these countries? (see *Mooij*, 1991: 278)?
- What are the legal regulations (e. g. regarding telephone marketing and fax usage)?

The advance of telecommunications, data highways, ISDN and the like will certainly provide interesting opportunities for the internationalisation of direct marketing measures. *Hewlett Packard*, for instance, intend to offer cleared stocks and products that have been removed from the product assortment via the Internet throughout Europe to specialist customers (see *Wißmeier*, 1997: 204).

11.6.4 Sponsorship

International sponsorship publicly supports events, teams or persons in various countries (see *Berndt*, 1993: 798). The most frequent forms of international sponsorships are:

- major sports events and organisations (e. g. World Championships; AOL-Arena),
- the music market in general as well as concerts and musical events (e. g. *Fernet Branca* and *Pavarotti)*,
- sponsorship of internationally renowned teams or celebrities

As there is little opportunity to present detailed information about products, brands and the sponsoring corporation itself, international sponsorships seek to create a positive corporate image and to make the sponsor well-known. If sponsorships are to be effective, they need to be backed up by additional communication measures and to form an integral part of the communications mix and thus of the standardisation or adaptation strategy.

The advantages and disadvantages of international sponsorships resemble those of national sponsorships (see *Berndt*, 1993: 801 p.). The **benefits** include the multiple usage opportunities offered by the mass media, a relatively high reach, and the possibility to bypass prohibitive advertising laws (e. g. TV advertising bans on certain products).

On the **downside** there are the limitations in presenting the object to be communicated, and the risks incurred by the image losses affecting supported teams or persons (a classic example being the sprinter Ben Johnson, who had signed sponsorship agreements running into millions of US dollars and who was found guilty of doping).

11.6.5 Product placement

Product placement means the deliberate insertion of a product into the plot of a movie or a TV production in exchange for financial compensation, whereas corporate placement integrates the name or the signature of a corporation. If these movies are broadcast in more than one country (e. g. *Ferrari* in the TV series *Magnum* or *Michelin, Renault, Nikon* and others in *James Bond* movies) we are dealing with international product or corporate placement.

International product placement needs to pay attention to the following items:

- Its reach level is higher than that of national measures.
- The compensation demanded is a lot higher.
- There are possibly national differences in the intended communications effects, and the product or corporation to be placed should already be known internationally.

11.6.6 Trade shows and congresses

There are a number of trade fairs, trade shows and congresses that have always drawn international crowds and the internationalisation trend in this important area of communications seems to be continuing.

International trade fairs and exhibitions serve, *inter alia,* the following purpose:

- They are important for companies which have entered into international activities and which now intend to focus on exports, and
- for international corporations which want to branch out into new national markets or economic regions.
- They are instrumental when products are to be launched internationally, and
- assist companies in building up and consolidating business relations.

A further reason for companies to attend internationally renowned fairs is the presence of their major competitors and their target groups. The communication means chosen ought to reflect the international significance and the prestige of the fairs. This includes the multi-lingual setup and support of stands and exhibits, invitations, product and service catalogues, newsletters tailored to the target groups as well as the choice of experienced staff.

11.7 Integration of international communication policies

If integrating national communications represents a daunting task to communications managers, this is all the more valid in the international arena. This process not only involves more people, it also requires that the specific characteristics of a large number of country markets should be taken into account. However, in view of the challenges faced by international marketers, e. g. a high level of market saturation, virtually indistinguishable products, information overload and low consumer involvement, increasingly segmented and internationalised markets, the growing closeness of foreign markets owing to consumer mobility and the advancement of telecommunications, there is no alternative to the continuous development of international of marketing communications.

Integrated marketing communications can refer to:

- the communications tools,
- the communications partners and
- the planning, information and monitoring processes.

One of the first empirical surveys investigating the effectiveness of integrated communication tools was published by *Brandt* (1993 b). It maintains that enforced interpenetration and standardisation of the routines and procedures that structure international communications will contribute to the effectiveness of market communications in general. Moreover, there will be a larger variety of communication instruments as some companies have started to develop their communications "kit" for each country they expand to.

The integration of partners will tackle the questions who the company should communicate with and how this should be achieved while paying due attention to the specific features of individual markets. Generally speaking, the most appropriate approach and the most suitable strategy depend on each company's particular situation and business environment relevant to this area.

11.8 Multiple choice questions

Question 11/1: Which of the following statements on international management orientations are correct?

(a)	Ethnocentric businesses make considerable efforts to tailor their market communications to the needs of their foreign markets.
(b)	The communications concepts of polycentric business organisations take the specific features of the host country into consideration.
(c)	Global corporations seek to hone their international competitive edge by integrating all corporate activities.
(d)	Transnational corporations find themselves in an area of contention where global competition collides with local needs.

Question 11/2: How can advertising be adapted to the international stage?

(a)	It can consider country-specific requirements.
(b)	It can comply with the formal requirements only.
(c)	It can be culturally adapted.
(d)	It can emulate competitive designs.

Question 11/3: Which statements argue in favour of standardisation strategies in international communications?

(a)	Heterogeneous markets and needs.
(b)	The need for a consistently communicated corporate image.
(c)	Cost advantages when advertisements are released.
(d)	The repeated usage of successful campaigns.

Question 11/4: Which of these arguments support adaptation strategies in international communications?

(a)	Translation and interpretation problems.
(b)	Different nature or degree of motivations.
(c)	Different media systems.
(d)	Different distribution systems.

11.9 Case study

For decades, *Cosmetics PLC* has enjoyed its reputation as a renowned producer of a broad range of quality hair cosmetics. Its international market-

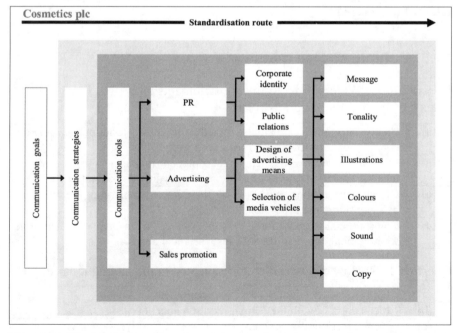

Fig. 11.20. The elements and stages of standardisation at *Cosmetics PLC* (adapted from *Backhaus, Büschken & Voeth*, 2000: 207 pp.)

ing manager assumes that, at least in the short and medium term, country markets will not be characterised by identical market situations "but by a long-term assimilation process". The coordination task companies need to meet does not so much arise from the question whether they should adopt a strategy of standardisation or adaptation but from the question **to what extent** they should adapt the standardised communications elements and **how** this process should be executed.

You have been requested to develop the "tools" that would elucidate and facilitate the decisions to be taken.

Solution

1. First and foremost, you outline the fundamental **coordination problem** faced by international corporations. In view of the dynamic development and interpenetration of country markets, *Cosmetics PLC,* too, needs to take a close look at standardisation approaches that hold the promise of profit maximisation. The above chart maps a standardisation process which reflects the specific communications policy suggested by *Backhaus, Büschken & Voeth* (1996: 190). Following their advice, *Cosmetics ·PLC* will first standardize its communication goals and follow this up by

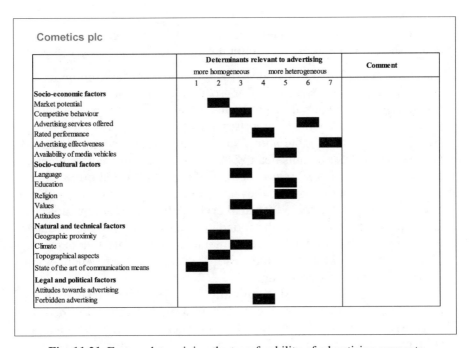

Fig. 11.21. Factors determining the transferability of advertising concepts

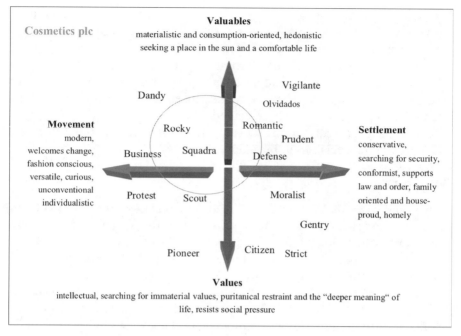

Fig. 11.22. *Cosmetics PLC's* cross-cultural target groups

the standardisation of its communication strategies and processes. At a later stage it will choose its communications tools accordingly.

2. The next stage will ensure the **transferability** of the communication concepts and of the advertising approach chosen. This is achieved by investigating the external determinants affecting a given region such as "Southern Europe" which comprises Italy, Greece, Spain and Portugal (see Fig.below). The table above shows that – independent of the consumer-related determinants dealt with below – standardised communications in the geographical region defined above is a **limited option**.

3. *Cosmetics PLC* believe that they can rely on the typology of "Euro-Socio-Styles" to determine **identical cross-cultural target groups**. This approach is designed to lay the foundation for a more pronounced standardisation of their international communications. This is independent of the fact that external factors restrict standardisation, whereas consumer-related factors encourage it.

4. By assessing all **external determinants** that affect the transferability of this concept, one can define the degree of **standardisation** at *Cosmetics PLC* (see Fig.overleaf). Internal factors, such as market development strategies, the significance of the company's international business ac-

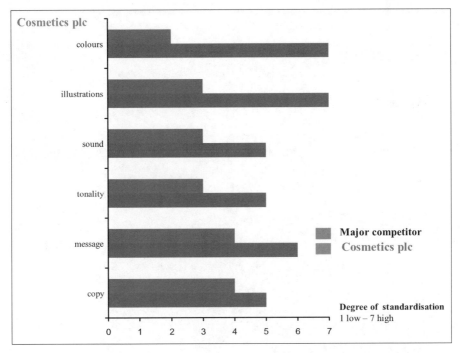

Fig. 11.23. Standardisation of advertising compared to that of the major rival

tivities and its organisational structure, underlie the relatively **low degree of standardisation of** *Cosmetics PLC*: its focused approach aims at the development of a few markets by means of adaptation. Subsequently, this will result in a deeper adaptation to country specific requirements. By contrast, the major competitor of *Cosmetics PLC* is pursuing a strategy of diversification and has been "forced" to standardise its market communications to a greater extent owing to its rapid acquisition of new markets. On the whole, *Cosmetics PLC's* adept coordination mirrors the company's greater market competency.

Additional reading and sources

1. Althans, J. (1982): Die Übertragbarkeit von Werbekonzeptionen auf internationale Märkte. Frankfurt am Main.
2. Argyle, N. (1982): Intercultural Communication. In S. Borchner (ed.), Intercultural communication, Oxford, pp. 61–69.
3. Asseal, H.(1992): Consumer behavior and marketing action. Boston.
4. Assael, H. & Poltrack, D. F. (1991): Using single source data to select tv programs based on purchasing behaviour. Journal of Advertising Research, vol. 31, no. 4, pp. 9–17.
5. Assael, H. & Poltrack, D. F. (1993): Using single source data to select tv programs based on purchasing behavior, Part II. Journal of Advertising Research, vol. 33, no. 1, pp. 48–56.
6. Assael, H. & Poltrack, D. F. (1994): Can demographic profiles of heavy users serve as a surrogate for purchase behavior in selecting tv programs. Journal of Advertising Research, vol. 34, no. 1, pp. 11–17.
7. Assael, H. & Poltrack, D. F. (1996): Single versus double source data fort tv program selection. Journal of Advertising Research, vol. 36, no. 6, pp.73 – 81.
8. Auer, A., Kalweit, U. & Nüßler, P. (1988): Product Placement – Die neue Kunst der geheimen Verführung. Düsseldorf.
9. Backhaus, K., Büschken, J., Voeth, M. (2000): Internationales Marketing (3rd ed.). Stuttgart.
10. Bauer, H. H., Huber, F. & Hägele, M. (1998), Zur präferenzorientierten Messung der Werbewirkung. Marketing ZFP, vol. 20, no. 3, pp. 180–194.
11. Bauer, J. & Seidenspinner, M. (2001): Betriebswirtschaft. Übersetzungsübungen. Berlin.
12. Bente, K. (1990): Product Placement. Wiesbaden.
13. Berlyne, D. E. (1970): Novelty, complexity, and hedonic value. Perception & Psychophysics, vol. 8, pp.279–286.
14. Berndt, R. (1993a): Produet Placement. In R Berndt & R. Hermanns (eds.), Handbuch Marketing-Kommunikation, Wiesbaden, pp. 673–694.
15. Berndt, R. (1993b): Das Management der internationalen Kommunikation. In R. Berndt & A. Hermanns (eds.), Handbuch Marketing-Kommunikation. Wiesbaden, pp. 769–808.
16. Berndt, R., Altobelli, D. F. & Sander, M. (1995): Internationale Kommunikationspolitik. In Hermann, A. & Wissmaier, U. K. (eds.), Internationales Marketing-Management. Munich, pp. 176–224.
17. Bernhard, U. (1978): Blickverhalten und Gedächtnisleistung beim visuellen Werbekontakt. Frankfurt am Main.
18. Birkigt, K., Stadler, M.N. & Funk, H. J. (1995): Corporate Identity. Grundlagen, Funktionen, Fallbeispiele. Landsberg am Lech.

19. Blackwell, R. D., Miniard, P. W. & Engel, J. F. (2006): Consumer behaviour (10th ed.). Fort Worth.

20. Brehm, J.W. (1966): A theory of psychological reactance. New York.

21. Bruhn, M. (1993): Integrierte Kommunikation als Unternehmensaufgabe und Gestaltungsprozeß. In M. Bruhn & H. B. Dahlhoff, (eds.), Effizientes Kommunikationsmanagement. Stuttgart pp. 1–34.

22. Bruhn, M. (1998): Sponsoring. Systematische Planung und integrativer Einsatz. Frankfurt am Main.

23. Bruhn, M. (1999): Internes Marketing. Wiesbaden.

24. Bruhn, M. (2003b): Integrierte Unternehmens- und Markenkommunikation (2nd ed). Stuttgart.

25. Bruhn, M. (2003a): Kommunikationspolitik (2nd ed). Munich.

26. Busch, R., Dögl, R. & Unger, F. (2001): Integriertes Marketing. Wiesbaden.

27. Caillat, Z. & Mueller, B. (1996): Observation: The influence of culture on american and british advertising. Journal of Advertising Research, vol. 36, no. 3, pp. 79–88.

28. Cateora, Ph. R., Graham, J.L. (1999): International Marketing. Boston.

29. Cohen, D. (1981): Consumer behavior. New York, Toronto.

30. Chatelat, B. (1993): Socio-Styles. London.

31. Czinkota, M.R. & Ronkainen, I. A. (1993): International marketing. Orlando.

32. Czinkota, M.R., Ronkainen I.A., Moffett, M.A. & Moynihan, E.O. (1995): Global business. Fort Worth.

33. Danaher, P. J. & Beed, T. W. (1993): A coincidental survey of people say with what they do. Journal of Advertising Research, vol. 33, no. 1, pp. 86–92.

34. Dibb, S., Simpkin, L., Pride, W.M. & Ferrell, O.C. (2001): Marketing concepts and strategies. Boston, Houghton Mifflin.

35. Dichtl, E. & Müller, S. (1992): Merkmale erfolgreicher Exporteure. In B.N. Kumar, & H. Hausmann (eds.), Handbuch der Internationalen Unternehmenstätigkeit, Munich, pp. 429–446.

36. Dmoch,C. (1992): Die Entwicklung standardisierbarer Bilder für die erlebnisorientierte Ero-Werbung. Planung & Analyse, vol 23, no. 4, pp. 28–33.

37. Douglas, S. P. & Craig, C.S . (1995): Global marketing strategy. New York.

38. Durante, N.-V. & Unger, F. (2000): Mediaplanung. In F. Unger, N.-V. Durante & P.M. Rose, Komunikations- und Identitätspolitik. Colonge, pp. 77–97.

39. Fechler, C. (1982): Die Gestaltung und die Produktion der Fernsehwerbung. In B. Tietz (ed.), Die Werbung, Band II. Landsberg am Lech, pp. 1313–1376.

40. Festinger, L. (1957): A theory of cognitive dissonance. Stanford.

41. Fill, C. (2002): Marketing communications. Contexts, strategies and applications. Harlow.

42. Freeman, R. E. (1984): Strategic management. Boston.

43. Frey, M. & Gaska, A. (1993): Die Theorie der kognitiven Dissonanz. In D. Frey, & M. Irle (eds.), Theorien der Sozialpsychologie, vol. 1, (Kognitive Theorien), (3rd ed.). Bern, pp. 275–326.

44. Fritz, W. (1981): Informationsbedarf und Informationsbeschaffung alter Menschen beim Kauf rezeptfreier Medikamente. In H. Raffée, G. Silberer (eds.), Informationsverhalten des Konsumenten – Ergebnisse empirischer Studien, Wiesbaden, pp. 113–142.

45. Fuchs, W. (1995): Transkulturelle Werbung. Markenartikel, vol. 57, pp. 432–435.
46. Galbraith, J. K. (1958): The affluent society, Boston.
47. Goede, G. W. (1998): Marketing-Lexikon. Englisch-Deutsch / Deutsch Englisch. Munich.
48. Harris, G. (1996): International advertising: Implementational issues. Journal of Marketing, vol. 60, pp 551–560.
49. Hasebrink, U. (1995): Vergleichende Betrachtungen zur Fernsehnutung in Europa. in: L. Erbring (ed.), Kommunikationsraum Europa. Konstanz, pp. 190–202.
50. Hawkins, D. I., Best, R. J. & Coney, K. A. (1992): Consumer behavior – implications for marketing psychology. Homewood.
51. Hermanns, A. & Suckrow, C. (1995): Wissenschafts-Sponsoring in der Bundesrepublik Deutschland – Ergebnisse einer Basisstudie unter Einbezug von Hochschulen. In T. Tomczak, F. Müller, & R. Müller (eds.), Die Nicht-Klassiker der Unternehmungskommunikation, St. Gallen, pp. 126–137.
52. Hewstone, M. (1983): Attribution theory. Oxford.
53. Hill, C. W. L. (1994): International business. Boston.
54. Hite, R. E. & Fraser, C. (1988): International advertising strategies of multinational corporations. Journal of Advertising Research, vol. 23, no. 4, pp. 9–17.
55. Hoecklin, L. (1998): Managing Cultural Differences. Wokingham.
56. Hofstede, G. (1994): Cultures and organizations. London. Holscher, C. (1993): Product Publicity. In R Berndt & R. Hermanns (eds.), Handbuch Marketing-Kommunikation. Wiesbaden, pp. 695–703.
57. Hünerberg, R. (1994): Internationales Marketing. Landsberg am Lech.
58. Huth, R. & Pflaum, D. (2005): Einführung in die Werbelehre (7th ed.). Stuttgart.
59. Irle, M. (1975): Lehrbuch der Sozialpsychologie. Göttingen.
60. Irle, M. (1991): Die Theorie der Laienepistemologie (Kruglanski) und die (revidierte) Theorie der kognitiven Dissonanz. Bericht über den 37. Kongress der Deutschen Gesellschaft für Psychologie in Kiel 1990. Göttingen, pp. 84–91.
61. Izard, C. (1994): Die Emotionen des Menschen (3rd ed.). Weinheim, Basel.
62. Jeck-Schlottmann, G. (1988): Anzeigenbetrachtung bei geringem Involvement. Marketing ZFP, vol. 10. pp. 3–43.
63. Kaloff, B. H. (1982): Die Gestaltung von Hörfunkspots. In B. Tietz (ed.), Die Werbung, vol. 2, Landsberg am Lech pp. 1272–1299.
64. Keegan, W. J. (1995): Global marketing management. Englewood Cliffs.
65. Kleining, G. & Prester, G.-G. (1999): Familien-Lebenswelten, eine neue Marktsegmentation von Haushalten. Jahrbuch der Absatz- und Verbrauchsforschung, vol. 45., pp. 4–25.Koschnik, W. J. (2000): Marketing-Wörterbuch / Marketing Dictionary. Berlin.
66. Kotler, P. (1997): Marketing Management. McGraw Hill, London.
67. Kotler, P. & Bliemel, F. (2001): Marketing-Management. Stuttgart.
68. Kroeber-Riel, W. (1986): Die inneren Bilder der Konsumenten. Marketing ZFP, vol. 8, pp. 81–94.
69. Kroeber-Riel, W. & Weinberg, P. (2003): Konsumentenverhalten (8th ed.). Munich.
70. Kunczik, M (1992): Internationale Public Relations als Forschungsfeld. In H. Avenarius & W. Armbrecht (eds.), Ist Public Relations eine Wissenschaft? Opladen, pp. 335–370.

71. Lackman, C. & Lanasa, J. M. (1993): Family decision – making theory. An overview and assessment. Psychology and Marketing, vol. 10, pp. 81–93.
72. Langner, H. (1996): Marketing und Marktforschung in Europa: zwischen global und lokal Planung & Analyse, vol. 23, no. 4, pp. 9–13.
73. Lannon, I. (1991): Developing brand strategies across borders. Marketing Research Today, vol. 8, pp. 160–168.
74. Lasogga, F. (1999): Emotionale Werbung im Business to Business-Bereich. Jahrbuch der Absatz- und Verbrauchsforschung, vol. 45, pp. 56–70.
75. Lasserre, P. & Schütte, H.(1996): Managementstrategien für Asien Pazifik. Stuttgart.
76. Laukamm, T. & Steinthal, N. (1985): Methoden der Strategieentwicklung und des strategischen Managements – Von der Portfolio-Planung zum Führungssystem. In Arthur D. Little International (ed.), Management im Zeitalter der strategischen Führung, Wiesbaden, pp. 7–36.
77. Lefrancois, G. R. (1994): Psychologie des Lernens (3rd ed.). Heidelberg.
78. Levitt, T. (1983): The globalization of markets. Harvard Business Review, vol. 63, no. 3, pp. 92–102.
79. Levitt, T.(1995): The globalization of markets. In: R. D. Buzzell, J. A. Quelch, & C. A. Bartlett (eds.), Global marketing management. (3rd ed.), Reading. pp. 10–29.
80. Lilli, W. (1983): Perzeption, Kognition: Image. In M. Irle (ed.) Marktpsychologie, Göttingen, pp. 402–471.
81. Lilli, W. & Frey, D. (1993): Die Hypothesentheorie sozialer Wahrnehmung. In D. Frey & M. Irle (eds.), Theorien der Sozialpsychologie, vol. 1, (Kognitive Theorien), (3rd ed.). Bern, pp. 49– 80.
82. McFarlin, D. B, Sweeney, P. D. (1998): International management. Cincinnati.
83. Meffert, H. (2000): Marketing (9th ed.). Wiesbaden.
84. Meffert, H. & Wagner, H. (1986): Marketing im Spannungsfeld zwischen weltweitem Wettbewerb und nationalen Bedürfnissen. Arbeitspapier 27 der Wissenschaftlichen Gesellschaft für Marketing und Unternehmensführung e. V.
85. Milde, H. (1993): Single Source. Ein neuer Ansatz in der Marketing-Forschung macht Einkaufsentscheidungen transparent. Planung & Analyse, vol. 20. pp. 24–29.
86. Mooji, M. (1991): Advertising worldwide. New York, London.
87. Morrison, A. J., Ricks, D. A. & Roth, K. (1998): Globalization versus Regionalization. Which Way for the Multinational? In M.R. Czinkota & M. Kotabe (eds.), Trends in international business. Oxford pp 271–282.
88. Müller, S. & Kronmeier, M. (1996a): Global Marketing: Mythos oder reale Handlungsperspektive? Planung & Analyse, vol. 23, no. 4, pp. 14–23.
89. Müller, S. & Kornmeier, M. (1996b): Grenzen der Standardisierung im internationalen Marketing. Jahrbuch der Absatz und Verbrauchsforschung, vol. 38, no. 1, pp. 4–29.
90. Nieschlag, R., Dichtl, E. & Hörschgen, H. (2002) Marketing (19th ed.), Berlin.
91. Pepels, W. (1994): Kommunikations-Management, Stuttgart.
92. Peter, J. P., Olson, J. C. & Grunert, K. G. (1999): Consumer behaviour and marketing Strategy. McGraw-Hill, London.
93. Petty, R. E. und Cacioppo, J. T. (1986): Communication and persuasion, central and peripheral routes to attitudes change. Springer, New York.
94. Reber, A. S. & Reber, E. S. (2001): The penguin dictionary of psychology. London.

95. Rogers, M. & Smith, K. H. (1993): Public perceptions of subliminial advertising. Journal of Advertising Research, vol. 33, no. 2, pp. 10–18.

96. Raab, G. & Unger, F. (2005): Marktpsychologie (2nd ed.). Wiesbaden.

97. Raffée, H. & Silberer, G. (1975): Ein Grundkonzept für die Erfassung und Erklärung des subjektiven Informationsbedarfs bei Kaufentscheidungen des Konsumenten. Bericht aus dem Sonderforschungsbereich 24 der Universität Mannheim "Sozial- und wirtschaftspolitische Entscheidungsforschung". Mannheim.

98. Ries, A. & Trout, J. (1986): Positionierung: Die neue Werbestrategie. Hamburg.

99. Rosenberg, M. J. & Hovland, C. I. (1960): Cognitive, affective, and behavioral components of attitudes. In M. J. Rosenberg, C. I. Hovland, W. J. McGuire, R. P. Abelson, & J. W. Brehm Attitude organization and change. Westport.

100. Scherer, K. R. (1990): Theorien und aktuelle Probleme der Emotionspsychologie. In K. R Scherer (ed.), Psychologie der Emotion, Göttingen pp. 2–38.

101. Schub von Bossiazky, G. (1991): Psychologische Marketingforschung. Munich.

102. Seidenspinner, M. (2202): Volkswirtschaftliche Übersetzungsübungen. Berlin.

103. Soukop, B. (1993): Product Placement – Theoretische Ansätze zur Wirkungsweise und Einsatzmöglichkeiten für die Markenartikelindustrie (unpublished dissertation). Fachhochschule für Druck, Stuttgart.

104. Steffenhagen, H. (1984) Ansätze der Werbewirkungsforschung im Marketing. Marketing ZFB, vol 6, pp. 77–88.

105. Terpstra, V. & Sarathy, R (1997): International Marketing. Orlando.

106. Theis, H.-J (1994): Werbestrategien internationaler Handelsunternehmen. Jahrbuch der Absatz- und Verbrauchsforschung. vol. 40, pp. 391–413.

107. Tietz, B. (1990): Euro-Marketing – Unternehmensstrategien für den Binnenmarkt. Landsberg am Lech.

108. Tomczak, T. & Roosdorp, A. (1993): Positionierung – Neue Herausforderungen verlangen neue Ansätze. In T. Tomczak, T. Rudolph, & A. Roosdorp (eds.), Positionierung – Kernentscheidung des Marketing. St. Gallen, pp. 26–43.

109. Tostmann, T. (1985): Die Globalisierung der Werbung: Faktum oder Fiktion. Harvardmanager, vol. 7, no. 2, pp. 54–60.

110. Tybout, A. M. & Artz, N. (1994): Consumer psychology. In L. W. Porter & M. R. Rosenzweig (eds.), Annual review of psychology. Palo Alto, vol. 45, pp. 131–169.

111. Unger, F., Durante, N.-V., Gabrys, E., Koch, R. & Wailersbacher, R. (2006): Mediaplanung (5th ed). Heidelberg.

112. Unger, F. & Fuchs, W. (2005): Management der Marktkommunikation (3rd ed), Heidelberg.

113. van Bernem, T. (1999): Wirtschaftsenglisch-Wörterbuch. Munich.

114. von Keitz, B. (1983a): Der Test von TV-Werbung. Neue Ansätze auf der Basis der Aktivierungstheorie. Planung & Analyse, vol. 10. pp. 340–344.

115. von Keitz, B. (1983b): Wirksame Fernsehwerbung. Würzburg.

116. Weinhold-Stünzi (1996): Marktobjekte optimal positionieren. In T. Tomczak; T. Rudolph & A. Rootsdorp (eds.), Positionierung – Kernentscheidung des Marketing. St. Gallen, pp. 44–55.

117. Wells, W.; Burnett, J. & Moriarty, S. (1992): Advertising – principles and practice (2nd ed.). Englewood Cliffs.

118. Williams, T. G. (1982): Consumer behavior. Fundamentals and strategies. St. Paul.

119. Wilson, R., & Gilligan C. (2002): Strategic marketing management (2nd ed.). Oxford, Butterworth.
120. Wiswede, G. (1983): Marktsoziologie. In M. Irle (ed.), Marktpsychologie. Göttingen, pp. 151–224.
121. Wißmeier, U. K. (1997): Internationales Marketing im Internet. Jahrbuch der Absatz- und Verbrauchsforschung, vol. 43, no. 2, pp. 189–123.
122. Wundt, W. (1905): Grundzüge der physiologischen Psychologie, vol. 3, Leipzig.
123. Yip, G. S. (1992): Total global strategy. Englewood Cliffs.
124. Yip, G. S. (1995): Global Strategy – In a World of Nations? In R.D Buzzell, J. A. Quelch, C. A. Bartlett (eds.), Global Marketing Management. Reading, pp. 30–52.
125. Zajonc, R. B. (1968): Attitudinal effects of mere exposure. Journal of Personality and Social Psychology, vol. 9, pp. 1–27.
126. Zandpour, F. (1994): Global reach and local touch. Journal of Advertising Research, vol. 34, no. 5, pp. 35–63.
127. Zanger, C. & Sistenich, F. (1996): Eventmarketing. Marketing, ZFP, vol. 20. pp. 233–242.
128. Zimbardo, P. G. & Gerrig, R. J. (1999): Psychlogy and life (15th ed.). New York, Reading, Menlo Park.

Consolidated glossary of German and English key terms

The following definitions, where they are not defined by the authors, are taken from the information provided by the market research institutes, the reference works and dictionaries indicated in unit 11 or have been adapted from the glossary provided by Pickton & Broderick.

The terms considered below are mostly subject-specific terms or marketing jargon. In addition, we have included semantically ambiguous or complex items such as the proverbial "false friends (e. g. Kommission/commission, Format/format) and expressions that might not be self-explanatory.

Account executives: managers in charge of serving individual clients and of administering their communications accounts. They are assisted by → customer contact managers.

Adaptation strategy: marketing communications strategy that is partially or wholly tailored to meet the particular requirements of country or regional markets, renders *Differenzierungsstrategie.*

Advertising platform: the fundamental selling points that an advertiser wishes to include in the advertising campaign

Advertorials: print advertisements that are especially designed to look like press editorials.

Ad-wearout: the waning impact of advertisements due to the fact that they are placed repeatedly. Wearout occurs with all means of communications.

Agency (sales) pitch: presentation performed by short-listed competing agencies during which they present their ideas, proposals, designs and → roughs to a client's brief.

Artwork: the illustration and the layout of an advertisement.

Business organisation: collective term for all types of owned and administrated businesses, although – in its broader sense – it may simply refer to a group of people who come together for a specific purpose (e. g. the World Trade Organization). Business organisations (translates *Unternehmen, Gesellschaft*) are divided into "incorporated businesses" *(Kapitalgesellschaften)* and "unincorporated businesses" *(Personengesellschaften)*. Alternative terms are → businesses and → companies. Its US variant is "organization".

Businesses: commercially run establishments that seek to make profit, places of commerce.

Buying centre: → "decision making unit"

Capital goods: goods that are made or provided to produce other goods (e. g. raw materials, components) and thereby to increase a corporations assets. They do not satisfy a consumer's → want directly but are necessary to produce the goods that do. Synonymous expressions are **production goods**, or **producer's goods**.

Chart: semantically complex noun which refers to a) a table, detailed list or breakdown of figures, b) drawn geometrical figures (e. g. pie charts) or diagrams integrated in a → graph (e. g. bar charts). The verb means "to draw a map", "to plot a course" or "to make a structured and detailed list".

Classified ads: name of small adverts with no distinctive design that appear under a sub-heading in the columns of the classified sections of some print media *(Fließsatzanzeigen)*. They account for a significant part of the total advertising spend.

Cluster sample: units (usually geographically-based) selected from a subset, e. g. to research teenagers' attitudes to certain products in a certain region.

Commission: a) payment e. g. for sales representatives over and above their regular salary to boost trade (sales commission), b) a charge raised, e. g. for credit transfers, c) project by-project payment to **agents** for their services in buying or selling goods calculated as a percentage of the amount of the business generated (see also → mark-up). – Please note that in a business context the verb **to commission** means to place an order for something or to charge someone with a duty or task.

Companies: incorporated → business organisations, their US equivalent is corporations.

Conjoint analysis: analysis that includes two or more components each of which affects the objects of investigation. Many analytical variables (e. g. consumer preferences and product utilities) are conjoint.

Consumer panel: a permanent, syndicated and representative sample of consumers, who provide ongoing details of the fast moving consumer goods (FMCGs) they purchase. Using effective collection methods (EPOS, electronic or paper diaries, on-line sampling, till receipts, telephone) each panel member records the details of every item they have purchased.

Consumer typology: lay-psychological method to categorize and describe groups of people beyond their purely socio-demographic characteristics.

Contest: a sales promotion measure during which customers compete for prizes or money on the basis of skills or ability, entry requires a proof of purchase and the winners are "found" against a set of predetermined tasks such as identifying a product, see also → sweepstake.

Contribution in kind: payment in the form of goods and services, this term translates *Sachleistung*.

Copy: the verbal portion of an advert, this includes the headlines, subheadings, the body of the text (or body copy) and the corporate signature. Not to be confused with the "copy strategy" explained in section 6.4.

Corrective advertisement (piece of communication that is forced to corrects a previous advert on the grounds that this was deliberately or accidentally misleading (*irreführend*) or incorrect.

Cost per thousand (CPT) or **cost per mill (CPM):** the cost of achieving a given coverage in the media.The CPT is computed by dividing the cost of media placing by the vehicle's reach and by multiplying the result by 1,000. CPT is a widely used measure of media efficiency as it allows the agencies to compare the price of different media vehicles.

Coverage: → reach

Creatives: the team responsible for providing creative solutions, e. g. the art directors, designers and → copy writers.

Critical success factors (CFS): product features that are particularly valued by the customers. Companies need to outperform their competitors in the areas that sustain these factors.

Cross buying: buying other products from the same supplier.

Cross selling: selling a company's other products to the same customer.

Customer contact management (CCM): the strategic and tactical tasks involved in establishing a positive personal communication between an organisation and its customers. CCM is complementary to image and brand management, also referred to as **customer liaising**.

Decision Making Unit (DMU), also known as **Decision-Making Group** or **Buying Center** (US variant): the often sizeable group of people involved in the (purchasing) decision making process. The composition of this group may be coincidental or formally organized. The buying decision may be made ad hoc or follow prescribed routines as they occur in a B2B context. The DMU includes a number of 'players' that are typified as influencers, gatekeepers, specifiers (i. e. one of the major influencers who specifies the product, e. g. in at B2B market), deciders, buyers and end users.

Diagram: representation of isolated geometrical figure, such as cubes, cones or pyramids, that is drawn for demonstration and visualisation purposes, diagrams can be integrated into a → graph. The verb "to diagram" means "to mark out by lines".

Direct-response advertisements: contain items which invite the members of a targeted audience to respond immediately to the communication measure. These items can be reply cards, stamped addressed envelopes (SAEs), coupons, "tipped on" address stickers.

Duplication: the fact that media or seen or heard by same person. Duplication increases OTS/OTH and thereby → frequency.

Durable goods: items that are used over a period of time. They can be → capital goods or consumer durables.

Effective reach: refined → reach calculation which is based on a specified minimal frequency figure which achieves maximum impact.

Effectiveness: "doing things right", i. e. achieving the desired result.

Efficiency: "doing the right thing", i. e. completing a task in the most advisable way.

Enterprise: noun which denotes any business undertaking or organisation but is often used for business ventures that involve an element of risk requiring entrepreneurial initiative. Examples: small and medium-sized enterprises or SMEs, state enterprise.

EuroPanel™: international consumer research partnership owned by GfK and the British research company TNS (Taylor Nelson Sofres). It tracks the actual purchases on several individual markets in over 40 countries using a continuous representative sample of individuals (not households). Moreover, it measures consumer behaviour to understand market movements and their implications. The German GfK panel will be increased to include 17,000 households in 2004.

Experiential appeal: the product's ability to address the consumers' desire for cognitive or sensory stimulation and to turn the act of acquiring the product into a pleasant experience.

Exposure: the → insertion of a communications item in a medium which the members of the targeted audience are expected to see or to hear, used as an equivalent term to "opportunity to see" (OTS) and opportunity to hear (OTH).

Firm: strictly speaking, a non-incorporated business entity, such as a "legal firm" *(Kanzlei)* or a partnership of medical practitioners *(Gemeinschaftspraxis)*. However, this term is often loosely used for any business.

FMCGs: abbreviation for "fast moving consumer goods". These goods are usually sold at a low unit price.

Foldout, fold → gatefold

Format: collective term that denotes a large variety of design features such as the general style of an advert, its layout, size, colours, graphics, illustrations and typography. The English term does not exactly render the German *Format* which first and foremost refers to the size of an advertisement.

Frequency: like → reach and → impact a central concept used to measure the marketing success of an advertising measure. Although there is no general agreement of how often audiences should be exposed to communication messages to achieve at least adequate results, marketers define "ideal" or "optimal" rates. Frequency is measured in terms of OTS (opportunities to see) and OTH (opportunities to hear).

Full-service agencies, another name for **multi-service agencies:** companies which offer a complete range of communication solutions at all distribution levels and are therefore also referred to as **one-stop shops** or **through-the-line agents**.

Gatefold: this printing item is an oversize page in a book or magazine which is folded **in** and – in line with the inherent logic of natural languages – also called a **foldout** or simply a **fold**.

Global village: term coined in the early 1960's by the Canadian philosopher Marshall McLuhan to describe the fact that the world seems to be getting smaller owing to the interpenetration and merging of regional lifestyles into one.

Glocalisation: a somewhat flippant but common neologism for a global strategy that has been partially adopted to the needs of regional markets.

Goals: anticipated outcomes that are of a general, principal or superordinate nature. Goals are usually broken down into less broadly defined or more specific **aims** and narrowly defined and (always) quantified **objectives**. If these objectives are forecast figures, the term **target** is used synonymously (e. g. sales targets, production targets.

Graph: mathematical term that stands for **"graphic formula"**. Graphs portray the relationship of the variables of a functions and equations. Graphs usually form an integral part of a set of axes in which they take the form of plotted lines (i. e. line graphs or curves), clusters (scatter diagrams) or horizontal or vertical bar → charts. The verb "to graph" means "to draw a line or diagram expressing some degree of change, an equation or function." – Please not that the noun *graph* does not translate *Grafik,* nor is it synonymous with → diagram.

Gross rating points (GRP): measure for the performance and effectiveness of advertising means. GRPs are mostly determined by multiplying → reach by → frequency.

Heuristic decision models or **decision heuristics:** Owing to their "bounded rationality" defined by the American economist and philosopher *H.A. Simon*), human beings can never be in full command of a complex decision situation. One creative tool to overcome this obstacle is to use heuristic techniques. These constitute simple "rule of thumb" or "if ... then" approaches that facilitate decisions by reducing the complexity of the decision process, thereby making it more manageable. Heuristic methods are used in teaching when pupils are allowed to learn things for themselves, e. g. by trial and error.

Household panels: market-tracking vehicle which measures consumer purchasing behaviour, especially in → FMCG markets and delivers details for market analysis.

Icon: an image, picture or symbol that resembles or is analogous to the object it represents, a person or object that embodies a religious belief or cultural phenomenon. Thus, Paris uses the Eiffel Tower as its icon in most of its marketing communications.

Illustrations: visual portion of an advertisement which includes photographs, drawings → graphs, → charts, → diagrams, and tables (*Tabellen*).

Impact: 1) as a non-countable collective noun "impact" signifies "the strength of the impression created" by an advertisement or a marketing campaign. 2) **An impact** (as a countable noun) also signifies an exposure to a marketing item. This is achieved by multiple → insertions which provide contact opportunities (OTC) that can be measured. For this reason the impact is an essential concept in media planning as it allows the evaluation of advertising → effectiveness.

Individual panels: some markets are driven by the individual's needs and decisions, instead of the family's or the household's.

Infomercials: specially designed sales promotion activities that contain more information than ordinary advertisements and may merge the spots of several advertisers or for various products into one programme.

Insert: a printed sheet, especially one bearing advertising, placed loose between the leaves of a book, magazine, periodical or journal, 2) another name for → inset.

Insertion: refers to the fact that an advertisement has been placed in a medium.

Inset: 1) a small → illustration set within the borders of a larger one, 2) in loose usage another name for → insert.

Insetter: semantically ambivalent printing term which denotes a) the control device for inserting the separately produced colour sections into the normal high speed newspaper press thereby ensuring a perfect fit with the type area (*Satzspiegel*), and b) the → intaglio pre-printed illustrations themselves. This technique makes full use of the type area and chosen newspaper format. "Insetters" have evolved from → high fidelity techniques.

Intaglio method: any of the printing techniques in which an image or tonal area is printed from lines or textures scratched or etched into a metal plate (engraving, etching etc.). The plate is covered with ink, then wiped clean leaving ink in the incised lines or textures of the image. This plate is then printed in a press on moistened paper. The paper is forced down into the area of the plate holding ink, and the image is transferred to the paper.

Inter-media decision: choosing the main media or → media classes to be used in the media plan.

Jobbing: work or assignments performed on an occasional basis, on a project-by-project basis or by the piece.

Key account: a major customer or any customer seen as significant by an organisation, see also → account executive.

Landscape: format of publications whose width is greater than its height, see also → portrait.

Layout: essential part of the artwork of an advertisement, the way in which the illustrations and the copy of an advertisement are physically arranged.

Leverage: a) the action and force of a lever and the mechanical advantage gained by using a lever, b) as a business term leverage signifies "enhanced power". Supermarkets have grrater market leverage than corner shops, c) in finance, the synonym of gearing, i.e. the use of external loans rather than one's own financial assets.

Live spots or **live readers:** promotional commercials that are delivered by the speakers during regular radio programmes

Logo: short for logotype, → symbol

Marginal analysis: the examination of what happens to a company's cost and revenues when production or the sales volume are changed by one unit.

Marketing communications: In its narrow sense, this term refers to the "promotion" item of the classic four P's of the marketing mix which includes all marketing activities affecting a company's target audiences. From a broader perspective, marketing communications also comprise the "non-promotional" forms of the marketing mix. They can be directed at all company stakeholders, i. e. at target audiences other than customers and consumers. These multifarious forms of communication are summed up under the label communications. Marketing communications are vital for the success of all marketing ventures and for business performance in general.

Mark-up: percentage of the service price or any other sum added to the fee charged to an agency by a service supplier (e. g. a photographer).

Maslow's needs hierarchy: a popular theory which was developed by the US psychologist *Abraham H. Maslow* (1908–1970). His model suggests that human beings satisfy and prioritize their needs in a sequential order starting with sustenance driven needs (such as food, water and sex) and ranging through the intrinsically directed needs for safety (protection from harm) and belongingness (love, companionship) to the extrinsically directed need for esteem (prestige, respect of others) and self-fulfilment. The Problem of this model is, that it was never confirmed by empirical research; may be, it is an oversimplificated model of human behaviour. This oversimplification is surely the reason of its popularity.

Media class: a major category of communication means, such as the print media, radio, television, cinemas, posters, direct mail or the Internet.

Media vehicles: the actual media within a → media class that carry the advertising message. In the media class of television, for instance, a TV channel such as BBC 1 would be a vehicle. A press vehicle would be *The Times*.

Multi-service agencies: → full-service agencies

Need: the experience or imagined physiological, material, social, or personal lack that a person seeks to satisfy.

Net reach: total reach less the allowance for → duplication.

Noise: psychological term denoting any item that interferes with the communication of a message so that the decoded message is different from the encoded item. In a more general sense, noise can refer to any uncontrolled factor that contaminates a process.

Objective and task method: technique for setting an advertising budget which involves determining campaign objectives and then listing the tasks required to accomplish them.

Omnibus surveys: a) an → ad-hoc research method that includes several test groups, usually followed by post-hoc tests that specify the differences found between these groups, b) any test that includes generalized sub-items which are distributed throughout it. Such tests are designed to evaluate a number of related factors. c) In advertising jargon, the composite noun "omnibus programme" is used to denote TV programmes which consist of several broadcasts.

One-stop shop: → full-service agency

OTH: → frequency

OTS: → frequency

Penetration: → reach

Phylogenic: adjective that refers to the sequence of events involved in the evolution of a species or genus, identical with **phylogenetic**.

Pitch: → agency sales pitch

Portrait: a print format whose height is greater than it width, see also → landscape.

Pre-testing: the process of evaluating marketing communication elements at the start of a campaign, see also → pre-vetting

Pre-vetting: the process of checking and approving advertisements before they are released, not identical with → pre-testing

Prime position: an especially advantageous position for an advertisement e. g. on the front page or back cover of a newspaper

Probability sampling: → random sampling

Product adoption process: the five stages of acceptance of a product which comprise "awareness" (when customers notice that a product exists), "interest" (when they become motivated to obtain more information about this product), "evaluation" (when they decide whether the product will meet their needs), "trial" (when a test purchase is made) and "adoption" (when customers deliberately choose this product).

Product managers (persons responsible for a product, a product line, or interrelated groups of products in larger organisations that produce a multiple range of products. – Please note that the female form **"manageress"** refers to ladies who are in charge of small establishments such as canteens.

Production goods, producer's goods: → capital goods

Publics: in PR jargon this expression includes all → target audiences that communication measures can be directed at.

Random sampling: research method that draws → samples from the total population ensuring that each member has a non-zero chance of being included, a.k.a. **probability sampling**.

Reach (a.k.a. media reach or **audience reach):** a central concept of media planning and media research that measures the number of members or the percentage of an audience exposed to an advertising measure in a medium – or a combination of media – during an advertising campaign, synonymous with **coverage** or **penetration**.

Recall: The evaluation of message contents on the basis of prompted (aided) or unprompted (un-aided, spontaneous) recollection of an advertisement or any other stimulus material.

Recognition: evaluation of a communication message on the basis of the existing awareness (of a brand, a company). In order to define the recognition level achieved by an advertisement, it is shown to respondents whose reaction is recorded.

Reminder or **follow up advert:** a) brief advertising spot released as a follow-up to the main advertisement, b) a campaign of several brief mentions of a product that is supposed to be known to the audience (a.k.a. **remembrance advertising**).

Retainer: regular fee paid by the advertisers to their agents in order to retain their services over time. Retainers are calculated on the basis of the total assignment to be carried out.

Rolling sample: a sample whose structure and size remain constant over a longer period of time but whose participants change at regular intervals.

Run of paper adverts: advertisements which appear in the main text of a newspaper or magazine. They can occupy a full page or any proportion thereof and can be fully or partially inserted in the text of the newspaper articles.

Salience: signifies prominence, distinctiveness. Widely used term in the study of perception and cognition to refer to any aspect of the stimulus which stands out. In marketing, it denotes the ability of an advertising feature to "shout" at its audience. The salience concept is based on the premise that audiences respond positively to a persuasive product but also to the advertisement itself.

Sample: part of a population selected for research purposes, the selection process usually following determined procedure, in everyday language short for → random sample.

Satisfice: economic term deriving from the verbs "satisfy" and "suffice". The satisficing principle is demonstrated by companies which accept satisfactory (instead of maximised) profits if these can be realized with minimal or reduced efforts.

Scamps: drafts or "roughs" of creative ideas that are produced cheaply during the pre-vetting stage of advertising campaigns.

Self-concept: the way in which individuals and organisations describe themselves in as complete a way as possible, there is a semantic contrast with → self-image and the evaluative concept of self-esteem.

Self-image: a person's imaged (or rather imagined) self which is often incongruent with the "real self" or the image perceived by this person's environment, see also → self-concept.

Self-regulation: a business or industry' self-imposed principles too meet regulations, social or environmental obligations, to comply with certain standards (quality, safety) and pursue certain values.

Sign: an item, gesture or action that is a taken as a token of a fact or condition, the meaning a sign creates may be outwardly observable (e. g. road signs), but it may also be implied or be based on conventional interpretation.

Solus position: a) special position for an advertisement that is completely surrounded by editorial, classified ads or margin and, hence, appears without any other advertisement in its vicinity, b) a creatively designed advert placed in the middle of the → classified ads (*Fließsatzanzeigen*) section of a newspaper.

Stakeholders: can be "any group or individual who can affect or is affected by the achievement of an organisation's purpose" (*Freeman*, 1984) or who has a vested interest in an organisation. Stakeholders include suppliers, customers, consumers, investors, employees and the members of the communities in which the organisation is based or operates. They form relationships with the organisation and exert influence and power whose nature, intensity and duration vary.

Standardisation strategy: the employment of identical marketing communications across all country markets

Storyboard: series of miniature scenes (drawings, cartoons or illustrations) that show the sequence of the scenes in an advertising movie, it also includes comments on the sound and the voice-over to be provided.

Strategic business unit (SBU): self-contained business unit which serves a distinct market and enjoys strategic responsibility. That is much more, than the pure profit responsibility of profit centres. Often linked to a company's core competences and internal investments.

Stratified sampling: research method which divides the population (or samples) into mutually exclusive and exhaustive subsets, strata or sub-populations, e. g. people who live in high, medium or low income areas. Random samples are then taken from each subset.

Subliminal perception: the perception of stimuli below the "limen" (i. e. the threshold) of awareness. A stimulus is defined as **subliminal** if persons are completely unaware that they have received it.

Sweepstake: as a marketing term sweepstake denotes a sales promotion technique in which the participants and the winners of the "stake" or "prize" are drawn by chance. A proof of purchase is not required. In general English, this expression sometimes refers to the prize itself, see also → contest

Symbol: an artistically or artificially created → sign that embodies or implies a meaning which is usually attributed by (e. g. cultural) convention and/or definition. The two yellow arches, for instance, immediately recall McDonald's fast food restaurants. Symbols are often termed **logos**, **emblems** or **trademarks**.

Syndicated data services: market data of a general nature that are periodically collected from panels and sold to a number of clients, e. g. the purchasing and retail data collected by MRCA (Market Research Corporation of America).

Tachistoscope: electronic device that measures the ability of an advertisement shown to respondents to a point where they can identify the components of a message. This is instrumental in discovering the elements that viewers see first when an ad is exposed and thus facilitates the creation of impact based messages.

Target audience, synonymous with **target group:** the viewers, listeners and readers that have been identified as having a direct or indirect effect on media and product performance and have therefore been selected as recipients of marketing communications.

Teasers: a) any advert that relies on the concepts of → salience or alienation (*Verfremdung*) to attract attention. b) advertising spots whose main function is to incite the listeners' or viewers' curiosity for the ensuing centrepiece which carries the advertising message, see also → **reminder**

Through-the-line agency: → full-service agency

Tonality: design concept which includes the form of creativity desired, the atmosphere and the style of a market communication measure.

Trademark or brand mark: → symbol

Want: in economic theory the subjective desire for a commodity or a service that underlies demand. Wants are only of interest to the marketer if they can be converted into purchasing power, this term translates (*Bedürfnis* rather than *Bedarf,* see also → need.

Weighted ratings or **weighted rating points:** comparative scale to establish the importance or **weight** of a medium vis à vis its competitors.